Motivational Dialogue

D0060945

Motivational Dialogue explores the application of motivational interviewing in various contexts, with a view to enhancing understanding and improving practice.

The book describes the research and practice of motivational interviewing as a stand alone intervention, as an adjunct to further treatment, and as a style of delivery of social and behavioural interventions. The contributors draw on their expertise and experience as researchers, teachers and practitioners to encourage the reader to appreciate the broad applicability of motivational dialogue. The book is divided into 5 sections, which cover:

- reflections and a model
- the evidence base
- learning and practice
- four studies of motivational therapy in practice
- motivational dialogue and stepped care

Motivational Dialogue will be of great interest to psychiatrists, clinical psychologists and anyone in the social and health care professions who is involved in assisting people to challenge addictive behaviours.

Gillian Tober is Honorary Consultant in Addiction Psychology and Head of Training at the Leeds Addiction Unit and Associate Lecturer at the University of Leeds. She is President of the Society for the Study of Addiction.

Duncan Raistrick is Associate Medical Director of the Leeds Addiction Unit.

Contributors: Simon J. Adamson, Samuel A. Ball, Kathleen M. Carroll, Daryle D. Deering, Gian Paolo Guelfi, Susi Harris, Ronald M. Kadden, Rob Kenyon, Ian K. MacEwan, Steve Martino, Duncan Raistrick, Roger Roffman, Ian Russell, Belinda Scrivings, J. Douglas Sellman, Valter Spiller, Karen L. Steinberg, Gillian Tober, Valeria Zavan

Motivational Dialogue

Preparing addiction professionals for motivational interviewing practice

Edited by Gillian Tober and Duncan Raistrick

LONDON AND NEW YORK

First published 2007 by Routledge
27 Church Road, Hove, East Sussex BN3 2FA

Simultaneously published in the USA and Canada
by Routledge
270 Madison Avenue, New York, NY 10016

Routledge is an imprint of the Taylor & Francis Group, an Informa Business

Copyright © 2007 selection and editorial matter, Gillian Tober & Duncan Raistrick; individual chapters, the contributors

Typeset in Times by Garfield Morgan, Swansea, West Glamorgan
Printed and bound in Great Britain by TJ International Ltd, Padstow, Cornwall
Cover design by Design Deluxe, Bath

All rights reserved. No part of this book may be reprinted or reproduced or utilised in any form or by any electronic, mechanical, or other means, now known or hereafter invented, including photocopying and recording, or in any information storage or retrieval system, without permission in writing from the publishers.

This publication has been produced with paper manufactured to strict environmental standards and with pulp derived from sustainable forests.

British Library Cataloguing in Publication Data
A catalogue record for this book is available from the British Library

Library of Congress Cataloging-in-Publication Data
Motivational dialogue : preparing addiction professionals for motivational interviewing practice / edited by Gillian Tober & Duncan Raistrick.
p. ; cm.
Includes bibliographical references and index.
ISBN-13: 978-1-58391-295-9 (hardback)
ISBN-10: 1-58391-295-9 (hardback)
ISBN-13: 978-1-58391-296-6 (pbk.)
ISBN-10: 1-58391-296-7 (pbk.)
1. Substance abuse–Treatment. 2. Motivational interviewing. 3. Drug abuse counselors–Training of. 4. Alcoholism counselors–Training of. I. Tober, Gillian. II. Raistrick, Duncan.
[DNLM: 1. Behavior Therapy–methods. 2. Behavior, Addictive–therapy. 3. Interview, Psychological–methods. 4. Motivation. 5. Substance-Related Disorders–therapy. WM 425 M918 2007]
RC564.M683 2007
362.29–dc22

2007003288

ISBN: 978-1-58391-295-9 hbk
ISBN: 978-1-58391-296-6 pbk

Contents

Contributors

Editors

Gillian Tober PhD is Honorary Consultant in Addiction Psychology and Head of Training at the Leeds Addiction Unit and Associate Lecturer at the University of Leeds. She was Principal Investigator for Training in the United Kingdom Alcohol Treatment Trial. Her research is in the process of treatment delivery, the effectiveness of addiction treatment, and the nature and measurement of substance dependence. She was first editor and co-author of "Methadone Matters: evolving community methadone treatment of opiate addiction". Her clinical work includes development of and supervision in the use of treatment manuals. She is co-director of the RESULT Information Management System. She is the President of the Society for the Study of Addiction.

Dr Duncan Raistrick is Associate Medical Director of the Leeds Addiction Unit. He qualified in medicine from the University of Leeds in 1971; he trained at the Maudsley Hospital, London. He has been Medical Advisor on Alcohol to the Chief Medical Officer. He is co-director of the RESULT Information Management System and has published research papers and books including *Dealing with Drink* and *Tackling Alcohol Together*. Research interests are the nature of dependence, outcome measures and therapist characteristics.

Chapter authors

Simon J. Adamson PhD is Senior Lecturer and Deputy Director (Research) at the National Addiction Centre Aotearoa New Zealand and is a practising clinical psychologist in a government funded outpatient alcohol and drug treatment service. His research interests include prediction of treatment outcome, screening for cannabis misuse and co-existing conditions.

Samuel A. Ball PhD is Associate Professor in the Department of Psychiatry at the Yale School of Medicine and Coordinator of Psychology Training in the Division of Substance Abuse. His research focuses on the assessment and treatment implications of personality traits, subtypes and disorders among substance dependent patients.

Kathleen M. Carroll PhD is a Professor of Psychiatry at the Yale University School of Medicine and Scientific Director of the Center for Psychotherapy Development at Yale. The author of over 190 journal articles, chapters and books, Dr Carroll's research and clinical interests lie in the area of developing, specifying and evaluating behavioural and pharmacologic treatment for substance use disorders.

Daryle D. Deering, Registered Nurse, is currently a lecturer at the National Addiction Centre in New Zealand, and Director of Mental Health Nursing Practice for the Canterbury District Health Board. She has worked extensively as a clinician and clinical manager in alcohol and drug youth mental health services. She is currently completing a doctoral thesis on methadone treatment (client profile, health status, satisfaction with treatment and routine outcome evaluation).

Gian Paolo Guelfi is a psychiatrist, who worked in many psychiatric services, and was in charge of the Addiction Unit in Genova, Italy 1993–1999. Formerly President of the SITD (Italian Society of the Addictions), he founded and is at present President of the Centre for Motivation and Change (CMC-Italia), the organisation of trainers in motivational interviewing in Italy.

Susi Harris qualified in 1984 from Southampton Medical School and took up various hospital posts in London, Torquay and Burnley before eventually settling on GP training. She worked as a GP principal in Hebden Bridge in West Yorkshire for ten years. She became a facilitator for the local Shared Care for Drug Misuse scheme for two years and is now the Lead Clinician in Substance Misuse for Calderdale. She is also the Moderator for the Substance Misuse Management in General Practice Forum. She was part of the team which wrote the Part 1 Certificate in Drug Misuse for the Royal College of General Practitioners, and she recently co-edited the electronic modules for the course.

Ronald M. Kadden PhD is professor in the Department of Psychiatry at the University of Connecticut School of Medicine. His clinical orientation is cognitive-behavioural. He is an attending doctor in the Alcohol, Drug Abuse, and Psychiatric Day Hospital Program. His research focuses on treatment effectiveness for chemical dependence. He is co-author of two clinical manuals for treating alcohol and drug dependence.

Rob Kenyon BSc (Hons) DipHE is Associate Director, Primary Care Drug Treatment Directorate at Leeds Primary Care Trust, Honorary Lecturer at the Academic Unit for Primary Care at the University of Leeds and a member of the Higher Education Academy. He has worked in the addiction field for 14 years, has taught, supervised and accredited practitioners from a variety of professional backgrounds, and has published as both primary and contributory author. He was a trial trainer and supervisor for Motivational Enhancement Therapy in the United Kingdom Alcohol Treatment Trial.

Ian K. MacEwan's main activity is as Senior Project Manager, National Addiction Treatment Workforce Development Programme, Christchurch School of Medicine, New Zealand. He has 35 years of experience as a social worker, counsellor, teacher and supervisor.

Steve Martino PhD is an Associate Professor of Psychiatry (Psychology Section) at the Yale University School of Medicine. His work includes developing and studying adaptations of motivational interviewing (MI) for patients diagnosed with co-occurring psychiatric and substance abuse conditions, MI adherence and competence measures, and strategies for training community treatment program clinicians in MI.

Roger Roffman is Professor of Social Work at the University of Washington where he also directs the Innovative Programs Research Group. He is co-editor of *Cannabis Dependence: Its Nature, Consequences, and Treatment.*

Ian Russell has been Founding Professor of Public Health at the University of Wales, Bangor since October 2002. He is a career public health researcher who specialises in the design, conduct and analysis of pragmatic randomised trials to evaluate complex interventions. He was an early protagonist of both patient-assessed measures of health outcome within trials and systematic reviews to synthesise the findings of trials. Ian was educated at Cambridge and founded the Department of Health Sciences in York. He holds Fellowships in the Royal College of General Practitioners, the Royal College of Physicians of Edinburgh, and the Faculty of Public Health.

Belinda Scrivings has been a part-time GP for 13 years and has always been interested in the psychological aspects of family medicine. Recently she became a GP trainer and is using her motivational skills in training doctors to become general practitioners.

J. Douglas Sellman, psychiatrist, has been Director of the National Addiction Centre in New Zealand, since 1996. He has recently been promoted to a Personal Chair in Psychiatry and Addiction Medicine at the Christchurch School of Medicine & Health Sciences, University of Otago. Academic highlights include a national postgraduate training programme, a two-week Addiction Medicine block course for final year medical students, PhD supervision for nine students investigating a wide range of addiction-related topics, and internationally recognised research on the effectiveness of motivation interviewing. He has 67 peer-reviewed papers and book chapters published, as well as two books and 10 monographs.

Valter Spiller PhD is a psychologist and psychotherapist, working in the Italian National Health Service since 1986 and in the field of addiction since 1992. He is a specialist in Clinical Criminology and in Family Therapy. He is author of several published studies about motivation for change in Italy. He is also a founder member of CMC-Italia, the Italian Association of Motivational Interviewing Trainers.

Karen L. Steinberg is Assistant Professor of Psychiatry at the University of Connecticut Medical School and a clinical psychologist. She teaches and conducts research in psychotherapy and developmental psychopathology, has published articles on substance abuse treatment, and has recently edited a CSAT treatment manual focused on integrative psychotherapy for marijuana dependence.

Valeria Zavan is a psychiatrist and specialist in medical toxicology at the University of Padua. She has been working in an Addiction Service with clinical and research interests since 1992 on which she has published national articles.

Acknowledgements

Our thanks to Melanie Barker for her early role in organising the editorial management process, and to Paula Singleton and Belinda Savage for hours of meticulous and good-humoured attention in ensuring the completion of this book.

We also wish to acknowledge how much we owe to the patients and colleagues who have over the years stimulated our interest in, and expanded our understanding of, motivational interviewing.

Section I

Reflections and a model

Chapter 1

What is motivational dialogue?

Gillian Tober and Duncan Raistrick
with original dialogue from Belinda Scrivings

Introduction

This book is about *motivational dialogue* as a style of treatment delivery which is adaptable and applicable to interventions for addictive as well as many other problem behaviours. All of these behaviours can be characterised as things that people like to do or that have some utility – in psychological terms the consequences of the behaviours are reinforcing in some way, that is to say that the behaviour is likely to be repeated. The behaviour may be something relatively harmless, such as eating chocolate or playing golf, or may fall within those behaviours often described as addictions, such as injecting heroin or smoking. The whole spectrum of behaviours has the potential to be harmful but those coming under the umbrella of addictive behaviours are commonly associated with physical and mental ill-health, psychological or social problems, or a combination of these. Changing any behaviour that we like doing is difficult, involves the resolution of conflict or ambivalence about the behaviour and is likely to be unstable at least at first. Of course the wish or need to change a problematic behaviour is usually associated with the intention of improving health or social functioning, or sometimes with the aim of preventing health or social problems in the future. In order to avoid confusion with specific motivational treatments we refer to motivational dialogue as a style in which to deliver treatments and converse with people who are seeking help with addiction problems. In this book we will look at motivational therapies in general and specifically at the application of motivational dialogue as a style of delivering addiction treatment which practitioners may wish to consider for use with other conditions that are likely to be responsive, for example weight watching, compliance with diabetes management, or excessive sexual behaviour, but also outside the treatment setting, for example in supervision of therapists.

The book has taken shape over a number of years of experience in practising, teaching and supervising motivational therapies with different professional groups ranging from addiction treatment specialists, smoking cessation advisors, community and hospital psychiatric nurses and doctors, primary care doctors, nurses and counsellors, midwives, hospital accident and emergency staff, medical and surgical ward staff, the criminal justice system, teachers at secondary and tertiary education levels, and also from our experience in measuring its delivery and effectiveness. We have assembled examples of applications in different settings, examined the evidence we have assessed as being relevant to our task and discussed the relevant theory from which the approach is derived.

Some terminological considerations

Why have we called the book *Motivational Dialogue*? It is not our intention to change the name of motivational interviewing but this term has come to be associated with the delivery of a specific treatment modality. We think that at its most basic, motivational dialogue is a way of talking to people where the purpose and content are different from having a chat. Such purposeful talking is about helping a person to think in a different way. The general intention is to reduce harm and to maximise the potential for improving an individual's circumstances. The term motivational dialogue emphasises the essential two-way nature of the therapeutic exchange – it is more about the skills of the therapist than it is about an effective treatment. The principle central to motivational dialogue is of a two-way discussion with interdependent parts which progresses in an incremental way. The therapist (a term we will use in a generic fashion, whether we are referring to a physician, a counsellor or any other professional) is guided by the motivational state and progress made by the client (for simplicity we have used this term throughout whether we are referring to a patient, a teenager or any other kind of service user), continually gauging the mood and meaning of their statements and matching their responses to take the next step forward. Therapist activity is determined by the client. There is an overall plan, a guiding sense of direction, which the therapist pursues. But progress is possible only on the basis of the client's statements and expressions of feeling. Thus the term dialogue in the title refers to the essential to and fro, the interdependence of therapist and client in facilitating cognitive movement in the direction of change.

We also decided on the term motivational dialogue to distinguish what we are discussing as a style of consultation which can be applied to different structured psychosocial treatments, of which there are many including motivational interventions, or more generally as a style of doing what we do, whether this is behavioural change, harm reduction interventions, pharmacological treatments, after-care and so forth. Our aim is to promote the understanding of the approach as a style of dialogue, applicable in different settings, in differing motivational contexts, for a variety of ends with the variety of behaviours and to distinguish these from stand alone, structured motivational interventions such as motivational enhancement therapy or motivational interviewing.

What is it that informs our understanding of how we set the agenda for promoting motivational change? The stages of change model of Prochaska and DiClemente (1983) made a ground-breaking contribution to new thinking in the nature and design of treatments for addiction problems. It had an illuminating effect on the way that health and social care practitioners understood change in addictive behaviours by describing the commonly experienced challenges of resistance and ambivalence as an integral part of the change process. It has been applied beyond the bounds of addictive behaviours to the task of adopting new behaviours, whether these involve compliance with a treatment regimen following diagnosis, or to the adoption of a healthier lifestyle through exercise, diet and changing daily routines. In doing so the model was successful in giving optimism to therapists through an understanding that there were different tasks to be undertaken at different stages of change, that failure to change right away was not the same as failure to change, and that different interventions could profitably be performed by different people working in collaboration.

The model of change gave impetus to the debate on the nature of change, the prerequisites of change and the way that treatment might harness the naturally occurring processes of change. There is evidence from the assessment of stage of change that motivation is an important variable in predicting the outcome of efforts to change whether these efforts are channelled through self-determination or addiction treatments. Unfortunately the stages of change model has not led to stage-matched treatments. This has been disappointing since it makes intuitive sense to design and deliver treatments appropriate to the different stages. However, Tober (2002) has argued elsewhere that the ingredients of treatments which target stage of change might be more subtle than the comparisons of one treatment with another have allowed, as for example in Project MATCH where the treatment specifically designed to target motivation, namely MET, did not show greater efficacy in people less prepared for change than the two treatments thought better to serve those who were ready to change, namely cognitive behavioural coping skills training and a twelve step facilitation approach (Project MATCH Research Group 1997). Close scrutiny of those treatments reveals that they all contained components which addressed the client's motivational stage of change in the pursuit of motivational change. A 'heuristic device' the model of change may well be (Davidson 1998) but having engaged the practitioner in thinking about the question of motivation, does it then help in the making of an accurate assessment of motivation and in designing an intervention matched to that assessment? In our teaching we have found it both helpful and unhelpful. On the one hand, the model draws attention to the possibility that different motivational states determine different behavioural outcomes; on the other hand we have witnessed the way that practitioners may be encouraged to think of motivation in unrealistically simplistic terms. The model might encourage people to think about multiple levels of motivation, but not so much as a fluctuating balance, a process in which change occurs at quite different rates in different people, that rarely follows a uniform path and that is multi-layered. Some of the complexity and interactions between different components of motivation at each of the stages of change is shown up in evidence reported in Chapter 3. In the implications for practice in Chapters 12 and 13 we explore further the way that motivational dialogue can be harnessed to arrive at an understanding of motivational balance while avoiding the pitfalls inherent in assigning a categorical definition such as motivational stage. While the debate about the scientific integrity of the model is played out (Davidson 1992, Sutton 2005), practitioners will continue to be inspired by its use as a set of organising principles for determining the starting point of treatment and for setting the short-term goals of treatment.

What is the history of motivational interviewing?

A brief and selective history of motivational interviewing is presented here to highlight the simple, first and central principles of the approach, which have been elaborated over the years into a complex web of strategies, tactics, micro-skills, clinical principles, and numerous definitions of sub categories of each of these.

Motivational interviewing was initially described as a pragmatic solution to the problem of confrontation in counselling problem drinkers (Miller 1983). Miller observed that confrontation tended to elicit denial and avoidance of further discussion, and in his eloquent first description of the method he presented motivational interviewing more as a common sense and pragmatic approach based upon sound principles derived from evidence for effective counselling practice. Some of these principles, specifically accurate empathy, positive regard and a non-judgemental approach, described and evaluated as long ago as the 1950s by Carl Rogers (Rogers 1957), are shown time and time again to be associated with improved therapeutic outcomes, and can be harnessed to coax the client towards motivational change by eliciting client-perceived concerns and client-defined aspirations. While the client-centred approach described by Rogers has come to be associated with a 'non-directive' counselling style, Miller applied the principles to the development of an agenda-driven, directive style while maintaining a non-confrontational approach; the challenge for the practitioner has been in the reconciliation of these hitherto contradictory components of counselling, that is in combining a non-confrontational with a directive style.

The immediately positive response with which Rogers' paper was received prompted exploration of this style of counselling and a commitment to investigate the claims made in that early paper, namely that motivational interviewing would make a difference to treatment commitment, adherence and outcome. One early study was designed to investigate the impact of the awareness raising strategy of providing objective feedback, described in Miller's (1983) paper. A structured intervention, the Drinker's Check-up, consisted of an assessment session and a single session of feedback, with a follow-up appointment at six weeks (Miller *et al.* 1988). Here the point was that if people receive personalised, objective feedback delivered in a factual, non-judgemental way with the opportunity to explore their thoughts and feelings about the consequences of their drinking and what their options are without feeling forced into change, they would be more likely to engage in subsequent treatment of their alcohol dependence.

Studies designed to examine how the method performed in comparison to other established methods were conducted. An early example was the comparison with a confrontational style of counselling people with drinking problems (Miller *et al.* 1993) commonly used in the USA but probably also in the majority of those countries adopting an essentially disease framework of understanding. The components of the eliciting style included listening, restructuring and offering support, thus creating an atmosphere of a therapeutic alliance, whereas the components of the confrontational style included head on disputes, challenging, disagreeing, incredulity, emphasising negative client characteristics and sarcasm, leaving the reader wondering why anyone would come back to see counsellors working in this way. The investigators found that the more confrontational the therapist, the more resistant was the client in acknowledging their problems and thinking about change. They also found that more arguments between counsellor and client occurred in those sessions. Perhaps most important was that they found a difference in drinking outcomes a full 24 months later, with the clients experiencing less in-session conflict drinking significantly less than the clients experiencing more conflict with their therapist during their counselling sessions.

Many studies of motivational interviewing have followed on from these starting points and those which have a significant bearing on helping people to understand and practise the approach will be discussed further. Particularly we want to emphasise the studies in which motivational interviewing has been contrasted with other approaches because we want to know whether what therapists do makes any difference.

There is evidence in the form of meta-analyses that motivational interviewing or adaptations of motivational interviewing (AMIs) are effective. Comparisons have been made of motivational interviewing and AMIs against (1) no treatment or placebo, (2) active treatment or treatment as usual; and of motivational interviewing as a prelude to further treatment against further treatment alone. Motivational interviewing and AMIs have been used for the treatment of a variety of problem behaviours beyond alcohol and drug misuse including smoking, HIV risk and diet and exercise (see Dunn *et al.* 2001; Burke *et al.* 2003; Hettema *et al.* 2005).

Motivational interviewing and AMIs are as effective as other active treatments but generally briefer. In alcohol misuse treatment trials, effect sizes range from approximately 0 to just over 3.0 and in drug misuse treatment trials from approximately 0 to nearly 2.0, but most typically the effect sizes are in the middle range of 0.3 to 0.6. The best results have been found with weight reduction treatment and the least good with smoking cessation and reducing HIV risk behaviours.

There is considerable variation in effectiveness even within trials, suggesting variable treatment delivery across agencies. This highlights the need to evaluate training outcome and delivery of treatment, as discussed in Chapters 6 and 10, in order to understand the impact of therapist effects. Motivational interviewing and AMI effects occur early in treatment and tend to persist albeit with some diminution. These treatments are particularly good at engaging individuals and enhancing other treatments. There is some evidence of less effectiveness when delivery is manual driven. This latter finding may be explained by excessively rigid adherence to a manual and failure to respond to the client's motivational state. The purpose of a manual is better seen as a source of structure or a framework within which the therapist can work.

We conclude from the literature that if you practise well, with conviction, in the delivery of a treatment that has an evidence base, the likelihood is that you will do good (no, we do not mean 'do well', though that too). Motivational dialogue is one way of doing this.

The scope of the book

Much has been written about motivational interviewing and we wondered whether there was more to be said. We did, however, want to contribute to the debate on whether this is a style of delivery or itself a treatment. We have been particularly keen to broaden the application of motivational interviewing. A number of the authors of this book have been involved in teaching motivational interviewing for many years, either as a style of counselling or as a structured treatment or both, in the addictive behaviours and related fields. It has been our overwhelming impression that it is not easy to teach, and that there are those who learn it more easily than others. Many people want to practise motivational interviewing and they have a variety of professional backgrounds, educational careers and previous training experiences. The evidence derived from independent ratings of competence, and our experience in assessing competence in those we teach, tells us that some practitioners are better able to learn to practise; equally some methods of teaching are more effective than others in helping people achieve competence to practise. We learnt interesting lessons that we wish to share, lessons that go beyond reporting the results of those studies.

The rapid expansion of motivational interviewing practice over the twenty years since its initial description probably owes more to the popularity of the approach than it does to the strength of its evidence base. The breadth of application in the addiction treatment field, which we hope to illustrate, is one indication of its popularity; the sheer number of training events and courses that have been delivered in response to demand across the world are further testimony to this popularity. Later in this chapter and repeatedly throughout the book we will look at what we think it is that makes this style of counselling so popular.

What does this book aim to do? Primarily it is designed for practitioners in the field of addiction treatment with the purpose of increasing the understanding of motivational issues in treatment and facilitating practice through an appreciation of the use of motivational dialogue. One of the ways we want to encourage the reader in thinking about motivational dialogue is by referring to its broad applicability, not just across the domains of health related behaviour change but in everyday life. Thus while we have decided to focus our attention on subjects within the addiction treatment arena, we give the reader an example, at the end of this chapter, of the applicability of motivational dialogue in a domestic setting, thereby demonstrating its versatility. In Chapter 2, the second scene setter, we discuss the question of limitations and we explore a specific, and in our view insufficiently addressed, challenge in many cognitive treatments of addiction problems, namely the challenge of treating the substance dependence rather than just the use of the substance. We look at why we think that motivational dialogue is the best approach for addressing this most difficult of tasks. Chapter 3 describes research which develops the stages of change model in looking at motivational change and its relationship with behavioural change. It is included here as an aid to exploring different factors that affect readiness to change, its measurement and implications for targeting treatment endeavours more accurately.

The next section of the book examines the way the evidence base for motivational therapies might be approached. Chapter 4 provides an exploration of the question of developing and critically appraising the evidence base. How are we best able to assess the effectiveness and efficacy of the approach in a way that is meaningful, by being relevant and applicable, to routine practice in the UK and in countries with similar health and social care arrangements and institutions, as well as similar approaches to understanding the nature of addiction? Chapter 5 reviews the evidence for integrating motivational and other therapies and addresses the question 'Is motivational interviewing enough?' While much of the evidence does suggest that in general it is as effective as treatments of longer duration that include behavioural and social components, there is evidence that suggests that some groups of people, those with co-existing mental illness and multiple problems, might do better with additional treatments.

The third section of the book is concerned with learning and practising motivational dialogue skills. Chapter 6 reviews methods of training in a number of studies, providing the reader with case material for illustration, and explores methods of rating the delivery of treatment for the purpose of supervision and evaluation of its delivery. Chapter 7 describes a single case of individual supervision-based learning, illustrating the principle of practising supervision in the style of motivational dialogue when teaching the approach.

The fourth section of the book uses selected research reports to illustrate a range of motivational therapies. In Chapter 8 the authors describe evidence important for those who have been trained in a non-directive style of counselling, some of whom have found elements of motivational interviewing a particular challenge. Gaining an understanding of how motivational therapies differ from a non-directive approach when there are so many familiar components helps to answer the question 'How is this different from what I do already?' Chapter 9 describes a study of training social workers to deliver a motivational interviewing intervention in a criminal justice setting, picking up on the challenges and achievements of training staff who might previously have worked in a non-directive and non-coercive setting. In Chapter 10 we discuss our experience in the UK Alcohol Treatment Trial. Training and supervising practitioners across the spectrum of professional disciplines typically employed in the UK alcohol problems treatment field posed new challenges for teaching and maintaining consistent practice over time and some insights into meeting these challenges are discussed. Chapter 11 returns to the single case description format taking an example of smoking cessation intervention in a primary care setting.

The final section of the book is dedicated to examples of motivational dialogue in practice. We have taken the kinds of interventions currently proposed in the UK Models of Care for alcohol and for drugs (Models of care for alcohol misusers [MoCAM], NTA in development; Models of care for the treatment of adult drug misusers [MoCDM], NTA 2002) and written extensive 'scripts' illustrating how to deliver these in a motivational dialogue style. Chapter 12 is concerned with the core psychosocial therapies including assessment and Chapter 13 with special topics such as pharmacotherapies and working with people who suffer from mental health problems. There is nothing prescriptive about the therapist 'scripts', rather, therapists are expected to understand the principles involved and then adopt words and phrases that suit their personal style.

We have found that in order to practise motivational dialogue competently, it is essential to understand the underpinning principles, however, understanding is insufficient to guarantee competent practice. Indeed there is a bit of a discrepancy between the numbers of people who can engage in insightful discussion and who can practise consistently and to a high standard. Evidence for the outcomes of different styles of training (Miller *et al.* 2004; Miller and Mount 2001) supports the need to participate in observed supervised practice. The book as a whole makes extensive use of examples of motivational dialogue applied in many different circumstances.

An everyday example of motivational dialogue

Before moving on, we decided to include here an account of the everyday use of motivational dialogue which illustrates our point about its utility in day-to-day interactions. The example is given by a primary care physician, who attended training in motivational interviewing and decided to see what would come of a little homework. She applied what she had learned to a domestic situation. First she describes the setting:

> Sam, aged 14, is energetic, articulate and intelligent. He plays rugby, is passionate about mountain biking and is very competitive. Amy, aged 10, is quieter and more studious but equally intelligent and articulate although more reserved. She attends the Junior Department of the same school as her brother. She likes to play netball.
>
> The mother describes that during the past year the two children have been arguing a lot. Typically Amy might goad her brother, he would retaliate with verbal insults to which she would reply, and he would quickly follow with a physical assault. Alternatively a fight might break out over a minor dispute. Amy would invariably scream as loud as possible to attract her mother's attention and Sam would often be reprimanded as by now Amy would probably be crying. Family tensions have been rising and the mother feels all her interactions with her children involve discipline and no fun. The mother is beginning to realise that she is automatically telling Sam off before ascertaining the details of any particular conflict.
>
> Following a particularly nasty fight during a game of 'Risk', their mother decided to intervene using motivational dialogue techniques. She describes the purpose of the intervention thus: to improve the siblings' relationship and to reduce family tension. There follows a verbatim report of the dialogue under headings following the structure of a motivational interview and commencing with a description setting the scene.
>
> The school holidays bring particular difficulties. This Easter holiday was no exception. Fighting between Sam and Amy had become more aggressive and efforts from their mother to control the situation seemed to be exacerbating the situation. The game of Risk has the aim of world

domination and when Amy conquered the African continent Sam's self control broke down. He dived onto Amy, pinning her to the floor, pummelling her. The allied forces (aka the parents) separated the children and a desperate mother made a mental note to try a new approach. Later that day the following motivational dialogue occurred between the mother and Sam and Amy.

Bringing up the subject

Mother to children: You don't seem to be getting on very well at the moment and neither of you seem especially happy these days. What do you think the problem could be?

Sam: You always blame me for things I don't do. You always tell me off – never her. She gets me into trouble. You always believe her and she lies to you all the time.

Amy says nothing.

Eliciting benefits of the undesirable behaviour

The mother did not ask her children about this but rightly or wrongly made the assumption that each child was gaining something from their behaviour. She hypothesised that Amy was seeking attention and gained pleasure from getting Sam into trouble. Sam probably was able to release some tension by physically attacking his sister. He was getting revenge for her tale telling.

Eliciting the disadvantages

Mother to Amy: What is the problem about playing with Sam?

Amy to Mother: He makes me play with him and when I don't want to anymore. He's horrible to me.

Sam to Mother: She always gets me into trouble when I haven't done anything wrong. She gets away with everything and you always believe her – not me. I've never heard you tell her off.

Listing concerns

Mother to children: This is obviously very upsetting for you both but it's really good that we are talking about it . . .

Mother to Sam: Tell me how you feel about what is going on . . .

Sam to Mother:	I hate her – but she hates me (close to tears). You love Amy more than me.
Mother to Sam:	I'm sorry that you believe that – but it really isn't true. I love you both the same.
Mother to Amy:	How do you feel about all this?
Amy to Mother:	He hates me.
Sam:	No, I don't.

Eliciting self-motivational statements

Mother to children:	If you don't want to carry on like this, what do you want to do?
Sam to Amy:	I'd like to play with you and do things together.
Sam to Mother:	I'd like it if you would stop telling me off all the time.
Mother to Sam:	Yes, I'll try – how could you do things differently?
Sam replies:	Stop hitting her.
Mother to Sam:	And I'll try to stop presuming that you are always doing something wrong.
Mother to Amy:	What do you think that you could do to make things better between you and Sam?
Amy replies:	Stop saying horrible things and getting him into trouble.
Mother to Amy:	That sounds like a good idea – do you think you can do that?
Amy to mother:	Yes (she looks relieved).

The outcome of this intervention was that the relationship between brother and sister calmed down, as did the mother. Mother remembered to revisit the children's intentions by having short conversations every few days praising their good behaviour and repeating the negotiation when things seemed to be reverting to the previous pattern. This style of negotiation became the norm when there seemed to be a conflict brewing. The children appeared to get into it and would insist to each other that they had to negotiate.

This example of practice followed training in motivational interviewing as a means of treating addictive behaviours. This student was persuaded that she might consolidate what she had learned during the training course by commencing practice right away. Beyond that she was sufficiently convinced that motivational interviewing could be adapted as a way of dealing with the potential conflict that results from two or more people seeing things from a different point of view, having different perspectives; she saw the possible wider application of what she had learned. This illustrates why we are using the term motivational dialogue to describe the therapist style of working not the intervention. The temptation to tell another person what to do, especially when things are going wrong, is often difficult to resist; one of the greater challenges is getting people to practise resisting this temptation and to experience that the desired outcome can be achieved more reliably by using motivational dialogue.

We hope that this book will help practitioners to think about their style of treatment delivery. In describing motivational dialogue we have done no more than extract its key principles and describe how these might be applied to a wide variety of interventions or treatment modalities. We also hope that practitioners, trainers and researchers will be inspired to explore new methods for developing and evaluating its practice.

References

Burke, B.L., Arkowitz, H. and Menchola, M. (2003) 'The efficacy of motivational interviewing: a meta-analysis of controlled clinical trials', *Journal of Consulting and Clinical Psychology*, 71: 843–861.

Davidson, R. (1992) 'Prochaska and DiClemente's model of change: a case study?', *British Journal of Addiction*, 87: 821–822.

Davidson, R. (1998) 'The transtheoretical model: a critical overview' in W. Miller and N. Heather (eds) *Treating Addictive Behaviours*, 2nd edn, New York: Plenum Press.

Dunn, C., Deroo, L. and Rivara, F.P. (2001) 'The use of brief interventions adapted from motivational interviewing across behavioral domains: a systematic review', *Addiction*, 96: 1725–1742.

Hettema, J., Steele, J., and Miller, W.R. (2005) 'Motivational interviewing', *Annual Review of Clinical Psychology*, 1: 91–111.

Miller, W. (1983) 'Motivational interviewing with problem drinkers', *Behavioural Psychotherapy*, 11: 147–172.

Miller, W.R. and Mount, K.A. (2001) 'A small study of training in motivational interviewing: does one workshop change clinician and client behaviour?', *Behavioural and Cognitive Psychotherapy*, 29: 457–471.

Miller, W.R., Sovereign, R.G. and Krege, B. (1988) 'Motivational interviewing with problem drinkers: II. The Drinker's Check-up as a preventive intervention', *Behavioural Psychotherapy*, 16: 251–268.

Miller, W.R., Benefield, R.G. and Tonigan, J.S. (1993) 'Enhancing motivation for change in problem drinking: a controlled comparison of two therapist styles', *Journal of Consulting and Clinical Psychology*, 61: 455–461.

Miller, W.R., Yahne, C.E., Moyers, T.B., Martinez, J. and Pirritano, M. (2004) 'A randomised trial of methods to help clinicians learn motivational interviewing', *Journal of Consulting and Clinical Psychology*, 72, 1050–1062.

NTA (National Treatment Agency for Substance Misuse) (in development) *Models of care for alcohol misusers* (MoCAM), London: National Treatment Agency.

NTA (National Treatment Agency for Substance Misuse) (2002) *Models of Care for the Treatment of Drug Misusers: Promoting quality, efficiency and effectiveness in drug misuse treatment services in England*, London: National Treatment Agency.

Prochaska, J.O. and DiClemente, C.C. (1983) 'Stages and processes of self-change of smoking: toward an integrative model of change', *Journal of Consulting and Clinical Psychology*, 51: 390–395.

Project MATCH Research Group (1997) 'Project MATCH secondary a priori hypotheses', *Addiction*, 92: 1671–1698.

Rogers, C.R. (1957) 'The necessary and sufficient conditions for therapeutic personality change', *Journal of Consulting Psychology*, 21: 95–103.

Sutton, S. (2005) 'Another nail in the coffin of the transtheoretical model? A comment on West (2005)', *Addiction*, 100: 1044–1045.

Tober, G. (2002) 'Evidence based practice – still a bridge too far for addiction counsellors?' *Drugs: Education, Prevention and Policy*, 9: 17–20.

Chapter 2

Motivation and barriers to change

Duncan Raistrick

Introduction

This chapter is concerned with understanding possible limitations to motivational therapies and indeed motivational dialogue in general. The results of motivational interviewing studies have been mixed which is an indication of the complexity of interactions involved in building motivation and progressing to actual behaviour change (see Chapter 3) but also a caution that motivational therapies have their limitations. In a systematic review of 29 studies using motivational interviewing for the treatment of a variety of conditions, Dunn *et al.* (2001) found that three-quarters of the substance misuse studies had significant effect sizes, ranging from 0.30 to 0.95; treatments directed at weight reduction were most effective while those for smoking cessation were least effective. In the detail of some of these studies there is evidence that people not yet ready to change and those with a moderate severity of dependence benefit most from motivational interventions. It makes sense that people who are severely dependent on a substance may need more than motivation in order to change and that those who are already motivated do not need motivational therapies at all. This is the starting point for this chapter.

Apparently spontaneous change

Motivational dialogue is about helping people to decide that they want to change a particular behaviour. An essential part of this process is to increase the frequency of change talk on the grounds that people believe what they hear themselves say rather than believing what friends or professionals say. There is a good relationship between what people say they will achieve and what they actually achieve. People are constantly changing what they do with their lives and often do so without giving the change much thought. At some intellectual level, however, it must be the case that individuals create a decisional balance sheet, check this against their core values and, most of the time but certainly not inevitably, move to a logical and predictable shift in lifestyle. Many instances of change appear to be naturally occurring or spontaneous in that they follow an automated process of weighing up the good things and not so good things about the change.

Some examples of apparently spontaneous change will help to inform an understanding of the change process and barriers to change. Consider the following two situations:

> Jon is a 28-year-old man who has been married for two years and has a son aged 18 months. Jon has an average income working as a painter and decorator. His passion is to play football which he has done since being at school. He plays in the first team of an amateur club and his wife enjoys supporting the team. He has decided to hang up his boots next season.

> Michelle is a 32-year-old single woman. She has an 8-year-old daughter. Her partner has recently left and is living with a younger woman. Michelle works as a secretary and has an active social life, mainly with female friends. Her friends are fashion conscious but were surprised when Michelle came into work with her hair dyed red.

In the case of Jon the decision to stop playing football seems rational and a consequence of growing older. At 28, first team football is physically challenging and also he may now see it as more important to spend time with his family. Importantly there have been no negative consequences of playing football, rather the perception that the activity is at odds with his new and future lifestyle is the basis for Jon's decision to stop football now. If this interpretation is correct then it can be assumed that Jon has a core value about the quality of family life which takes precedence over other things he likes to do. Michelle's decision does seem to have been triggered by a negative life event, namely her partner leaving. She has made a decision based on wanting to feel good about herself. The fact that she has chosen to dye her hair red as the means of achieving this may seem irrational, even to Michelle's friends, but may denote an attitude that, having been hurt in the way she has, she wants to present herself as being independent and unconcerned with conventional attempts to appear attractive to the opposite sex.

These two cases illustrate how important lifestyle decisions might be reached in everyday life. In both cases the driving force is a mismatch between core beliefs, that is 'what sort of person do I want to be?', and present circumstances, 'what sort of person am I now?' Individuals do not tolerate this kind of psychological imbalance and need to resolve the mismatch either by a change in their core beliefs so that 'who I want to be' comes into line with 'the person I am now' or the other way about. The fact that core beliefs may be aberrant does not diminish this drive, rather it leads to seemingly irrational decision making.

In both of these examples it is probable that there will have been talk about making the changes before the commitment to change was actually made and carried out. The change talk might have been with family and friends, or it may have been that both Jon and Michelle talked to themselves as the means of deciding that they wanted to change and were able to do so. The desirability of a new behaviour or lifestyle is typically confirmed by others such as family or friends, the media and advertising, or local culture, but may also be a decision reached alone.

Addiction careers

If using or not using alcohol or other psychoactive drugs was as simple as reaching a rational decision and then acting upon it there would be no field of study called addiction and no practitioners engaged in the treatment of addictive behaviours. That said, a remarkable amount of apparently spontaneous change does occur in just the same way as any other behaviour change such as in the examples of Jon and Michelle. Without recourse to any kind of formal treatment, people move in and out of substance use categories such as abstinence, social, hazardous or harmful use, and dependence. This movement between substance use categories, with or without formal treatment, is referred to as a substance use career. This is not a career in the sense that someone may aspire to be a teacher or a footballer but rather in the sense that drinking or drug taking similarly becomes a dominant and sometimes defining part of the individual's life.

The influences over the use of or abstinence from different psychoactive substances change over the life cycle. For young people, substance use has a whole range of functions – it is about experimenting, rebelling, having fun and coping with problems. For young people the choice of substance has much to do with fashion, affordability and legality. Legality is something of a relative concept – for example, cannabis is so widely used and the subject of such ambivalence by the legislature that many consider its use to be socially acceptable. Use of more definitely illicit drugs, such as cocaine or heroin, tends to be associated with anti-social behaviours and the younger the age at which this kind of illicit drug use commences, the later into life it will persist.

As in the example of Jon, maturity is usually associated with giving up behaviours that are incompatible with new responsibilities and new aspirations – this applies to substance use as much as football. Those adults who continue to drink too much or misuse other drugs tend to move in and out of problem use. The number of adults remaining as problem drinkers or drug users steadily declines because of the increased mortality rate and a shift into stable (permanent) abstinence. Individuals with severe problems or dependence are more likely to move to stable abstinence because they are more likely to recognise the need for behaviour change and are more likely therefore to be help seekers. Similarly people with mild problems or dependence are likely to move to very occasional use or stable abstinence because they are readily attracted by alternative activities. It is those individuals with a moderate severity of problems or dependence that tend to continue with problematic levels of drinking or substance misuse. The 60-year follow up by Vaillant (2003) illustrates these generalisations. He tracked two socially distinct cohorts in the USA – 268 Harvard undergraduate students and 456 disadvantaged Boston adolescents and for each decade of follow-up found movement between abstinence, controlled use and harmful use. Paradoxically the disadvantaged Boston cohort were more likely to achieve stable abstinence – they had a greater severity of dependence and were unable to sustain periods of controlled drinking whereas the Harvard cohort coped with longer periods of harmful drinking which were associated with a higher mortality rate.

So, it is the severity dimension for both problems and dependence that limits how likely it is for people to make changes in their substance use behaviour simply because they have decided to do so or, put another way, by motivation alone. So-called spontaneous recovery from problem drinking or drug taking is often triggered by some life event that is inconsistent with such behaviour: marriage or the establishment of an important relationship, employment especially involving promotion or a work ethos intolerant of alcohol or drug use, financial restrictions, geographical relocation, religious or other group activity intolerant of alcohol or drug use, and adequate housing provision. The experience of additional positive life events is important to prevent relapse. The power of major life events to trigger change dramatically illustrates that even severely dependent drinkers or drug takers have the capacity for a repertoire of behaviours and that for many people formal treatment is not the vehicle for changing their substance use. This should not be interpreted as meaning that treatment does not work rather that treatment is one of a number of routes out of damaging substance use.

Motivational interventions

There is a substantial evidence base, including at least 14 meta analyses or systematic reviews, all of which reach the conclusion that brief interventions, which include 5 minutes of simple advice through to 30 minutes of more structured therapy, are effective at delivering improvements across the major outcome domains for hazardous or harmful drinkers. The evidence base for the effectiveness of brief interventions applied to the use and misuse of illicit drugs is less extensive but nonetheless generally positive. What is remarkable is that the effect of brief motivational interventions persists: in a meta analysis of 72 clinical trials Hettema *et al.* (2005) found a mean effect size for motivational interviewing when averaged across all reported outcome variables, was 0.77 up to one month later, 0.39 at 1–3 months, 0.31 at 3–6 months, 0.30 at 6–12 months and this has been found for both alcohol and some illicit drug use. In other words initial treatment gains are substantial but quickly fall to about half and then are maintained for at least a year.

Typically motivational interventions are brief and rapidly effective. Given what has been said about spontaneous movement in and out of different categories of substance use and misuse there is no surprise here. One of two things happens while people are waiting for treatment – either the waiting period is seen as the last opportunity to drink or take drugs in which case people indulge as much as they are able, alternatively the waiting time is used to start changing behaviour in which case there are marked reductions in substance use if not abstinence by the time treatment begins (Rosengren *et al.* 2000). As many as 20 per cent of people referred to a specialist treatment centre will be abstinent from alcohol or other drugs at initial assessment. In other words people who are motivated to come for treatment are at least primed if not already embarking on the change process before they ever attend. If the demand on the service is such that a waiting list is inevitable then the waiting time can be constructively used, for example by giving people self-help tools or directing them to online help.

It is a common finding that psychosocial treatments for addiction problems, as with other psychotherapies, tend to produce similar outcomes – this has been referred to as the dodo bird effect. This generalisation holds true for treatments of different intensity, for example, both Project MATCH (Babor and Del Boca 2003) and the UK Alcohol Treatment Trial (UKATT Research Team 2005) found the briefer motivational treatment to be as effective as the more intensive treatments investigated. It is a mistake to conclude either that any treatment is as good as another or that there is no place for longer or more intensive interventions, rather the dodo bird effect is largely an artefact of trial design.

In *Alice in Wonderland* the dodo bird declared that all the animals had won the race and so all should have prizes, hence the expression 'dodo bird effect'. There is a scientific underpinning to the reason why psychotherapies tend to deliver the same results:

1 It is usual to compare a new treatment against a gold standard treatment, such as motivational enhancement therapy. If the new treatment is at least as good as the gold standard then the repertoire of effective treatments is extended – if it is better then it may become the new gold standard. The point is that clinicians will not invest in a trial of a new treatment unless there is good reason to suppose that it is effective.

2 The amount of outcome variance that can be attributed to the specific treatment is quite modest. Other variables, notably therapist characteristics, are important.
3 Most behaviour change occurs within the first three months of treatment and maintaining the change may then have more to do with exposure to positive life events and new sources of reinforcement than any specific treatment effect. Those individuals who have better education, more cohesive families, financial and psychological stability are more likely to have more positive life events.

The stages of change model might help to make sense of some possible limitations to using a motivational approach alone (see Chapter 3). What has come to be known as the precontemplation stage of change is characterised by a psychological equilibrium achieved by denial or rationalisation of any substance misuse problem – it follows that motivational strategies are the best therapy choice having the aim of creating some discrepancy between an individual's core values and the reality of their substance use here and now. By definition this discrepancy, or psychological conflict, already exists at the contemplation stage – again motivational interventions are the therapy of choice with the aim of moving to a good quality decision to change the substance misuse behaviour in order to match up to core values. The determination stage is characterised by consolidation of the decision to change in the form of an action plan. It is at the action stage that some barriers may present and prevent further progression. The hallmark features of the action stage are self efficacy and positive outcome expectancy for the specific change and self-esteem: in plain language, an individual must believe that they are able to change, that life will be better if change happens, and that change is worth bothering about. A barrier in any one of these areas might be unblocked by the use of motivational techniques, or might better be unblocked by behavioural methods in which the individual has the opportunity to experience the benefits of change with the attendant increase in confidence to achieve it, and improved self esteem as a result of having done so. The Stages of Change model (Joseph *et al.* 1999) gives helpful guidance in deciding which intervention to choose on the basis of an understanding of the tasks that need to be accomplished for motivational and behavioural change to occur and facilitates communication with other therapists. The model should not, however, be taken too literally as some behaviour change will occur before reaching the action stage, some barriers in the action stage may be overcome if motivation to change is strong enough, and sustaining motivation is important through the action and maintenance stages as well as in the earlier stages. Thus, in the action stage the main treatment may be a 12-step programme, a behavioural programme, a community reinforcement programme or a pharmacological detoxification programme. The point of motivational dialogue is that it can be integrated into the style in which all of these very different treatments are delivered (see Chapter 12) as a means of optimising the treatment delivery.

The therapist as a potential barrier to change

Therapists have the potential to do harm as well as good. Around 10–15 per cent of people entering treatment programmes actually get worse – how much this is a consequence of the treatment rather than client characteristics is not certain. Factors that seem to predict deterioration are lack of bonding, confrontation, high emotional arousal, deviancy modelling, lack of monitoring and low expectations from therapists (Moos 2005). The concept of a therapeutic alliance is now widely used as shorthand for describing the quality of relationship between therapist and service user (Meier *et al.* 2005).

Carl Rogers defined a school of therapy, variously known now as person or client centred, which depended upon the therapist, rather than a specific treatment, as the main agent of change – in essence he described the ingredients of what is now called a therapeutic relationship (Rogers 1957). There exists an accumulation of evidence from psychotherapy which both supports the characteristics described by Carl Rogers as important and also demonstrates that some therapists are more effective than others. More effective therapists are characterised as empathic, supportive, goal directed, helping and understanding, encouraging client autonomy and able to mobilise external resources. These characteristics are at the core of the motivational dialogue style of delivery. Less effective therapists are characterised as psychologically distant, overwhelmed, belittling and blaming, intrusive and controlling, avoiding difficult issues and self interested (Najavits and Weiss 1994). There is evidence that it is not the therapist alone who is the change agent rather it is the combination of the therapist and their ability to deliver a specific treatment (Carroll 2001). Whatever the treatment, the evidence suggests that there will be benefits from using a motivational dialogue delivery style.

Estimates as to how much of the outcome variance is accounted for by therapist characteristics range from 10 per cent to 60 per cent. The reason for this wide range is that recent studies, such as Project MATCH or the UK Alcohol Treatment Trial, have been designed in such a way as to minimise therapist variation which has been achieved by means of rigorous pre-trial training, supervision and use of manual guided therapy – nonetheless both trials had one or two therapists described as outliers. It is the older uncontrolled studies, which would now be considered unethical, that show up large differences in therapist performance. In one study, for example, on the outcome measure 'drug use' the best therapist achieved 34 per cent improvement and the worst therapist a 14 per cent worsening; on 'psychiatric status', the best an 82 per cent improvement, the worst a 1 per cent worsening averaged across their caseloads (Luborsky and O'Brien 1985). In part these differences are accounted for by the range of therapist styles and in part by therapists drifting from the therapy task.

Unsurprisingly those clients who have a positive perception of their therapist are more likely to stay in treatment and are more likely to improve across a number of outcome domains. It may be that individuals who are most committed to change will be positive about treatment irrespective of the therapist. This is certainly not the whole story – in any group of therapists it is usual to find one or two who have poor follow-up attendances. Therapist performance is a sensitive matter and needs to be handled with due care, however, when the therapist is so pivotal to a successful outcome poor performance cannot be ignored.

All clinical sessions, including initial assessment, should be predicated by the assumption that the client may not be seen again. It follows that the therapist needs to be skilled at quickly building a therapeutic alliance. Carl Rogers identified empathy as a main plank of the therapeutic relationship – this is not a variant of sympathy but means understanding what is happening from the client's perspective and making sure that the client is at the centre of the treatment process. The therapist can convey empathy by the way that they greet the client and convey warmth and positive regard from the outset. Attention to simple things can make an important difference. For example, when is it right to use first names, is it all right to wear traditional dress, what kind of religious symbols are acceptable, what kind of jewellery or body piercing is appropriate and what sort of overall dress code will avoid causing offence? An important expression of empathy is ensuring that the focus of attention is on the client not the therapist, hence the need for a neutral appearance. It may be true that a particular client will identify with a therapist who dresses and talks in a similar way to themselves but identifying too closely is not the same as showing empathy and, moreover, risks losing the objectivity that help seekers expect from professionals. Given that the one way in which the therapist presents him or her self has to work for all clients it is prudent to opt for something that is universally acceptable.

It is unlikely that a poor therapist will deliver good therapy or that use of a manual will transform the poor therapist, whereas an ineffective treatment may be rescued by an effective therapist. In other words therapists play a central role both in engaging individuals, particularly those who are least motivated, and in effectively delivering specific treatments. Some people are naturally gifted therapists, most others can be taught to be good therapists, and a few people will never make effective therapists. It follows that the training of therapists is important. The UK Alcohol Treatment Trial was noteworthy for undertaking a prospective study of therapist training. In this trial Tober and colleagues (2005) showed that therapists from a range of disciplines and educational achievement levels could be trained to be competent at both a motivational and social therapy. However, the time taken to achieve competence varied: motivational therapy required an average 244 days of training that included introductory sessions and real case practice (range 64–405 days), and social therapy an average of 181 days (range 81–303 days). The time taken was measured in days spent in the normal workplace, thus, as well as therapist characteristics, the timescales reflect organisational commitment to learning and availability of clients.

Psychological barriers to change

A logical limitation of motivational interventions is that they can only be expected to go as far as reaching the good quality decision to make changes – the determination stage of change. For some people, those with more social stability and psychological strengths, stopping or controlling drinking or drug use may automatically follow. Motivational interventions are not, however, restricted to early stages of change and they may also assist people to get through actual behavioural change, because motivation may flag when change seems too difficult, and to maintain change once it is achieved. For others, however, additional treatment will be indicated. So, motivational change is a likely prerequisite to behavioural change and motivational interventions may, therefore, form the initial element of an integrated treatment package. Equally motivational dialogue can be incorporated into other elements of an integrated treatment package (see Chapter 12). For example, the cognitive behavioural family of therapies and 12-step facilitation can readily be conducted using motivational dialogue. The purpose of doing so is to maintain and build on motivation throughout active treatment – if motivational strategies are used only in the initial phase of treatment then there is a risk that the strength of the decision to change will decay in amongst the ups and downs of the treatment programme.

Core beliefs

Core beliefs are an essential part of motivational dialogue. It is the discrepancy between current substance using behaviours and a person's core beliefs about their preferred or ideal behaviours that creates the potential for change. Core beliefs are generally hard to shift because they are most commonly seeded in childhood. Core beliefs are handed down from family values, cultural and religious teachings, and, in adolescence and later life, they are fed by the social norms accepted by friends and colleagues at work. The process of growing up forces core beliefs to be tested so that the mature adult acquires a balanced rather than absolute set of beliefs. For example, the childhood belief that *All mothers are nurturing* may in adult life become

Mothers are usually nurturing or *Drunken men are violent* becomes *Sometimes drinking leads to violence*. It may be that core beliefs do not soften but persist unattenuated into adulthood. This is likely in circumstances where a young person has been seriously traumatised: for example sexual abuse or being unable to rouse a parent injecting drugs are experiences that may shape core beliefs well into adulthood.

For those individuals where brief motivational interventions are most effective it is likely that core beliefs will be positive and functional. For example:

- A good mother is there for her children when she is needed – I am not there for my children when I am using heroin – I need to stop using heroin.
- Other people are at risk if I drink and drive – I do not want to kill anyone in a road accident – I need not to drink if I am driving.
- To progress at work I need to be focused and get on with people – using cocaine makes me productive but also makes me distractible and irritable – I need not to use cocaine at work.
- Drinking over 35 units a week will inevitably cause health problems – even though I don't feel drunk my average daily intake is approximately 50 units of alcohol – I need to stop drinking.

For individuals with longer substance misuse histories or with an accumulation of problems or with pre-existing mental health disorders the dominant core beliefs may well be negative and dysfunctional. For example:

- People who drink too much always end up as failures – I drink too much – I am a loser.
- Heroin users are all liars and thieves – I am a heroin user – no one will ever trust me.
- Benzodiazepines make people feel calm and cheerful – the situation I am in makes me feel nervous and depressed – I will feel better taking some drugs.
- I do not know anybody with a heroin habit that has ever got better – my habit is as bad as anybody I know – I am never going to stop needing heroin.

Motivational techniques depend upon finding a positive core belief which is incompatible with drinking or drug taking. A question such as 'what do you mind most about your drinking (or drug taking)?' may be helpful. Therapy in practice is often more difficult than expected from theory. It may require considerable skill to elicit any psychological conflict with core beliefs, it may be that the dominant core beliefs are so dysfunctional that they need to be avoided or worked upon, or it may simply be that the client has priorities that are more important than making a change in drinking or drug taking which, although desired, has yet to move to the top of their personal agenda.

Change beliefs

Social learning theory (Bandura 1977) underpins recent developments in most mainstream substance misuse treatment programmes. Foremost in the original description of social learning is the concept of *self-efficacy* which is 'the belief that a particular behaviour can be accomplished in order to achieve a particular outcome'. More recently outcome expectancy which is 'a belief that a given behaviour will lead to a particular outcome' has assumed greater importance. It is important to separate the two beliefs because an individual may be wholly confident that they can undertake a particular behaviour and that it will deliver a particular result, but if the result is not highly valued then it is unlikely that the behaviour will ever be executed. Self-efficacy beliefs vary in terms of how difficult a task might be – for example, cutting down on drinking may be seen as easily achievable whereas achieving total abstinence is not only a difficult but also a frightening prospect. Equally outcome expectancies vary in strength – to take the earlier example, cutting down a bit may be accurately assessed as having few positive benefits as compared to achieving abstinence. Unsurprisingly there is a relationship between success at more difficult tasks and greater rewards.

An important general principle of social learning theory is that self-efficacy is more strongly learned and mastery of the new behaviour more durable where an individual is an active participant in behaviour change. Alternative but less potent ways of building self-efficacy are: (i) *modelling* – demonstration of a particular behaviour, for example drink or drug refusal, by a therapist or another client; (ii) *talking* – any form of communication, notably motivational dialogue, which seeks to strengthen belief in being able to undertake a particular behaviour, for example a harm reduction behaviour such as using clean needles and syringes and then disposing of them safely; (iii) *anxiety control* – ensuring that fear of the unknown does not lead to incapacitating anxiety and failure to go through with a particular behaviour, for example undertaking adequate preparation for a detoxification.

Self-efficacy is the belief that a particular change of behaviour, in this case achieving abstinence or controlled use of alcohol or other drugs, can be achieved. If self-efficacy is low then the probability of successful treatment is also low. At an individual level self-efficacy may be low for a number of reasons – first, an individual may have made repeated attempts to give up an addictive behaviour which have failed; second, an individual may mix only with other current drinkers or drug users who reaffirm the belief that change is impossible; third, there may be dependence on a substance or substances which, by definition, presents a barrier to change.

Expectancy theory (Jones *et al.* 2001) has a strong evidence base. Expectancies are beliefs about the likely outcome of a particular action or behaviour being positive or negative. Almost all the substance use work in this field has been with alcohol. A consistent finding is that positive outcome expectancies of drinking, for example 'a drink will cheer me up', are associated with drinking whereas the opposite is true for negative outcome expectancies, for example 'if I get drunk I am neglecting my child' might be associated with abstinence. Expectancies are credited with contributing a major component of motivation which depends on the overall balance between positive and negative expectancies. At the stage where people enter into treatment, drinking outcome is predicted more by pre-treatment negative outcome expectancies than positive outcome expectancies; positive outcome expectancies but not negative outcome expectancies for drinking reduce during treatment.

Successful and repeated completion of a behaviour, for example going out for a meal with a partner or friend and not drinking, will lead to mastery of the behaviour and possibly generalisation to other similar behaviours. The converse is also true and therapists must take care not to lead people into failures. Positive outcome expectancies are a necessary accompaniment to moving into the action stage of change – if positive expectancies become reality then a virtuous cycle of reinforcement and more change is established. The positive expectancies need to be achievable, meaningful and be truly positive rather than not negative – for example, not injecting heroin may not of itself be rewarding whereas buying some new clothes or going out for a meal probably will be.

Dependence

The nature and the significance of dependence are both somewhat controversial. There are numerous descriptions, going back to ancient history, of some kind of altered state of mind induced by regular use of alcohol or other drugs and associated with an inability to stop using those substances. The early scientific descriptions of dependence emphasise the physical consequences of regular use, especially of alcohol or opiates, and attach importance to the manifestation of withdrawal symptoms to the extent that withdrawal symptoms and dependence or addiction became pretty much synonymous. A better question is whether dependence is best seen as a purely psychological phenomenon or, as in the traditional model, a psychobiological state. The view taken here is that tolerance and withdrawal are consequences of regular substance use and should be thought of as separate from dependence albeit that they are closely linked. In-depth discussions on the nature of dependence can be found in *Problem Drinking* (Heather and Robertson 1997, pp. 52–64) and *Theory of Addiction* (West 2006, pp. 123–145).

Substance dependence, conceptualised as a psychological phenomenon, is most fully explained in terms of learning theory. Dependence is an over learned behaviour driven by desire or need. In conditioning terms the behaviour is over learned by repeated positive reinforcement, for example from experiencing the desired drug effect, or negative reinforcement, for example by experiencing the avoidance of withdrawal. The cues, or triggers, for taking a substance quickly become multiple and complex as they generalise and it is the fact that the user is not always aware of the whole gamut of circumstances that have been conditioned to elicit thoughts or craving about substance use which creates difficulties for a purely cognitive approach to changing a person's addiction. A common manifestation of severe dependence is that time and again an individual gets to the point of change or gets half way through change or achieves change but then relapses.

Dependence on a psychoactive substance is, in principle, very similar to any other strong attachment or habit. For example, some people find it difficult to control the amount of physical exercise that they take, to eat normally or adhere to an agreed diet, or to set limits on their gambling. In a slightly different example, young people are particularly fashion conscious and will display mood change and irritability if they are not allowed to wear the same clothes as their friends; equally they will completely change what they wear if there is social pressure to do so, namely a change of fashion. There are many similarities between these examples and dependence on psychoactive drugs. The essential difference is that psychoactive drugs have profound effects on neuro-chemistry which may lead to tolerance, to withdrawal symptoms, and to irreversible changes in brain function so that substance dependence is both qualitatively different to behavioural dependencies and also quantitatively different in terms of the magnitude of patho-physiological disturbance that is induced.

In principle, the way that individuals react to drinking and drug using cues can be modified by changing social and environmental factors thus altering outcome expectancies. Cue avoidance techniques are based upon the premise that some cues are too difficult to resist and cue exposure techniques are based upon the premise that not all cues can be avoided. The question of why in the addictive behaviours these strategies so often fail is a more complex question than one of faulty decision making. Dependence operates on a substrate of intertwined physiological and psychological events that are not easy to unravel. For example it is possible to alleviate withdrawal symptoms when these result directly from the physiological consequences of repeated drug use. What about those withdrawal symptoms that are environmentally cued (Siegel 1988; 1999)? What about the challenge of being able to resist triggers for use when the predominant drive is to experience the positive effects of alcohol or other drugs? It is difficult to anticipate and plan cognitive and behavioural responses to environmentally triggered biological events that are interpreted as a 'need' or as a craving. It is therefore difficult to raise self-efficacy, to develop belief in the ability to deal with these events. A psychobiological model of dependence would predict that detoxification and abstinence would markedly reduce dependence, however, the experience of addicts is that dependence, a strong urge to drink or take drugs, persists even after months or years of abstinence. It may be that in such circumstances a purely motivational approach will encourage individuals to engage in thoughts about change and in attempts to change, but it may equally be that in order to enhance belief in the success of change attempts, other treatments, such as pharmacological adjuncts will be necessary. The delivery of these in the style of motivational dialogue is described in the final two chapters of this book.

Substitute prescribing, usually for opiate dependence, is an interesting intervention in that it is designed to reduce drug-related harms but, at the same time, it prolongs and may increase dependence (Tober 2003). A substitute prescription, typically methadone or buprenorphine, produces an opiate effect which is less intense than that from heroin and which is long lasting so that the experience of withdrawal is removed. Other negative consequences, such as criminal activity to fund the heroin addiction, are also removed. Additional social benefits accrue, partially as a result of crime reduction but also reduced family conflict and increased ability to lead a 'normal' life result in reduction in the experience of 'discrepancy' and thus reduction in an important source of motivation to change. In these circumstances the therapist working in the style of motivational dialogue may be hard pressed to find grounds upon which to initiate thoughts about further change. Thus, substitute prescribing can be a useful means of creating some stability for an otherwise chaotic drug user and of reducing many of the negative consequences of drug use but is, of itself, a barrier to change.

Although many people may find that severe dependence will be a barrier to successful treatment by motivational interventions alone, a combination of motivational interventions and mobilising their own resources – family, friends and others in their social network – will lead on to a successful outcome. Some people find their strength from outside of themselves, perhaps through spiritual enlightenment, or through a mutual aid programme such as a 12 Step approach which offers participants self-efficacy through the idea of a 'higher power' and many people do overcome their addictive behaviour with the help of religious affiliation.

Self-esteem

Self-esteem is an imprecise construct which, some would argue, has now been superseded by developments in cognitive-behavioural psychology. In clinical practice, however, self-esteem endures as a concept that has some meaning for both clients and health care professionals. It is fair to question whether this woolly notion actually has utility either in terms of improving assessment, leading to a meaningful formulation of a particular case or in terms of improving the focus of treatment.

Self-esteem can be thought of as an individual's comfort zone where comfort is an expression of autonomy and security. People with material comforts, such as housing and good income, or security in their role as a parent, in a relationship or in their employment, may derive high levels of self-esteem and benefit from the self-perpetuating consequences. There is then a danger that self-esteem simply separates the 'haves' and 'have-nots', but this would be too crude – 'having' is a likely but not essential accompaniment of self-worth. Self-esteem reflects the extent to which an individual feels him or herself to be significant, capable and worthy of respect. Healthy or high self-esteem has been described as an essential requirement for effective behaviour both in the general sense of healthy psychological functioning and also in the specific senses of social and employment success. High self-esteem is also thought to protect the individual against social and environmental stressors.

It follows that low self-esteem is maintained and reinforced through an individual's repeated experience of ineffectiveness and, therefore, powerlessness. Additionally low self-esteem is associated with depression, anxiety and poor physical health. There is an obvious and self-perpetuating link between low self-esteem and substance misuse: people drink or take drugs because they have low self-esteem and they have low self-esteem because they drink or take drugs. People who do not perceive their substance misuse as a problem or who reject the need for treatment are more likely to maintain higher levels of self-esteem. Women are more likely to experience exceptionally low levels of self-esteem as compared to men. This is often the case for women who misuse alcohol or other drugs because of social disapproval of intoxicated females, especially if they have dependent children.

People with low self-esteem may defend themselves by displaying hostility to others. Common characteristics associated with low self-esteem are the habit of denigrating others, passive hostility, helplessness, a reduced ability to make positive decisions and a tendency to accept unfavourable assessments as accurate. High self-esteem is more likely to lead to objective assessment of positive and negative characteristics of others because there is no need to distort perceptions in self-defence. Raising an individual's self-esteem will in turn strengthen motivation to change, increase self-efficacy, and encourage positive outcome expectancies. All of these are important elements of effective behaviour change.

Low self-esteem is not a mental illness but it may be difficult to distinguish it from depression and indeed the one feeds the other. A helpful distinction might be that low self-esteem can be thought of in terms of an expected reaction to an expected and measured response to life circumstances whereas depression is seen in terms of an abnormal and excessive response. The distinction is somewhat academic, at least for mild to moderate severity of depression, in that the general thrust of treatment is likely to be similar. It is usual to assume that improvement in self-esteem will be one outcome from any psychosocial intervention whether or not the intervention includes specific exercises directed at self-esteem. Some problems leading to low self-esteem, for example domestic violence, poor housing, unemployment, may be intractable at least in the short term, but people will not change their substance misuse behaviour unless they have a sense of self-worth.

One of the benefits of motivational interviewing is the way that communication of respect for the client is a central principle: it is a product of asking open questions, thus demonstrating interest in what the client has to say, and reflective listening which places emphasis on the value of what the client has to say. Integral to the approach is the avoidance of confrontation and conflict with the client, both likely to result in feelings of inadequacy and low self-worth on their part. These methods are the means of communicating empathy, warmth and positive regard; there is then the communication of optimism which gives the client the feeling that the therapist believes in their ability to effect change. Thus the components of motivational dialogue are generally designed to enhance self-esteem in the face of serious challenges to it.

Summary and conclusions

People can change their drinking, smoking or drug use and the causes of change are much the same regardless of the particular substance used. It is easier to change a behaviour that is towards the 'bad habit' end of the spectrum than it is to change when a severe dependence on a substance has developed. Naturally occurring events and social pressures are sufficient to bring about change where problems are few and dependence is low but as problems and dependence increase then so too does the need for more intensive intervention successfully to achieve stable change.

People tend to use a psychoactive drug for one of two general reasons – either they like it or it has some utility. Similarly people tend to think about stopping or reducing their substance use for one of two general reasons – the realisation that life could be better following a change which may or may not be coupled with an accumulation of negative consequences. The challenge for therapists is to move from the first set of thoughts to the second set and it is in bringing about this shift of thinking that motivational dialogue, or indeed any specific motivational therapy, is used. Where the possibility of changing adverse social circumstances is bleak or where the substance use alleviates psychological problems it may be difficult to secure any real sense of motivation to change.

Wanting to change is not the same as changing. Overcoming the addiction, or dependence, itself can be a formidable task which often requires specialist treatment. After successful treatment there is usually a period of adjustment which includes both relapse prevention work and some practical sorting out of problems. The whole process may take many months and several attempts during which time therapists and members of the social network may help or hinder progress depending upon their ability to build a therapeutic alliance with the client. Motivational dialogue is a style of treatment delivery that is likely to facilitate the change process however tortuous and difficult this may be, not least because of the way it requires the therapist continually to identify those factors described in the next chapter as constituting the motivational steps through the cycle of change.

References

Babor, T.F. and Del Boca, F.K. (eds) (2003) *Treatment Matching in Alcoholism*, Cambridge: Cambridge University Press.

Bandura, A. (1977) 'Self-efficacy: towards a unifying theory of behaviour change', *Psychological Review*, 84: 191–215.

Carroll, K.M. (2001) 'Constrained, confounded, and confused: why we really know so little about therapists in treatment outcome research', *Addiction*, 96: 203–206.

Dunn, C., Deroo, L. and Rivara, F.P. (2001) 'The use of brief interventions adapted from motivational interviewing across behavioural domains: a systematic review', *Addiction*, 96: 1725–1742.

Heather, N. and Robertson, I. (1997) *Problem Drinking*, Oxford: Oxford University Press.

Hettema, J., Steele, J. and Miller, W.R. (2005) 'Motivational Interviewing', *Annual Review of Clinical Psychology*, 1: 91–111.

Jones, B.T., Corbin, W. and Fromme, K. (2001) 'A review of expectancy theory and alcohol consumption', *Addiction*, 96: 57–72.

Joseph, J., Breslin, C. and Skinner, H. (1999) 'Critical perspectives on the transtheoretical model and stages of change', in J.A. Tucker, D.M. Donovan and G.A. Marlatt (eds) *Changing Addictive Behavior: Bridging Clinical and Public Health Strategies*, New York: Guilford Press.

Luborsky, L. and O'Brien, C.P. (1985) 'Therapist success and its determinants', *Archives of General Psychiatry*, 42: 602–611.

Meier, P.S., Barrowclough, C. and Donmall, M.C. (2005) 'The role of the therapeutic alliance in the treatment of substance misuse: a critical review of the literature', *Addiction*, 100: 304–316.

Moos, R.H. (2005) 'Iatrogenic effects of psychosocial interventions for substance use disorders: prevalence, predictors, prevention', *Addiction*, 100: 595–604.

Najavits, L.M. and Weiss, R.D. (1994) 'Variations in therapist effectiveness in the treatment of patients with substance use disorders: an empirical review', *Addiction*, 89: 679–688.

Rogers, C.R. (1957) 'The necessary and sufficient conditions for therapeutic personality change', *Journal of Consulting Psychology*, 21: 95–103.

Rosengren, D.B., Downey, L. and Donovan, D.M. (2000) '"*I already stopped*": abstinence prior to treatment', *Addiction*, 95: 65–76.

Siegel, S. (1988) 'Drug anticipation and drug tolerance', in M. Lader (ed.) *The Psychopharmacology of Addiction*, Oxford: Oxford University Press.

Siegel, S. (1999) 'Drug anticipation and drug addiction', *Addiction*, 94: 1113–1124.

Tober, G. (2003) 'Dependence on methadone: the danger lurking behind the prescription' in G. Tober and J. Strang (eds) *Methadone Matters: Evolving Community Methadone Treatment of Opiate Addiction*, London: Martin Dunitz.

Tober, G., Godfrey, C., Parrott, S., Copello, A., Farrin, A., Hodgson, R., Kenyone, R., Morton, V., Orford, J., Russell, I. and Slegg, G. (2005) 'Setting standards for training and competence: the UK Alcohol Treatment Trial', *Alcohol and Alcoholism*, 40: 413–418.

UKATT Research Team (2005) 'Effectiveness of treatment for alcohol problems: findings of the randomised UK alcohol treatment trial (UKATT)', *British Medical Journal*, 331: 541–544.

Vaillant, G.E. (2003) 'A 60-year follow-up of alcoholic men', *Addiction*, 98: 1043–1051.

West, R. (2006) *Theory of Addiction*, Oxford: Blackwell.

Chapter 3

Motivation and change: a three dimensional continuum

Valter Spiller, Valeria Zavan and Gian Paolo Guelfi

Introduction

The importance of assessing motivation to change in people with behavioural problems, such as substance misuse, is widely acknowledged. The assessment of motivation to change affects how the professional deals with the problem presented by the client: to a certain extent it influences the choice of treatment, expectations of compliance and expectations of the outcome of the treatment (Miller 1989; Miller *et al.* 1992; Connors *et al.* 2001). Most of the assessment tools for motivation in the addiction literature refer, either directly or indirectly, to the concept of readiness to change as described by Prochaska and DiClemente (1982) in their stages of change model. Motivational change in this model is understood to be affected by putative factors that trigger or are the result of specific processes of change and it is these processes that are of particular interest to clinicians.

The available assessment tools can be used to allocate a client to a dominant stage of change taken from a profile of scores across all of the stages. The stage of change has become a proxy for motivational state with regard to the presenting problem behaviour although the model itself is actually a mixture of cognitive and behavioural elements. Examples of tools that are commonly used in clinical practice to assess readiness to change are the URICA (McConnaughy *et al.* 1983; DiClemente and Hughes 1990), the Readiness to Change Questionnaire (Rollnick *et al.* 1992; Heather *et al.* 1999) and the SOCRATES (Miller and Tonigan 1996). Recent versions of readiness to change instruments have been critically reviewed by Carey and colleagues (1999). Merely identifying that a person is in a dominant stage of change or even creating a profile of the stages is only partially useful since it does not account for the interaction of other important factors that might impact on the change process.

Miller and Rollnick (2002) describe two factors that they consider to be important components of readiness to change, namely the constructs of *discrepancy* and *self-efficacy*. The concept of discrepancy, based upon Festinger's cognitive dissonance (Festinger 1957), focuses on a perception of the contradiction between how a person sees him or herself currently and how he or she would like to be in order to come into line with their ideal self-image, value systems and expectations. Similarly, numerous cognitive-behavioural theories refer to the concept of self-regulation where motivation to change is based upon the comparison between the goal to be pursued and the perception of the current situation (Kanfer 1987). Thus, behaviours, situations and conditions that are incongruous with self-image are perceived as threats (Steele and Liu 1981; 1983; Steele 1988) and can trigger a change in behaviour. So, fully to understand discrepancy there is a need to explore the concerns, dissatisfaction and distress that an individual is experiencing with regard to their current situation, in this case substance misuse or related consequences, as well as appreciating the importance of change and a realignment to match up to personal values.

There is an extensive literature (see Chapter 2) on the concept of self-efficacy (Bandura 1977; 1982; 1995) and its influence on the process of change in the field of dependence (Rollnick and Heather 1982; DiClemente *et al.* 1995). A person's conviction about his or her ability to achieve and maintain a specific goal is considered one of the most predictive factors in the outcome of behaviour change attempts (DiClemente 1986). In the study of alcohol dependence, self-efficacy is mainly evaluated in an operative manner as the perceived ability, meaning confidence, to deal with high-risk situations. Therefore, the tools focus on evaluating self-efficacy with regard to a specific objective, such as avoiding heavy drinking or the ability to achieve total abstinence. Some of them, for example the Situational Confidence Questionnaire (Annis and Graham 1988) or the Alcohol Abstinence Self-Efficacy Scale (DiClemente *et al.* 1994), explore predetermined situations, while others, like the Individual Self-Efficacy Survey (Miller *et al.* 1994), take the form of personalised semi-structured interviews. Many instruments have been proposed and validated for such purposes (Donovan 2003).

The literature does not provide an example of a questionnaire specifically designed to evaluate discrepancy albeit that there are tools that refer to similar constructs. Discrepancy can be related to motivational processes and evaluated through an analysis of the positive and negative consequences of an individual's substance use (Brown *et al.* 1987; McMahon and Jones 1993; Donovan 2003), or to costs and benefits of substance use (Sobell *et al.* 1996; Cunningham *et al.* 1997; DiClemente 1999; Noar *et al.* 2003). More integrated with and closer to discrepancy is an analysis of the concerns, stress and dissatisfaction and their impact on attitudes towards the use of alcohol as described by Cox and Klinger (1988) using the Motivational Structure Questionnaire (MSQ) (Klinger and Cox 1985).

In our view, the clinical usefulness of a multi-dimensional model is based on the ability to integrate an evaluation of (i) readiness, (ii) self-efficacy and (iii) discrepancy into a single, easy-to-administer tool which more accurately reflects components of motivation to change. The need to integrate the assessment of these three variables into a single tool capable of providing an overall view of a person's motivation, consistent with the proposed theoretical model, led to the creation of the Motivazione Al Cambiamento 2 – Alcool (Motivation To Change 2 – Alcohol) (MAC2-A) an English version of which is reproduced at the end of this chapter.

Brief description of the MAC2-A

The MAC2-A was designed to evaluate motivation to change in people judged to suffer from alcohol misuse or alcohol dependence. The questionnaire was successfully validated in adults who received a recommendation, requested, completed or were undergoing specific professional therapy for problem drinking (Spiller *et al.* 2006), and was based on a sample of 419 Italian adults. The instrument had good internal consistency, reliability and validity. The MAC2-A consists of 36 statements that are answered using a 7-point Likert scale (from *Not true at all* to *Completely true*), and there are six questions that are answered using a graduated analogue scale with values ranging from 0 to 100.

The MAC2-A evaluation covers all the stages described in Prochaska and DiClemente's Transtheoretical Model. Six stages of change totals are obtained so as to produce a profile of values representing precontemplation, contemplation, determination, action, maintenance and termination (not in recent versions of the model). Properly combining the totals relative to the stages of change produces two summary numerical values: the first one indicates the *readiness to change*, that is how close is the individual to reaching the decisional threshold for change, and the second one indicates *stabilisation*, that is the degree of consolidation of any change made in substance misuse behaviour. The questionnaire provides separate assessments of *discrepancy* and of *self-efficacy*.

The MAC2-A includes analogue summary scales that provide second ratings of readiness to change, stabilisation, discrepancy, and self-efficacy and therefore provide a check on the same constructs that were previously assessed. In addition importance attributed to changing substance use, described by Miller and Rollnick (2002) and thc level of temptation to use were measured using analogue scales added to the MAC2-A. These last two scales taken together provide an alternative way to think about the evaluation of discrepancy.

In summary, the MAC2-A produces 16 numerical scores that constitute the motivational assessment. It is not the intention to use this chapter to describe the detailed design and methodology used to validate MAC2-A (Spiller *et al.* 2006), rather to draw out some key findings and discuss the practical implications of taking a multidimensional view of the nature of motivation.

Relationships between motivational factors

The observations that follow are based on an analysis of the data from the sample used to validate the MAC2-A. Findings from administration of the questionnaire highlighted links between the motivational factors investigated and basically confirmed what has already been described in the literature. Some interesting results that associate the various aspects of motivation may provide pointers to more in-depth analyses. The information presented should be considered as initial data that require further verification and provide food for thought concerning the interactions between the motivational factors, rather than evidence of the application of a mature explanatory model. The data were analysed mainly by using the distributions of two variables and by studying the curve of interpolation obtained utilising the Distance Weighted Least Square method. The sections below are divided into before and after substance use change as well as stages of change.

Before substance use change – precontemplation to contemplation

The profile of the stages prior to behaviour change is summarised in the questionnaire by the *readiness to change* score (abbreviated to *readiness* hereafter). People with less than a week of alcohol abstention were included in this subgroup (N = 147) on the grounds that the period of abstinence was too short to be considered stable change. The relationship between *discrepancy*, *importance* and *readiness* is shown in Figure 3.1. Since discrepancy seems to have a very powerful effect during the initial phases of the change process, it is likely to be the determining factor in starting off thoughts about change, namely the transition from precontemplation to contemplation. This process occurs with rather low discrepancy values. Its initial and even relatively small increase is associated, on the average, with a rather appreciable increase in readiness. Conversely, very high levels of discrepancy are not necessarily associated with an additional increase in readiness.

The validation exercise found that participants rated importance of changing substance use more strongly on the MAC2-A components that reflected their value systems and personal expectations, rather than on their perception of concerns or dissatisfaction with their current circumstances. According to the theoretical assumptions of MAC2-A, importance and discrepancy should develop in parallel in the pre-behaviour change phase. This assumption is basically confirmed by the data in Figure 3.1; there is an evident association between the increases in importance and discrepancy. The association between importance and readiness shows a more constant trend and indicates that higher degrees of importance attributed to change

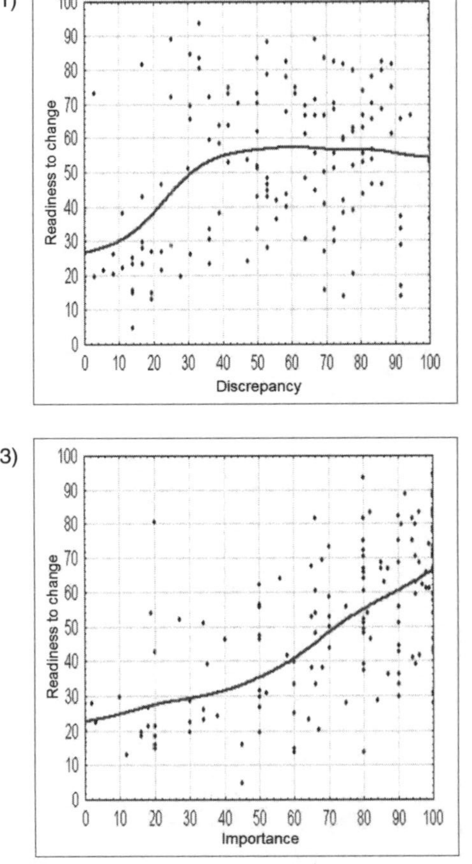

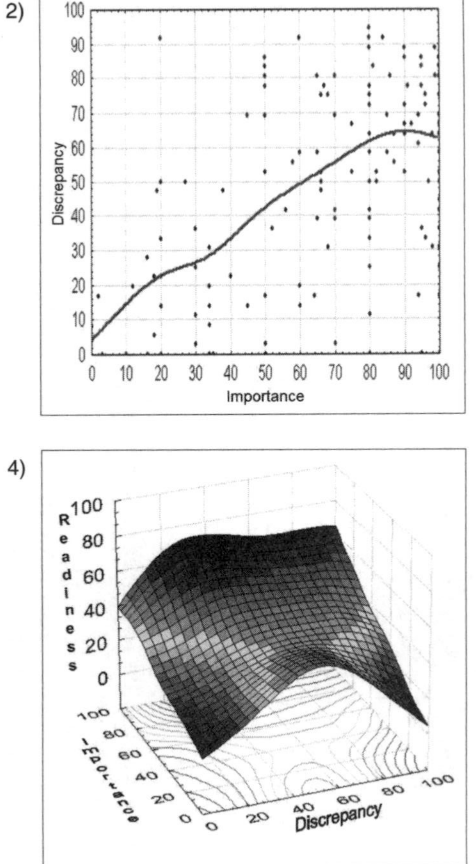

Figure 3.1 Readiness, discrepancy and importance

are associated with what is basically a linear and continuous increase in readiness. Therefore, such an increase would seem to be greater the higher the importance scores.

The relationship of the two elements, discrepancy and importance, to readiness would appear to demonstrate that, for those individuals approaching the threshold of actual behaviour change, it is relatively unhelpful to pursue actions aimed at amplifying concerns and dissatisfaction, rather there is greater benefit in focusing attention on personal values and positive outcome expectancies involved in the behaviour change. In summary, it can be stated that there is a two-phase increase in readiness in relation to discrepancy and importance. The distribution of these three variables can be used to generate a three dimensional graph which illustrates this assumption (see Figure 3.1).

Crossing the threshold into substance use change – determination and action stages of change

There is evidence (DiClemente and Hughes 1990; DiClemente *et al.* 1995) that, in general, an increase in *self-efficacy* is associated with an increase in *readiness*. High and increasing self-efficacy scores are associated with a more decisive increase in readiness scores. At first sight self-efficacy appears to be the key to the transition from contemplation to determination and subsequently to action stages of change. In line with clinical experience, however, we found that self-efficacy decreases rather significantly with an increase in discrepancy. This would seem to support the fact that very high discrepancy is not associated with an increase in readiness since the effect generated by the simultaneous trend toward a decrease in self-efficacy would prevail. It is evident that the maximum level of readiness, that is readiness which is on the cusp of the change from the determination to the action stage, is associated with high levels of self-efficacy and with intermediate levels of discrepancy (see Figure 3.2 overleaf).

There are some interesting additional interactions to be found at these stages of change. As is to be expected, temptation and self-efficacy have a strong inverse correlation, as often indicated in the literature (DiClemente *et al.* 1994). As temptation increases, the trust in one's ability to abstain from substance use decreases sharply, in a rather linear manner. For very high levels of temptation, the association between the two variables tends to become rather random. From the data obtained, it would seem that people who experience high levels of temptation cross a threshold and partially lose the ability to maintain their previously high perceptions of self-efficacy (see Figure 3.2 overleaf).

In addition, an increase in temptation is associated with an increase in discrepancy up to moderately high scores; very high scores on temptation are no longer associated with an additional increase in discrepancy, but

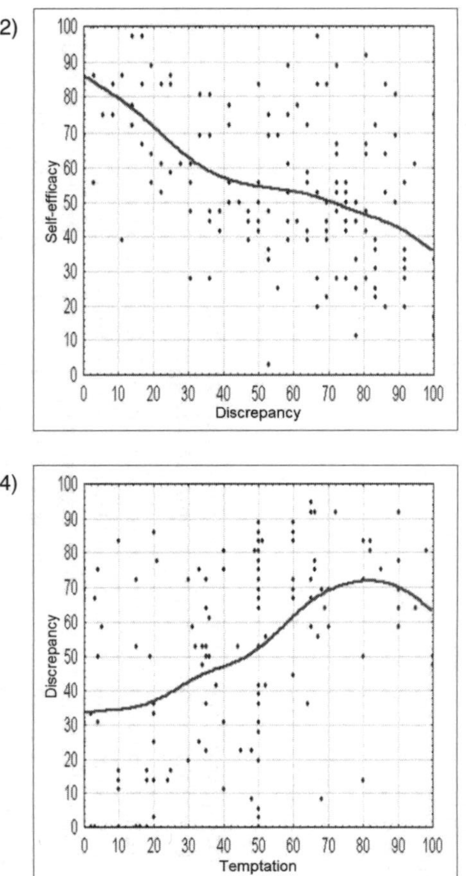

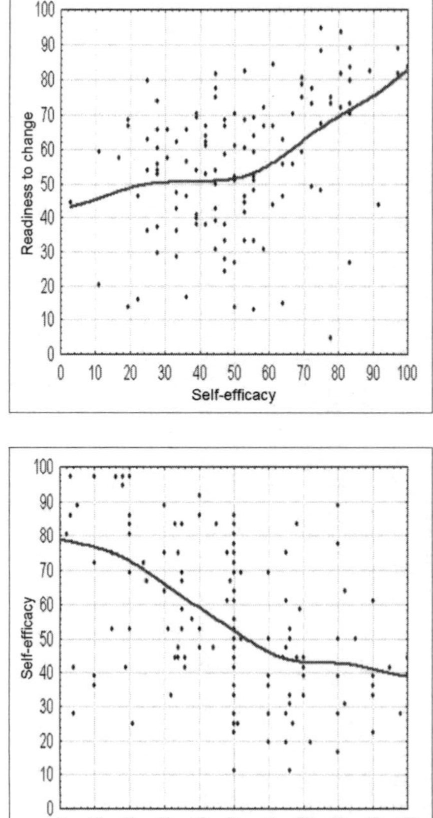

Figure 3.2 Self efficacy, readiness, discrepancy and temptation

with its relative reduction. A similar trend is noted also for readiness. Thus presumably there is a point when temptation to use is so great that confidence in resisting it is diminished as is readiness to change. From what was previously reported it would seem that in the presence of a very high level of temptation the cognitive aspects of self-evaluation self-efficacy, discrepancy and readiness are by-passed by the intensity of the desire. High temptation to drink seems to neutralise the influence of the previously described motivational factors. In any case, this aspect requires more in-depth research.

After substance use change – maintenance and exit from the cycle of change

In the period following a change in substance misuse, the *stabilisation* variable of the MAC2-A questionnaire comes into play. In this part of the change cycle, the different variables indicated by the MAC2-A can be correlated to the referenced duration of the abstinence period. This part of the sample includes subjects with at least one week of abstinence. The relationships between the motivational factors and abstinence provide data that essentially confirm previous findings in the literature and the predictions of the theoretical model. With regard to progression through the stages of change, most of the increase in stabilisation takes place in the first 3–6 months of therapy. This is a common finding of treatment outcome research and is in accord with the early descriptions of time spent in the action stage of the stages of change model (Prochaska and DiClemente 1983). After 3–6 months, consolidation, usually of abstinence, increases much more gradually. A similar trend can be observed for self-efficacy. Initially, it increases rather quickly and constantly up to about one year from the beginning of abstinence, a period in which it seems typically to reach the maximum value. In contrast, the trends for discrepancy and importance, after the change threshold, are appreciably divergent. While importance tends to remain very high and stable over time, discrepancy tends to decrease, first rapidly and then more slowly, while always remaining at detectable levels even after almost two years of abstinence. Over time, even temptation tends to decrease more and more (see Figure 3.3 overleaf).

Some interesting trends emerge based on an analysis of the associations of stabilisation with the other motivational factors. In the MAC2-A, very low stabilisation values are indicative of people who, despite abstinence from drinking alcohol, still have high precontemplation and contemplation and low maintenance and termination scores on their stages of change profiles. The trends of stabilisation and self-efficacy are directly proportional. For low values of stabilisation the distribution appears to be basically random, while as change consolidates, self-efficacy increases with an almost perfectly linear association. Increasing stabilisation is associated

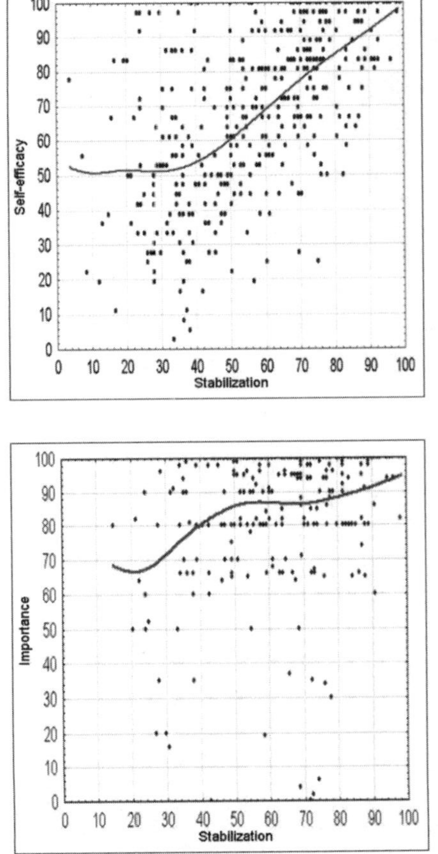

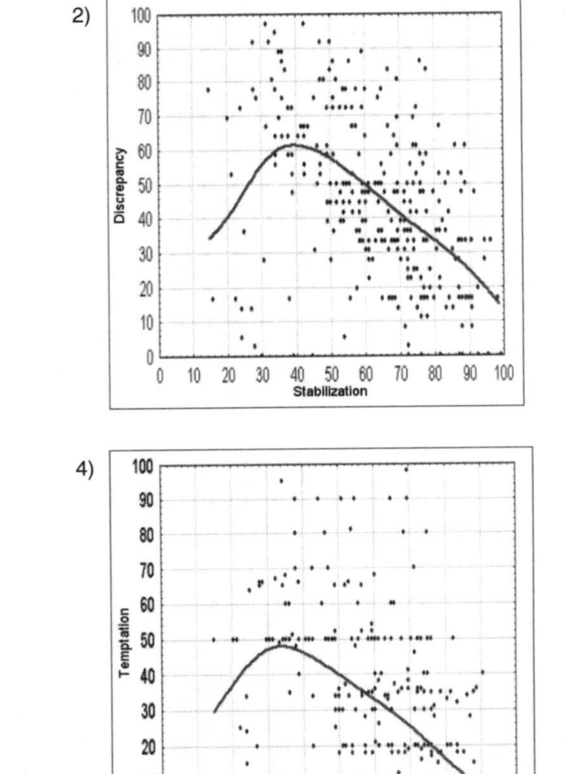

Figure 3.3 Stabilization, self efficacy, discrepancy, temptation and importance

with a progressive reduction in the degree of temptation, up to its disappearance at the maximum values. Thus, the research data confirm the common perception that consolidation of change is associated with the maximum possible reduction of desire or, better still, its extinction.

It can be expected that those individuals who feel that change has been adequately consolidated tend not to perceive any more contradictions, dissatisfaction or concerns for their situation with regard to substance use. However, the association between these two aspects is not linear: up to average values of stabilisation, the perception of discrepancy tends to increase. Such a result merits additional analysis and verification. As the consolidation of change continues, discrepancy decreases with an almost perfectly linear association. In relation to stabilisation, importance tends to increase with very high scores, indicating that attaining and consolidating the behaviour change is associated with what tends to be a high value placed on the goals achieved. The partial overlapping of the evaluation of discrepancy and importance, which was indicated as a significant factor for that part of the change process that occurs prior to the transition to action, is not confirmed after the decision-making threshold: in fact, discrepancy and importance have very different diverging trends.

Clinical implications of multidimensional motivational assessment

The stages of change model is best thought of as being about changes in thoughts and not behaviours. The stages have come to be loosely associated with variable strengths of motivation to change pivoted around, on one side, a desire to carry on, and, on the other side, a desire to stop or change substance use (or other problem behaviours). There is a point at which the balance shifts in favour of actual behaviour change. The data gathered from the MAC2-A validation project add new elements to the original stages of change model and quantify their influence on the change process. These are preliminary data which are intended to help clinicians better to understand the change process. The interactions described below are derived from MAC2-A data but are thought to be consistent with other research in this area.

The process leading to actual behaviour change

The process of changing thoughts about substance use appears to be triggered by an increase in discrepancy, that is by the initial concerns and dissatisfaction flowing from an individual's current situation. The drive produced by becoming aware of these negative consequences decreases and has less importance as the process continues in the transition from contemplation to determination and on to action stages of change. There is a shift in focus onto the positive aspects of change, positive outcome expectancies, which start to have resonance with the individual's personal value system or core beliefs. This shift is reflected in the greater importance attached to change behaviours. The process results in growth of the readiness scores. Transition into action is associated mainly with a sharp increase in self-efficacy. It follows from this formulation that the strategy behind motivational therapies regarding discrepancy amplification should be different depending on an individual's level of readiness: more emphasis on the disadvantages of substance use in the initial phases and greater attention to the advantages of change in the later stages.

As actual change in substance use approaches then *self-efficacy* becomes a determining factor. In fact, the sample data indicate that readiness and self-efficacy are directly related but only for moderately high scores of self-efficacy. Generic and poorly developed trust in one's ability to change seems to be associated randomly to any level of readiness. Thus, progress towards the decision-making threshold that brings actual behaviour change is dependent upon self-efficacy. In the transition from determination to action the development of self-efficacy is decisive. There is a potential trap here. There exists an inverse relationship between self-efficacy and discrepancy (Spiller *et al.* 1996; Spiller and Guelfi 1998; Guelfi *et al.* 1999): too much amplification of discrepancy at this point will damage growth of the all-important self-efficacy, hence, the previous recommendation to focus on positive outcome expectancies at this stage.

A further problem that the therapist must manage is the influence of *temptation*. As temptation increases, up to medium or slightly higher levels, self-efficacy and readiness decrease and discrepancy increases. This confirms the 'counter-motivational' effect of temptation which is well known from clinical experience. For very high values of temptation the relationship with motivational factors appears to be almost random indicating that temptation, certainly at very high scores, clinically detectable as 'craving', might best be treated as an independent variable, that cannot easily be influenced by cognitive-behavioural interventions other than avoidance strategies or may respond to pharmacological treatments. On the other hand it appears that lower values of temptation can be managed with appropriate therapy. Temptation appears again in a very similar fashion after actual change.

The process following actual behaviour change

The roles of *importance* and *self-efficacy* seem to be critical in supporting the actual changes made and in preventing relapse. Maintaining the importance of the goals achieved is helpful in consolidating change. Over time discrepancy tends to decrease naturally, although at a rather slow rate. The therapist may need to manage an appreciable level of discrepancy;

discrepancy may be helpful, indeed necessary, to consolidate change provided that levels are not so high as to undermine self-efficacy. This seems to be confirmed by the fact that in the first part of this phase of the cycle, for rather low values of stabilisation, discrepancy still tends to increase. Only the perception of a sufficient consolidation of the change should be expected to be associated with a decrease in the subjective perception of discrepancy.

A very similar trend involves temptation, which decreases only after achieving significant stabilisation scores. Over time and as stabilisation progresses, self-efficacy and temptation are completely divergent, indicating how values for these variables tend to evolve and the need for specific actions if this does not occur. Therefore, the therapist should be ever vigilant for the persistence of temptation or a low level of self-efficacy, even with high levels of stabilisation or extended abstinence, and be ready to take remedial action.

Conclusions

This chapter describes findings from the analysis of MAC2-A results in a sample of 419 Italian adults. While additional research and in-depth studies are needed, broadly speaking the findings are consistent with previous research and with clinical experience. The MAC2-A questionnaire can be used to carry out multidimensional motivational assessment, and thus evaluate the relationships between the key variables thought to influence the process of change. The MAC2-A questionnaire can be used at an individual case management level but the purpose here has been to use aggregate data to develop insights into the process of change for people with substance misuse problems and thereby refine the application of the stages of change model. The interpretation of the data as presented in this chapter is intended as an aid to clinicians and in particular to suggest some refinements to the application of the stages of change model and the use of motivational therapies.

References

Annis, H.M. and Graham, J.M. (1988) *Situational Confidence Questionnaire (SCQ) User's Guide*, Toronto: Addiction Research Foundation of Ontario.

Bandura, A. (1977) 'Self-efficacy: toward a unifying theory of behavioral change', *Psychology Review*, 84: 191–215.

Bandura, A. (1982) 'Self-efficacy mechanism in human agency', *The American Psychologist*, 37: 122–147.

Bandura, A. (1995) *Self efficacy in changing societies*. Cambridge: Cambridge University Press.

Brown, S.A., Christiansen, B.A. and Goldman, M.S. (1987) 'The Alcohol

Expectancy Questionnaire: an instrument for the assessment of adolescent and adult alcohol expectancies', *Journal of Studies on Alcohol*, 48: 483–491.
Carey, K., Purnine, D., Maisto, S. and Carey, M. (1999) 'Assessing readiness to change substance abuse: a critical review of instruments', *Clinical Psychology: Science and Practice*, 6: 245–266.
Connors, J.G., Donovan, D.M. and DiClemente, C.C. (2001) *Substance Abuse Treatment and the Stages of Change*, New York and London: The Guilford Press.
Cox, W.M. and Klinger, E. (1988) 'A motivational model of alcohol use', *Journal of Abnormal Psychology*, 97: 168–180.
Cunningham, J.A., Sobell, L.C., Gavin, D.R., Sobell, M.B. and Breslin, F.C. (1997) 'Assessing motivation for change: preliminary development and evaluation of a scale measuring the costs and benefits of changing alcohol or drug use', *Psychology of Addictive Behaviours*, 11: 107–114.
DiClemente, C.C. (1986) 'Self-efficacy and the addictive behaviors. Special Issue: Self-efficacy theory in contemporary psychology', *Journal of Social and Clinical Psychology*, 4: 302–315.
DiClemente, C.C. (1999) 'Alcohol (and Illegal Drugs) Decisional Balance Scale', in *Enhancing Motivation for Change in Substance Abuse Treatment, Treatment Improvement Protocol (TIP) Series 35*, Rockville, DHHS Publication No. (SMA) 99–3354.
DiClemente, C.C. and Hughes, S.O. (1990) 'Stage of change profiles in outpatient alcoholism treatment', *Journal of Substance Abuse*, 2: 217–235.
DiClemente, C.C., Fairhurst, S. and Piotrowski, N. (1995) 'Self efficacy in the addictive behaviours', in J. Maddux (ed.) *Self efficacy, adaptation and adjustment: theory, research and application*, New York: Plenum Press.
DiClemente, C.C., Carbonari, J.P., Montgomery, R.P.G. and Hughes, S.O. (1994) 'The Alcohol Abstinence Self-Efficacy Scale', *Journal of Studies on Alcohol*, 55: 141–148.
Donovan, D.M. (2003) 'Assessment to aid in the treatment planning process', in *Assessing Alcohol Problems. A Guide for Clinicians and Researcher*, 2nd edn, NIH Publication No. 03–3745.
Festinger, L. (1957) *A theory of cognitive dissonance*, Evanston, IL: Row and Peterson.
Guelfi, G.P., Spiller, V. and Scaglia, M. (1999) 'La valutazione della motivazione al cambiamento nel tabagismo: il questionario MAC/T', Poster al Convegno: 'A fuoco il fumo', 1° congresso nazionale sul tabagismo, Padova, 1999.
Heather, N., Luce, A., Peck, D., Dunbar, B. and James, I. (1999) 'Development of a treatment version of the Readiness to Change Questionnaire', *Addiction Research*, 7: 63–83.
Kanfer, F.H. (1987) 'Self-regulation and behavior', in H. Hechhausen, P.M. Gollwitzer and F.E. Weinert (eds) *Jenseits des Rubikon*, Heidelberg: Springer-Verlag.
Klinger, E. and Cox, W.M. (1985) 'Motivational Structure Questionnaire', available from Eric Klinger, Division of Social Sciences, University of Minnesota, Morris, MN 56267.
McConnaughy, E.N., Prochaska, J.O. and Velicer, W.F. (1983) 'Stages of change in psychotherapy: measurement and sample profiles', *Psychotherapy: Theory, Research and Practice*, 20: 368–375.

McMahon, J. and Jones, B.T. (1993) 'The Negative Alcohol Expectancy Questionnaire', *Journal of the Association of Nurses on Substance Abuse*, 12: 17.

Miller, K.J., McCrady, B.S., Abrams, D.B. and Labouvie, E.W. (1994) 'Taking an individualized approach to the assessment of self efficacy and the prediction of alcoholic relapse', *Journal of Psychopathology and Behavioural Assessment*, 16: 111–120.

Miller, W.R. (1989) 'Increasing motivation for change', in R.K. Hester and W.R. Miller (eds) *Handbook of Alcoholism Treatment Approaches*, Needham Heights, MA: Allyn and Bacon.

Miller, W.R. and Tonigan, J.S. (1996) 'Assessing drinkers' motivation for change: The Stage Of Change Readiness and Treatment Eagerness Scale (SOCRATES)', *Psychology of Addictive Behaviour*, 10: 81–89.

Miller, W.R. and Rollnick, S. (2002) *Motivational Interviewing: Preparing People for Change*, 2nd edn, New York: The Guilford Press.

Miller, W.R., Zweben, A., DiClemente, C.C. and Rychtarik, R.G. (1992) *Motivational Enhancement Therapy Manual: A Clinical Research Guide for Therapists Treating Individuals with Alcohol Abuse and Dependence*, Project MATCH Monograph 2, Rockville, Maryland: National Institute on Alcohol Abuse and Alcoholism.

Noar, S.M., Laforge, R.G., Maddock, J.E. and Wood, M.D. (2003) 'Rethinking positive and negative aspects of alcohol use: suggestions from a comparison of alcohol expectancies and decisional balance', *Journal of Studies on Alcohol*, 64: 60–69.

Prochaska, J.O. and DiClemente, C.C. (1982) 'Transtheoretical therapy: toward a more integrative model of change', *Psychotherapy, Theory, Research and Practice*, 19: 276–288.

Prochaska, J.O. and DiClemente, C.C. (1983) 'Stages and processes of self-change of smoking: toward an integrative model of change', *Journal of Consulting Clinical Psychology*, 51: 390–395.

Rollnick, S. and Heather, N. (1982) 'The application of Bandura's self efficacy theory to abstinence oriented alcoholism treatment', *Addictive Behaviors*, 7: 243–250.

Rollnick, S., Heather, N., Gold, R. and Hall, W. (1992) 'Development of a short "readiness to change" questionnaire for use in brief, opportunistic interventions among excessive drinkers', *British Journal of Addiction*, 87: 734–754.

Sobell, L.C., Cunningham, J.A., Agrawal, S., Gavin, D.R., Leo, G.I. and Singh, K.N. (1996) 'Fostering self change among problem drinkers: a proactive community intervention', *Addictive Behaviors*, 21: 817–833.

Spiller, V. and Guelfi G.P. (1998) 'La valutazione della motivazione al cambiamento: il questionario MAC/E', *Bollettino delle Farmacodipendenze e Alcoolismo*, 2: XXI.

Spiller, V., Zavan, V. and Guelfi, G.P. (2006) 'Assessing motivation for change in subjects with alcohol problems: the MAC2-A questionnaire', *Alcohol and Alcoholism*, 41: 616–623.

Spiller, V., Scaglia, M., Zaccardi, M. and Guelfi, G.P. (1996) 'Il test dei ritratti: uno strumento per la valutazione della motivazione al cambiamento', Atti del convegno SITD 'Dipendenze: i confini e l'orizzonte', Padova.

Steele, C.M. (1988) 'The psychology of self-affirmation: sustaining the integrity of the self', in L. Berkowitz (ed.) *Advances in Experimental Social Psychology*, New York: Academic Press.

Steele, C.M. and Liu, T.J. (1981) 'Making the dissonant act unreflective of the self: dissonance avoidance and the expectancy of a value-affirming response', *Personality and Social Psychology Bulletin*, 7: 393–387.

Steele, C.M. and Liu, T.J. (1983) 'Dissonance processes as self-affirmation', *Journal of Personality and Social Psychology*, 45: 5–19.

Appendix
English version of the MAC2-A

1. Response choices

0	1	2	3	4	5	6
Per niente vero	**Pochissimo** vero	**Poco** vero	**A metà** vero	**Abbastanza** vero	**In gran parte** vero	**Del tutto** vero

Scale: Not true at all – Not true – Not so true – Half true – Quite true – Mostly true – Completely true.
2. Place a cross over the number that most accurately reflects what you think with reference to each of these statements

1. Da una parte vorrei continuare a bere e dall'altra penso che sarebbe meglio che smettessi
   On the one hand I would continue drinking, and on the other I think I'd better quit
2. Riesco a non bere anche quando ho voglia o bisogno di farlo
   I can stop drinking even when I feel like, or need, to drink
3. Penso che il problema di bere, a questo punto, sia per me una questione risolta
   I think that at this point, drinking for me is a closed question
4. La mia situazione attuale con il bere non mi preoccupa
   My present drinking does not concern me
5. Penso che continuerò a bere
   I think I'll go on drinking
6. Se penso alla mia attuale situazione con il bere, sono molto insoddisfatto/a di me
   If I think about my present drinking, I'm very dissatisfied with myself
7. Ho smesso di bere da tempo e mi sto impegnando per continuare così
   I've quit drinking a long time ago, and I'm strongly committed to keep on like that
8. Non sono capace di resistere alla tentazione di bere, in certe situazioni
   In some circumstances I can't resist the temptation to drink
9. Ho davvero iniziato a fare qualcosa per smettere di bere
   I really started doing something to stop drinking

10. Bevo e mi va bene così
    I drink, and it's OK like that
11. Adesso ho deciso di provare seriamente a smettere di bere
    At present I have seriously decided to stop drinking
12. Ho iniziato a farmi aiutare davvero per il mio bere
    I started getting really helped for my drinking
13. A volte i miei problemi con il bere mi fanno pensare che dovrei smettere
    Sometimes my drinking problems make me think that I should quit
14. Penso che bere sia una cosa che ormai non mi riguarda più
    I think that at this point drinking does not affect me any more
15. Adesso mi sento davvero determinato/a a trovare il modo per smettere di bere
    At present I feel I'm really resolved to find a way out of drinking
16. Bere mi piace così tanto che non sono sicuro di riuscire a farne a meno
    Drinking pleases me so much that I'm not sure I'll be able to get rid of it
17. Non bevo più da tempo e sto cercando di mantenere questo risultato
    I've not been drinking for a lot of time, and I'm trying to stick to this outcome
18. Sto bevendo e non ho bisogno di nessun aiuto in relazione a questo
    I'm drinking, and don't need any help for this
19. Riuscirei a dire di no anche se mi invitassero a bere
    I could say 'no' if someone invited me to drink
20. Posso dire che ormai l'idea di bere è davvero lontana da me
    At the moment I can say that the thought of drinking is really far away
21. Sono soddisfatto/a della mia attuale situazione con il bere
    I'm satisfied with my current drinking status
22. Ogni tanto penso di avere bisogno di un aiuto per smettere di bere
    Every now and then I think I need some help to quit drinking
23. In questo momento sono veramente preoccupato/a per le conseguenze del mio bere
    At this moment I'm really concerned about the consequences of my drinking
24. Mi sto facendo aiutare da tempo per il mio bere
    I've been getting help for my drinking for a long time
25. Con il bere, penso di non essere capace a dire di no anche se volessi
    I think I'm not able to say no to drinking even if I want to
26. Ho recentemente iniziato a non bere più
    I've recently stopped drinking
27. Sto cercando un aiuto concreto per affrontare i miei problemi con il bere
    I'm looking for real help to deal with my drinking problem

28. Qualcuno pensa che sarebbe meglio che smettessi di bere, ma a me non sembra il caso
    Some think I'd better quit drinking, but I don't think so
29. E' poco che ho smesso di bere e sto facendo tutto il possibile per continuare così
    I've recently stopped drinking, and I'm doing my best to continue this way
30. La mia situazione con il bere, in questo momento, va bene così
    At this moment my drinking status is OK
31. Ogni tanto penso di smettere di bere
    Every now and then I think of stopping drinking
32. Non ho più bisogno di aiuto per mantenere la mia attuale situazione con il bere
    I don't need help any more to maintain my present drinking status
33. Credo di saper resistere al desiderio di bere
    I believe I can resist the desire to drink
34. Ora che ho deciso di smettere di bere, sto cercando il modo per farlo davvero
    Now I have decided to stop drinking, and I'm looking for the way to actually do that
35. Mi disturba pensare che il bere mi faccia diventare così diverso da come vorrei
    I'm annoyed that my drinking makes me so different from what I'd like to be
36. Anche se non bevo da tempo penso di dover fare ancora attenzione
    Although I have not had a drink for a long time I think I must still be careful

3. The analogue summary scales

'Now we ask you to answer the six questions below.
Use the 0 to 100 scales you find below each sentence.
Check the point that best describes your present condition.'

Scale: Not at all – Very few – Few – Average – Much – Very much – Extremely

GF – How unhappy and concerned do you feel about your drinking condition?
GA – How confident do you feel about being able to quit drinking?
GD – How ready and resolute do you feel not to drink anymore?
GS – How stable and steady do you feel in your abstention from drinking?

GT – How strongly do you feel the temptation to drink?
GI – How important do you feel it is to abstain from drinking?

4. Duration of abstinence

Not drinking for . . . . days . . . . months . . . . years

Section II

The evidence base

Chapter 4

Towards evidence-based practice through pragmatic trials: challenges in research and implementation

Ian Russell, Duncan Raistrick and Gillian Tober

Introduction

Why has it proved difficult to find the best psychological treatment for substance misuse problems or dependence? Project MATCH and the UK Alcohol Treatment Trial are examples of large studies which found close similarity between different treatments. These findings were not entirely unexpected since researchers are bound to compare the most promising treatments available to them. Moreover the outcomes of psychological interventions are influenced by the therapeutic alliance between therapist and client as well as by the intrinsic effectiveness of those interventions. In the face of these challenges there is concern that previous policy and purchasing decisions for substance misuse treatment have been based upon sub-optimal research designs. This chapter discusses the methodological issues behind the choice of research design in this field.

Evidence-based practice

It is more than ten years since David Sackett, the eminent US clinical epidemiologist, initiated the campaign for evidence-based clinical practice. Not surprisingly early definitions related to evidence-based medicine (EBM); for example, Sackett *et al.* (1996, p. 71) described it as 'the conscientious, explicit and judicious use of current best evidence in making decisions about the care of individual patients'. While we have no quarrel with this as a definition, it does focus on EBM as a tool to inform decisions about the care of individual patients. Over recent years, however, health policy and central guidance have highlighted the need for decisions about health care to take account of the best available evidence. The concepts of evidence-based practice (EBP) for all health care professionals and evidence-based policy in the NHS give more weight to patients' values and NHS costs, and focus upon broader issues of resource allocation rather than individual clinical practice.

Attractive though the concept of EBP is, there are caveats to the evidence-based approach, of which we mention three. First, taken too far, EBP can place a disproportionate emphasis upon manuals and protocols and a generally mechanistic approach. Clinical practice is not an exact science, but has to cope with uncertainty, which is difficult to encompass within rigid guidelines and protocols. Secondly the implementation of EBP requires fundamental shifts in thinking and culture, which take time to achieve. Although performance assessment is important, initiatives to improve quality have less chance of success if they stress the 'stick over the carrot'. Incentives have to encourage a climate of learning rather than 'naming and shaming' clinicians whose performance ignores evidence. Finally EBP emphasises clinical effectiveness and cost-effectiveness, thereby seeking to maximise total health gain within available resources. However such an approach does not address the distribution of health benefits across society. Paradigms which place most weight on equity and entitlement are likely to lead to policies different from those based mainly on clinical effectiveness and cost-effectiveness.

Notwithstanding these limitations of EBP, we believe the approach has much to offer in making decision making more explicit and reducing the scope for unacceptable variations in practice. Critical to its success is the creation of an environment which rewards measurable improvements in health care, and in which there is a genuine focus on the health of patients and the general public.

Deriving evidence about effectiveness

To randomise or not to randomise?

In exploring what constitutes good evidence, we start with a paraphrase from Professor Archie Cochrane's seminal monograph (Cochrane 1989):

> The development of cost-effective health care needs hard evidence, preferably from randomised trials, that the use of each therapy either alters the natural history of the condition or otherwise benefits many patients at a reasonable cost.

Why was Cochrane so strong an advocate of randomised trials for all forms of health care? Consider for example the issue of the best design for evaluating the most effective form of psychotherapy for alcohol problems. In the USA, Project MATCH compared three manual-guided psychological treatments for alcohol dependence and problems: Cognitive Behavioural Therapy (Kadden *et al.* 1992), Twelve-Step Facilitation Therapy (Nowinski *et al.* 1992) and Motivational Enhancement Therapy (MET) – a 'brief' intervention lasting four sessions rather than 12 (Miller *et al.* 1992). There was no difference on average between these treatments in either of the principal outcome measures – clients' percentage of days abstinent or their number of drinks per drinking day (Project MATCH Research Group 1997). Thus MET, apparently the least expensive of these three therapies, is the most cost-effective, at least in the USA (UKATT Research Team 2005b).

Later the UK Alcohol Treatment Trial (UKATT) compared an anglicised version of MET with the newer Social Behaviour and Network Therapy (SBNT), based on the philosophy that people with drinking problems have the best chance of good outcomes when they have the support of 'social networks' of one or more people willing to help them to abstain from or reduce drinking (Copello *et al.* 2002). The UKATT Research Team (2001) faced the issue of how best to compare these two therapies. Suppose they had chosen an observational study comparing the outcomes of clients in Birmingham treated by SBNT with those of clients in Leeds treated by MET. There are many differences between Birmingham and Leeds, not only in the epidemiology of drinking problems, but also in the structure of the alcohol treatment services and the characteristics of the clients who use them. Hence it would have been impossible to attribute any significant difference in outcome between SBNT and MET clients to the difference in therapy rather than to the inevitable differences in the characteristics of clients or their therapists (Russell 1983).

While accepting the intrinsic weakness of the observational approach, many critics of randomised trials argue that quasi-experimental research designs (Cook and Campbell 1979) can ameliorate, if not resolve, the fundamental problem of attributing differences in outcome to their true cause. In health care evaluation the most common of the rigorous forms of quasi-experiment is the controlled before-and-after study. In evaluating alternative therapies for alcohol problems, this design would be feasible if the standard therapy delivered by services in Birmingham changed from MET to SBNT, while that delivered by services in Leeds remained MET throughout. Such a design would compare clients treated before the change in Birmingham with clients treated after, controlled by clients in Leeds treated before and after the date of the change in Birmingham. While the risk of bias in such a study is certainly less than in the previous observational design, this risk is very difficult, if not impossible, to eliminate (Russell 1983). In this example there would be many potential sources of bias. For example the change of standard therapy is likely to lead to a change in the characteristics of patients referred for treatment, reflecting the brief nature of the old therapy and the social nature of the new therapy. The resulting bias would be difficult to detect, and even more difficult to correct with confidence by statistical analysis.

In contrast randomisation protects against selection bias in health care evaluation. Its other main advantage, less well known, is that it provides a sound mathematical basis for subsequent analysis (Russell 1983). Even so there are several objections to randomisation. Professor Raymond Illsley expressed two of the more common objections at the time when he was Chairman of the Scottish Health Services Research Committee. First he argued that randomised trials were seldom feasible in health services research (Illsley 1982). Since he was excluding drug trials, he was right at the time. Stimulated by the NHS Research and Development Programme, however, the number of trials in health services research has been increasing ever since. In particular the UKATT Research Team (2001) followed the example of Project MATCH (1997) in adopting a randomised trial design. Thus Illsley's first objection no longer holds, even in a complex field like psychotherapy.

Explanatory trial or pragmatic trial?

Research methods for evaluating drug therapies are well established and have been widely used in the field of addictive behaviours. The double-blind placebo-controlled randomised controlled trial is often described as the 'gold standard'. Such trials allocate trial participants at random to one of two (or more) treatments. The control or 'placebo' treatment is manufactured so that neither participants nor researcher are aware of what treatment they are taking. So Illsley's second concern was that, even where randomised trials were feasible, the constraints of such artificial experiments would limit the relevance of the findings. Since patients in clinical practice take only active drugs, Illsley was questioning whether the use of double-blind placebos could provide evidence for the real world.

In the addictions field, for example, drug therapies are commonly used as adjuncts to psychosocial therapies, which are generally seen as the main interventions. However the double-blind placebo-controlled trial is less than ideal for evaluating psychosocial therapies, for four main reasons. First, psychological factors, notably motivation and self-efficacy, generally have a greater influence on outcomes for these therapies than for drug therapies. Secondly, it follows that the delivery of treatment, in particular therapist style, may be as important as the specific treatment. Thirdly, an untreated control group may be more difficult to justify on both ethical and practical grounds. Finally, it is more difficult to 'blind' participants and researchers to the psychotherapy given than it is for drug therapies. Studies comparing the efficacy of motivational interviewing with that of other approaches are particularly sensitive to the choice of research design, as the approach focuses on client motivation and self-efficacy, and the style of treatment is at the very heart of the approach.

As the number of trials increases across the world, the concern about practical relevance becomes critical in health services research. To address this concern we explore the distinction between explanatory trials (also called 'fastidious') and pragmatic trials – first drawn by Schwartz and

Table 4.1 Differences between fastidious and pragmatic trials

	Fastidious trials	*Pragmatic trials*
Objective	To draw *conclusions* about therapies by testing defined scientific hypotheses	To make *decisions* between therapies in clinical practice
Experimental conditions	Laboratory conditions	Normal clinical practice
Definition of therapies	1 Rigid 2 Equalised – therapies are defined to achieve the *same* placebo effect	1 Flexible 2 Optimal – each therapy is defined to make the *best* of any placebo effect
Definition of patients	1 Patients eligible for the trial (i.e. for all therapies) are strictly defined a priori and may be redefined a posteriori 2 Patients who withdraw from therapy are *withdrawn* from the trial	1 Patients eligible for the trial (i.e. for all therapies) are flexibly but irrevocably defined a priori 2 Patients who withdraw from therapy *remain* in the trial for analysis
Number of criteria	Single or multiple	Single criterion, if necessary by combining multiple criteria
Method of analysis	Traditional significance test for each hypothesis, but no formal relationship between significance tests	Select therapy that gives best weighted criterion (no formal significance test)
Number of patients	Traditional calculation based on *type 1 and type 2 errors* for each hypothesis; the total number of patients should be the maximum of these calculations	Calculation based on the weighted criterion and on *type 3 error*, i.e. concluding that therapy A is superior to therapy B when the opposite is true

Source. Russell (1983). 'The evaluation of computerised tomography: a review of research methods', in A.J. Culyer and B. Horsberger (eds) *Economic and medical evaluation of health care technologies*, Berlin: Springer-Verlag.

Lellouch (1967) and now summarised in Table 4.1. Explanatory trials try to draw conclusions about defined scientific hypotheses, while pragmatic or 'real world' (Simon *et al.* 1995) trials try to choose between therapies in clinical practice. This distinction is similar to that between Phase II drug trials – 'small-scale investigations into (efficacy and) safety' and Phase III trials – 'rigorous and extensive trials to compare a drug with standard therapy for the same condition' (Pocock 1983, p. 3).

The first implication of this distinction is that explanatory and pragmatic trials need different experimental conditions (Table 4.1). In seeking information about defined scientific hypotheses, explanatory trials need strict laboratory-like conditions to eliminate as many potential sources of bias as possible. To this end most explanatory drug trials are both double-blind and placebo-controlled. While experimental patients receive the active drug, control patients receive a placebo, that is an inert drug identical to the active drug in every other respect. 'Double-blind' means that neither the patient nor the doctor knows whether the patient is receiving the active drug or the placebo. Together these two ploys aim to eliminate the 'placebo effect' – the non-specific therapeutic effect that comes from the belief on the part of both doctor and patient that the patient is receiving an effective drug, rather than the intrinsic pharmacological effect of the active drug. Because placebo effects inflate estimated pharmacological effects, they are correctly regarded as biases within explanatory trials. In contrast pragmatic trials should use normal clinical practice to reflect the real world in which the resulting decisions are taken, rather than the artificial world of the laboratory. Furthermore there is no reason to eschew placebo effects that enhance the intrinsic effect of the basic intervention.

The second implication of the distinction between explanatory and pragmatic trials is that trial protocols should define the therapies to be compared in different ways (Table 4.1). Since explanatory trials test hypotheses about the intrinsic properties of therapies to the exclusion of placebo effects, they need rigid protocols that define therapies precisely and equalise placebo effects. Conversely pragmatic trials seek to identify the better therapy for routine clinical practice. Though this spans a range of clinical circumstances, therapists in each context aim to do the best for each patient who consults them, in particular by optimising the non-specific effects of the therapies they use. It follows that pragmatic trials need protocols that are flexible enough to permit therapists to adapt therapies to the needs of individual patients, as they do in the routine clinical practice to which the findings of the trial will apply. At the same time, however, these protocols must be explicit enough to ensure that all therapists deliver a consistent package of care, so that the conclusions of the trial stem from a homogeneous therapy rather than a heterogeneous collection of procedures.

To illustrate this clear distinction between explanatory and pragmatic trials, consider a randomised trial to compare naltrexone, a new alcohol treatment that needs only a single dose each day, with acamprosate, which is taken three times daily – an issue reviewed by Hotopf and colleagues (1997). To equalise the non-specific effects of the different dose frequencies (once versus three times a day), and thus focus on their pharmacological effects, the explanatory version of this trial would need to be double-blind. If research doctor or participating patients knew the identity of the prescribed drug, that would activitate the placebo effect of the different dose frequencies. It follows that all patients would have to take some dose, either active or placebo, three times a day. While patients randomised to acamprosate would receive the active drug within every dose, patients randomised to naltrexone would receive the active drug only in their first dose each day and a placebo in the other two doses.

The pragmatic version of this trial would be far more natural as argued by Simon *et al.* (1995; 1996). Though control patients randomised to acamprosate would again receive the active drug three times a day, they would know why. Hence their doctors would be able to make the best of the placebo effect by emphasising the benefit of receiving a drug whose performance was proven, even if the interval between doses was short. Experimental patients randomised to naltrexone would also know, with the result that they would need no interpolated placebo, and would merely take the active drug once a day. Hence their doctors would be able to make the best of the placebo effect by emphasising the benefits of leaving medication at home.

This example highlights two methodological problems faced by those who plan explanatory drug trials. First, how effective will the trial be in equalising the placebo effect between experimental and control groups? In particular what proportion of patients in each group would infer the identity of the drug to which they had been randomised? The answer to this crucial question depends on the nature of the drugs being compared. Each trialist needs to be confident that the trial under consideration will 'blind' almost all patients, and that the artificiality illustrated by this example is a price worth paying.

The planners of most explanatory trials respond to this dilemma by giving control patients only a placebo. Whether this procedure increases the proportion of patients who cannot tell whether they have the active drug or the placebo, it is likely to increase recruitment by reducing artificiality. Nevertheless the use of placebos on their own brings a second methodological problem. Trials that focus on the absolute efficacy and safety of a single therapy impede the study of the relative efficacy of therapies that are real alternatives to each other, for example naltrexone and acamprosate. This question is at the heart of evidence-based psychotherapy as much as pharmacotherapy. To use a pair of placebo-controlled trials, one of naltrexone and the other of acamprosate, to infer the relative effectiveness of these two drugs is tantamount to using an observational, or at best quasi-experimental, design – designs that are inherently susceptible to bias, as we have shown. The case-study of naltrexone versus acamoprosate shows that explanatory trials need not be placebo-controlled. Indeed the only patients in that hypothetical trial to receive a placebo would be in the experimental group, not the control.

The third implication of the distinction between explanatory and pragmatic trials is that the trial protocol should also define the patients to be studied in different ways (Table 4.1). The protocol for an explanatory trial should specify strict criteria to determine whether each patient is eligible for both therapies – criteria that are easier to fulfil if one of the therapies happens to be a placebo. Furthermore patients who fulfil these criteria but fail to comply with the strict therapy regime cannot contribute to the testing of the defined scientific hypotheses. So they are withdrawn from the trial and excluded from analysis. In contrast a pragmatic trial is intended to replicate normal practice, where the choice of therapy is based on clinical criteria and patients often fail to comply. Thus the protocol should specify explicit but flexible inclusion criteria. Furthermore patients who do not adhere to the recommended therapy, in part or in whole, nevertheless remain in their allocated group for analysis, because non-adherence is endemic in the real world where the results of the trial will be used.

The fourth implication of this distinction is that explanatory and pragmatic trials differ in the number and type of criteria that they use to compare the therapies under review (Table 4.1). An explanatory trial can in principle test an unlimited number of narrow scientific hypotheses provided that they are all precisely defined in advance. However a pragmatic trial should in principle have only one criterion since the choice of the better therapy has to be unequivocal. Hence that criterion has to include and weight as wide a range as possible of the advantages and disadvantages, both short-term and long-term, of the therapies being compared. Examples of such a criterion include cost per quality-adjusted life year (QALY) and the more sophisticated cost–benefit ratio (Drummond and McGuire 2002).

The last two implications of the distinction between explanatory and pragmatic trials concern the statistical issues of analysis and trial size. These follow directly from the difference in the nature and number of the criteria that these trials use. Since an explanatory trial typically has many well-defined hypotheses to test, it applies a traditional significance test to each. These tests are meaningful only if they ensure that statistical significance closely reflects scientific importance, expressed in biomedical or clinical terms. This will be true for each hypothesis only if the number of patients available for analysis achieves a target identified in advance on the basis of a traditional sample size calculation. The key feature of such a calculation is the specification of the size of difference between the two therapies that should be regarded as pharmacologically or clinically worthwhile (Altman 1991). As each hypothesis gives rise to a different estimate of the sample size needed, the trial will achieve all its aims only if the eventual trial size is at least the maximum of these estimates.

In contrast the corresponding pragmatic trial has but one comprehensive and therefore complex criterion by which to compare the alternative drug therapies. Since this trial is designed to decide between these two therapies, analysis is deceptively simple: the analyst merely has to choose the therapy that performed better according to the single weighted criterion. To ensure that this choice is as robust as the conclusions of the traditional hypothesis tests, however, the planning of the pragmatic trial should be at least as painstaking as that of the explanatory trial. The latter specifies the differences between the two therapies that are to be regarded as critical. It also puts limits on the probabilities of two types of inferential error: type 1 error – that is concluding by chance that the two therapies differ when they do not; and type 2 error – that is concluding by chance that the therapies do not differ when they do.

Although the process of trading off these two types of error receives widespread coverage in the statistical literature (e.g. Altman 1991), neither type is relevant to the planning of pragmatic trials. Type 1 errors are irrelevant because, if the two therapies do not differ, it does not matter which is chosen. Type 2 errors are impossible because the requirement that one of the therapies be chosen ensures that one cannot conclude that they do not differ. Instead the planning of pragmatic trials depends crucially on the need to limit the probability of type 3 error – concluding by chance that one therapy is superior to the other when the opposite is true. Although statistical tables linking the sample size needed to limit the probability of type 3 error to the inherent variability of the single criterion are rare, they can be found in Schwartz and colleagues (1980), elaborating on the original paper by Schwartz and Lellouch (1967). However the main difficulty in planning truly pragmatic trials lies not in the paucity of relevant statistical tables, but in estimating the variability of the single comprehensive criterion. There have been few complete cost–benefit and cost–utility analyses of alternative psychotherapies (Tolley and Rowland 1995). Even fewer have reported estimates of the variability of the cost–benefit or cost–utility ratios needed to inform the design of future pragmatic trials.

In summary there is increasing recognition that the randomised trial is the method of choice for evaluating the effectiveness of psychological therapies. Other designs are too prone to bias. Nevertheless many problems remain – logical, practical and ethical. More use of pragmatic trials would overcome many, but not all, of these problems. Of course we need preliminary research, often in the form of a fastidious trial, to establish the intrinsic properties of therapies, and their efficacy under ideal conditions. However the need for subsequent pragmatic trials to evaluate effectiveness in clinical practice is even greater. Though pragmatic trials create their own methodological problems, we are more likely to achieve evidence-based therapy if we tackle these problems directly. It is easier to increase the precision of answers to more relevant pragmatic questions than manipulate precise answers to less relevant fastidious questions.

Case-study: the UK Alcohol Treatment Trial (UKATT)

We again use UKATT to illustrate methodological issues. Observational and quasi-experimental designs are especially prone to bias when services differ between and within centres. Such differences are common in the treatment of alcohol and drug problems in particular and, we judge, in psychotherapy in general. So the UKATT Research Team (2001) was quick to adopt a randomised design. As UKATT aimed to generate evidence to guide commissioning decisions for services in the UK, there was a prima facie case for a pragmatic trial. Nevertheless the detailed design of the trial involved many choices between methods characteristic of pragmatic trials and others typical of explanatory trials. One example will suffice.

Project MATCH (1997) had shown that in the USA brief Motivational Enhancement Therapy (MET) was as effective as more extensive treatments, and therefore more cost-effective. Thus its popularity in the UK has increased over time. In particular it was the natural comparator for a trial to evaluate the newly developed Social Behaviour and Network Therapy (SBNT). However the manuals developed in the UKATT feasibility study concluded that in the NHS three sessions would suffice for MET, rather than the four used in MATCH (UKATT Research Team 2001). In contrast Copello and colleagues (2002) argued that SBNT would need eight sessions to cover its syllabus in full.

An explanatory trial design would advocate the construction of a brief version of SBNT, or even an extended version of MET, so that the resulting trial focused on the intrinsic merits of each therapy by devoting the same resources to each. However such a trial would have been of less use to the NHS, which wanted to know whether there was a therapy more effective or cost-effective than MET. The designers of UKATT therefore adopted the pragmatic design of comparing three sessions of MET with eight sessions of SBNT. If the full SBNT were to prove no more effective than MET, then MET would be confirmed as 'best buy'. In the event, however, the treatments were equally effective in reducing drinking and related problems and improving mental health (UKATT Research Team 2005a). Furthermore rigorous economic analysis showed that there was no difference in cost-effectiveness because the greater savings in health and social costs in the SBNT group made up for the lower cost of MET (UKATT Research Team 2005b). Hence the next question to answer is whether a brief version of SBNT, costing approximately the same as MET, would generate equal savings, and therefore be more cost-effective.

Implementing evidence-based practice

The implementation of evidence-based practice poses a challenge in all fields of health care, not least because this includes four distinct tasks. First there is the largely epidemiological task of creating the evidence base by reviewing and synthesising the rigorous evidence relevant to the issue in question. Scientific bodies like the (world-wide) Cochrane Collaboration and governmental bodies like the (British) National Institute of Health and Clinical Excellence demand that review and synthesis should achieve a high level of scientific rigour. In particular they require that the sub-tasks of finding, selecting and extracting evidence should be systematic, and that the subtask of analysing the resulting evidence should be statistically robust, preferably through meta-analysis (NHS Centre for Reviews and Dissemination 2001).

Secondly, there is the largely clinical task of developing guidelines, manuals, protocols or even frameworks. Ideally the evidence base created through the first task will provide a rich source of clinical material for the developers of guidelines and the like. Where the evidence is weak, however, developers must fall back on expert consensus. Though such weaknesses in evidence are inevitable in all fields, it is important that guidelines make this explicit, not only by grading the available evidence, but also by highlighting gaps in need of future research.

Thirdly, there is the largely psychological task of persuading clinicians to change their current practice and adopt the resulting evidence-based guidelines, both in principle and in their daily work. The Cochrane Collaboration has long since recognised that the work of the majority of its groups, who focus on clinical topics, was of no practical value unless the evidence they synthesise changes clinical practice. So they established an Effective Practice and Organisation of Care (EPOC) group to review and synthesise the evidence about changing clinical behaviour in the same way that most of their other groups address clinical issues.

Finally there is the largely information-scientific task of monitoring adherence to these evidence-based guidelines once implemented. The trials that underpin guidelines generally develop and use a portfolio of sophisticated, and therefore costly, outcome measures to generate the evidence that one therapy is more effective and more cost-effective than another. To use the same portfolio for monitoring adherence would be both inefficient and irresponsible. Instead the challenge is to devise a much smaller and therefore cheaper portfolio of routine measures that is sufficiently valid and reliable to detect inadequate levels of adherence to the evidence-based guidelines. Where there is evidence that adherence to a few process or intermediate outcome variables leads to good outcomes, those will often serve as good proxies to monitor the quality of implementation.

Though all four of these tasks are difficult in almost all fields of health care, they are even more difficult in the delivery of psychosocial therapies than in the delivery of drug therapies. Once a patient is known to have received a given drug, the investigator knows precisely what therapeutic substance(s) are acting upon the patient. Even if there is doubt whether the patient has taken the medicine, one can usually monitor blood levels. Thus it is feasible to deliver the drug in line with the evidence base. For psychosocial therapies in general and motivational therapies in particular, however, knowing what the client has received is more difficult. The therapist's behaviour and the client's attitude both contribute to the dose of treatment delivered and received. In the more behavioural of the psychosocial therapies, independent raters can monitor delivery by recording treatment components delivered by the therapist and, for example, homework tasks returned by the client. In rating motivational interviewing, the question whether the open questions, reflective statements and eliciting style of the therapist elicited 'change talk' and thus enhanced motivation to change is more complex. So Carroll and Nuro (1996) developed the technology model of psychotherapy research into addiction to overcome this difficulty by observing the delivery of treatment, thus mimicking the monitoring of drug therapy.

In Chapter 6 Martino and colleagues describe the resulting instruments. The Yale Clinical Trials Network developed the Yale Adherence and Competence Scale (YACS) to monitor the delivery of motivational interviewing, MET and other specific psychosocial therapies (Ball *et al.* 2002). Project MATCH used it to measure, monitor and supervise the delivery of three treatments. Tober *et al.* (2005) adapted the YACS to contribute to the evaluation of MET and SBNT in UKATT. More specifically the Process Rating Scale (PRS) enabled UKATT to measure manual adherence independently, and thus to facilitate continuing supervision and the assessment of competence. In particular PRS-based supervision after training enabled UKATT to address the habit of therapists to 'drift' from treatment manuals over time.

Summary

Achieving evidence-based practice faces at least six challenges in all clinical fields:

- to use robust research designs to generate rigorous evidence about (cost) effectiveness;
- to use pragmatic research designs to generate relevant evidence about (cost) effectiveness;
- to develop an evidence base by reviewing and synthesising rigorous and relevant information;
- to develop clinical guidelines or manuals from this evidence base;
- to persuade clinicians to change current practice by adopting these resulting guidelines; and,
- to monitor adherence to these evidence-based guidelines once implemented.

Though all these tasks are difficult in almost all fields of health care, they are even more difficult in the delivery of motivational interviewing than in the delivery of drug therapies. Motivational interviewing poses particular problems because of variations in practice and the wide range of therapist variables that influence outcome.

References

Altman, D.G. (1991) *Practical statistics for medical research*, London: Chapman and Hall.

Ball, S.A., Bachrach, K., DeCarlo, J., Farentinos, C., Keen, M., McSherry, T., Polcin, D., Snead, N., Sockriter, R., Wrigley, P., Zammarelli, L. and Carroll, K.M. (2002) 'Characteristics of community clinicians trained to provide manual-guided therapy for substance abusers', *Journal of Substance Abuse Treatment*, 23: 309–318.

Carroll, K.M. and Nuro, K.F. (1996) *The technology model: an introduction to psychotherapy research in substance abuse*, Training Series No.1, New Haven, Connecticut: Yale University Psychotherapy Development Center.

Cochrane, A.L. (1989) *Effectiveness and efficiency: random reflections on health services*, London: British Medical Journal and Nuffield Provincial Hospitals Trust.

Cook, T.D. and Campbell, D.T. (1979) *Quasi-experimentation: design and analysis issues for field setting*, Chicago: Rand McNally.

Copello, A., Orford, J., Hodgson, R., Tober, G. and Barrett, C. (2002) 'Social Behaviour and Network Therapy: basic principles and early experiences', *Addictive Behaviors*, 27: 345–366.

Drummond, M.F. and McGuire, A. (2002) *Economic evaluation in health care: merging theory from practice*, Oxford: Oxford University Press.

Hotopf, M., Lewis, G. and Normand, C. (1997) 'Putting trials on trial – the costs and consequences of small trials in depression: a systematic review of methodology', *Journal of Epidemiology and Community Health*, 51: 354–358.

Illsley, R. (1982) 'Research and the NHS', *Health Bulletin*, 40: 54–57.

Kadden, R.M., Carroll, K. and Donovan, D.M. (eds) (1992) *Cognitive behavioural coping skills therapy manual: a clinical research guide for therapists treating individuals with alcohol abuse and dependence*, Project MATCH Monograph 3, Rockville, Maryland: National Institute on Alcohol Abuse and Alcoholism.

Miller, W.R., Zweben, A., DiClemente, C.C. and Rychtarik, R.G. (1992) *Motivational enhancement therapy manual: a clinical research guide for therapists treating individuals with alcohol abuse and dependence*, Project MATCH Monograph 2, Rockville, Maryland: National Institute on Alcohol Abuse and Alcoholism.

NHS Centre for Reviews and Dissemination (2001) *Undertaking systematic reviews of research on effectiveness: CRD's guidance for carrying out or commissioning reviews*, 2nd edn, CRD Report 4, York: NHS CRD.

Nowinski, J., Baker, S. and Carroll, K. (1992) *Twelve step facilitation manual: a clinical research guide for therapists treating individuals with alcohol abuse and dependence*, Project MATCH Monograph 1, Rockville, Maryland: National Institute on Alcohol Abuse and Alcoholism.

Pocock, S.J. (1983) *Clinical trials: a practical approach*, Chichester: Wiley.

Project MATCH Research Group (1997) 'Matching alcoholism treatments to client heterogeneity: Project MATCH post-treatment drinking outcomes', *Journal of Studies on Alcohol*, 58: 7–29.

Russell, I.T. (1983) 'The evaluation of computerised tomography: a review of research methods', in A.J. Culyer and B. Horsberger (eds) *Economic and medical evaluation of health care technologies*, Berlin: Springer-Verlag.

Sackett, D.L., Rosenberg, W.M., Gray, J.A, Haynes, R.B. and Richardson, W.S. (1996) 'Evidence-based medicine: what it is and what it isn't', *British Medical Journal*, 312: 71–72.

Schwartz, D. and Lellouch, J. (1967) 'Explanatory and pragmatic attitudes in clinical trials', *Journal of Chronic Diseases*, 20: 637–648.

Schwartz, D., Flamand, R. and Lellouch, J. (1980) *Clinical trials*, London: Academic Press.

Simon, G., Wagner, E. and Von Korff, M. (1995) 'Cost-effectiveness comparisons using "real world" randomized trials: the case of new antidepressant drugs', *Journal of Clinical Epidemiology*, 48: 363–373.

Simon, G.E., VonKorff, M., Heiligenstein, J.H., Revicki, D.A., Grothaus, L., Katon, W. and Wagner, E.H. (1996) 'Initial antidepressant choice in primary care: Effectiveness and cost of fluoxetine vs tricyclic antidepressants', *Journal of the American Medical Association*, 275(24): 1897–1902.

Tober, G., Godfrey, C., Parrott, S., Copello, A., Farrin, A., Hodgson, R., Kenyon, R., Morton, V., Orford, J., Russell, I. and Slegg, G., on behalf of the UKATT Research Team (2005) 'Setting standards for training and competence: The UK Alcohol Treatment Trial', *Alcohol and Alcoholism*, 40: 413–418.

Tolley, K. and Rowland, M. (1995) *Evaluating the cost-effectiveness of counselling in health care*, London: Routledge.

UKATT Research Team (2001) 'The United Kingdom Alcohol Treatment Trial (UKATT): hypotheses, design and methods', *Alcohol and Alcoholism*, 36: 11–21.

UKATT Research Team (2005a) 'Effectiveness of treatment for alcohol problems: findings of the randomised UK alcohol treatment trial', *British Medical Journal*, 541–544.

UKATT Research Team (2005b) 'Cost-effectiveness of treatment for alcohol problems: findings of the randomised UK alcohol treatment trial', *British Medical Journal*, 544–548.

Chapter 5

Motivational enhancement therapy: stand-alone and integrated interventions

Ronald M. Kadden, Karen L. Steinberg and Roger Roffman

This chapter considers several clinical trials that studied motivational enhancement therapy (MET) as either a stand-alone intervention or integrated with additional treatment components. We begin with a discussion of several key definitions and concepts, followed by illustrative clinical trials.

Key definitions and concepts

Motivational interviewing is a counselling style that is client-centred and intended to support individuals in resolving ambivalence and enhancing their commitment to change. *Motivational enhancement therapy* is a brief intervention modality (generally 1 to 4 sessions) involving an assessment interview, personal feedback of assessment results, and exploration of problems the client has experienced, with the interviewer utilising motivational interviewing skills. *Stand-alone motivational enhancement therapy* can be of two types: (1) a brief treatment that may be sufficient in itself, or (2) a motivational catalyst designed for the non-treatment seeker at an early stage of readiness for change. *Integrated motivational enhancement therapy* is an intervention involving multiple treatment elements (e.g. assessment and feedback utilising a motivational interviewing style, cognitive-behavioural skills training, case management) with the purpose of enhancing commitment and supporting the achievement and maintenance of change.

MET as a stand-alone intervention

When MET is delivered as a stand-alone brief treatment, the basic assumption is that clients may already possess the personal resources and strengths needed to achieve behaviour change, and what they need is to become motivated to mobilise them and put them into action. In this model, the role of the counsellor is to help clients resolve their ambivalence about making changes, by providing empathic reflection in response to clients' statements, delivering feedback from an assessment of client behaviours and attitudes, providing information to clients regarding their personal risk, emphasising their personal responsibility for change, encouraging them to consider various change options, and facilitating their optimism and self-efficacy (Miller *et al.* 1992). This reflective and supportive counsellor style has been found to generate less resistance from clients, to be more successful in engaging them in the therapeutic process, and to predict better outcomes than a more directive, confrontational style (Miller *et al.* 1993). Later in this chapter, two examples of MET as a stand-alone brief treatment (Project MATCH, Marijuana Treatment Project) will be presented. In settings that utilise a stepped-care approach, failure of this minimal level of care to induce change would be followed by a longer, more intensive intervention.

MET may also be delivered as a motivational catalyst for individuals who are not seeking treatment and are in an early stage of change. The intention is to provide an intervention that is perceived as a non-demanding and meaningful service by individuals who are ambivalent about change and unlikely to enter treatment. Three examples of MET as a motivational catalyst (Marijuana Check-Up, Teen Marijuana Check-Up, Sex Check-Up) will be discussed.

MET in integrated interventions

There has been considerable interest in the integration of MET with other treatment approaches. Undoubtedly some of that interest arises from the problems of poor motivation and lack of adherence to treatment recommendations that are so common among clients in addictions treatment. MET is a natural for consideration as a brief add-on at the beginning of other treatment approaches to strengthen client commitment and prevent some of the problems that could otherwise impede treatment effectiveness.

In what is perhaps the most clearly articulated example of this reasoning, Baer, Kivlahan and Donovan (1999) make the case that skills training is not an adequate intervention by itself, because clients first have to accept the necessity of change and then have to develop enough motivation to engage in the process of actually making changes.[1] They reason that providing a motivational intervention prior to skills training is likely to enhance clients' engagement in treatment and reduce dropouts, and may result in better substance use outcomes. They also emphasise the necessity of continuing to use an empathic style throughout the course of skills training to maintain client motivation.

1 Baer *et al.* also reason the converse. That is, motivation to change, by itself, is often insufficient. Skills deficits exist in many clients, and therefore skills-training is frequently necessary to develop clients' personal coping resources.

Empirical tests of motivational interventions combined with other treatment approaches have found that when compared with control groups, clients assigned to a preparatory motivational intervention often had better substance use outcomes (Connors *et al.* 2002; Bien *et al.* 1993; Brown and Miller 1993), but not always (Donovan *et al.* 2001), fewer substance-related problems (Saunders *et al.* 1995), better motivation to change (Dench and Bennett 2000; Saunders *et al.* 1995), and improvements in both substance use and psychiatric symptoms among dual-diagnosis patients (Barrowclough *et al.* 2001). In a review of studies that specifically examined the effects of motivational interventions on adherence to subsequent treatment, Zweben and Zuckoff (2002) found that in many but not all studies, the motivational intervention improved adherence to subsequent treatment, an effect that often mediated improved treatment outcomes. However, findings of reduced attrition from treatment (Saunders *et al.* 1995) have not been consistent across studies (Dench and Bennett 2000; Donovan *et al.* 2001), and positive outcomes following a motivational intervention were not always maintained at subsequent assessments (Bien *et al.* 1993; Baker *et al.* 2002).

Reviews of randomised trials of motivational interventions for substance use disorders or for health promotion (Dunn *et al.* 2001; Resnicow *et al.* 2002) have found that the most supportive evidence was obtained when motivational sessions were added as an enhancement before more intensive treatment. In commenting on the findings of Dunn and colleagues, Miller (2001) suggested 'perhaps MI amplifies the effect of other treatment, exerting a synergistic effect that is larger than its effect as a stand-alone intervention.'

Clinical trials

Stand-alone MET: Project MATCH

An important test of MET as a stand-alone intervention was provided in Project MATCH, a multi-site study of patient-treatment matching that was the largest clinical trial of treatments for alcoholism ever mounted (Babor and Del Boca 2003). Although brief motivational treatment approaches were relatively new at the time Project MATCH was designed, it was decided that there already were a sufficient number of studies demonstrating efficacy and effectiveness to warrant inclusion of a motivational enhancement intervention in the trial.

Project MATCH studied two separate cohorts of alcohol dependent clients, 952 who received one of three treatments (one of which was MET) on an outpatient basis and 774 who received those treatments as aftercare following inpatient or intensive day hospital treatment. MET was developed by Project MATCH investigators (Miller *et al.* 1992) around the time the first edition of the Miller and Rollnick (1991) book on motivational interviewing was published. The MET manual includes some material that appeared in the earlier volume, but it is much more a treatment manual than its predecessor. It provides considerably more detailed information regarding implementation of the motivational interviewing style and its use in a clinical trial, in order to enhance counsellor adherence to the approach and minimise differences in its implementation among counsellors and across sites. The other two treatments in Project MATCH were Cognitive Behavioural Coping Skills Therapy (CBT) and Twelve-Step Facilitation Therapy (TSF), both involving weekly sessions over a 12-week period.

The MET intervention in Project MATCH consisted of four sessions occurring over the same 12-week time frame as the other two therapies in the trial. The treatment manual specified that MET counsellors should employ an empathic style as they ask clients about problems they have encountered, and explore discrepancies between clients' current behaviour and personally important goals and values. The manual also specified that counsellors should avoid confrontation, arguments and labelling, should 'roll' with resistance, and facilitate client optimism and self-efficacy. In the first MET session, structured feedback was provided based on pre-treatment assessments of alcohol consumption and its medical, psychological and social consequences. The Personal Feedback Report included a comparison of the individual's drinking to national norms, estimates of blood alcohol peaks, and feedback regarding risk factors, negative consequences of drinking, and results of liver function and neuropsychological tests. The intent was to increase participants' awareness of specific problems associated with their drinking and provide an opportunity for them to express concern and develop a commitment to change. The second MET session focused on enhancing the commitment to change and developing a plan for making behaviour changes. To enhance support for efforts to change, the client's spouse or significant other was invited to attend one of the first two sessions. The last two sessions, at weeks 6 and 12, monitored progress in implementing the change plan, considered ways of coping with obstacles encountered, and provided encouragement to continue working toward the specified goals.

During the 12-week treatment period there were no differences in efficacy between the 4-session MET and the two 12-session treatments among clients in the aftercare arm of the trial. However, in the outpatient arm, MET was less effective than the other treatments in limiting drinking and its consequences during the 12-week treatment period. Subsequently, during the year following treatment, outcomes were excellent in all three treatment conditions, with few differences among them for both aftercare clients and outpatients, and no significant differences among treatments emerged at a 3-year follow-up of outpatients.

Among the large number of client-treatment matching hypotheses tested, very few were supported, and only two of the supported ones involved the

MET intervention. In one of these, outpatient clients who were high in anger at intake had better drinking outcomes at both the 1-year and 3-year follow-ups if assigned to MET, compared to those in CBT and TSF, whereas outpatients who scored low on the anger measure had worse drinking outcomes if treated with MET. In another supported hypothesis, outpatient clients whose social network was supportive of drinking fared better at the 3-year assessment if they had been treated with TSF than with MET.

Overall, these results indicate that MET may not result in drinking reductions during the course of outpatient treatment that are comparable to those with CBT or TSF, but following treatment MET may be comparable in efficacy to the other two. In one positive matching finding, MET was more effective, following treatment, for those high in anger, but it was not differentially beneficial on a number of other matching dimensions, and was worse than TSF among clients whose social network was supportive of drinking.

Stand-alone MET: 'Check-Up' interventions

As noted in the introduction, one type of a stand-alone MET intervention is tailored for the non-treatment seeker. MET interventions publicised as 'check-ups' are intended to reach individuals at an early stage of readiness for change and engage them in an in-depth personal assessment of their behaviour, its consequences and their future goals.

The Marijuana Check-Up

Stephens and Roffman conducted a clinical trial ('The Marijuana Check-Up', MCU) with 188 non-treatment-seeking adult marijuana smokers who were randomly assigned to a motivational enhancement intervention (Personal Feedback, PF), a marijuana educational intervention (Multimedia Feedback, MMF) or a brief waiting period (Doyle *et al.* 2003). This experimental intervention was adapted from a brief motivational enhancement intervention ('The Drinker's Check-Up') in the alcoholism field (Miller and Sovereign 1989).

A variety of recruitment strategies were used to attract participants, including posters, radio and newspaper advertisements, and outreach at various community events. Project publicity targeted adults over the age of 18 who used marijuana and had concerns or were interested in obtaining information. The recruitment messages highlighted the objective, non-judgemental and confidential approach of the study, and emphasised that the MCU was not a treatment programme. Those who inquired were told that the programme didn't offer counselling but was aimed at helping participants better assess their experiences with marijuana.

The motivational enhancement (PF) intervention consisted of two sessions. The first was a structured interview to assess the individual's use patterns, perceived benefits and adverse consequences associated with use and with reductions or cessation of use, and self-efficacy for accomplishing cessation. In the second session, feedback was presented to the client based on the initial assessment, comparing the participant's use to national norms. Utilising motivational interviewing skills, the counsellor elicited the client's views concerning benefits and costs associated with his or her current marijuana use pattern and with various pathways of change. When appropriate, the discussion turned to goal setting for reduction or cessation of use and the identification of behaviour change strategies.

Participants in the MMF condition had an initial assessment session as in the previous group, and a second session that consisted of a videotaped documentary and a PowerPoint presentation on the health and behavioural effects of marijuana. Counsellors delivering the presentation were trained to answer the participant's questions regarding research findings on the effects of marijuana, but they avoided conversing on the details of the participant's personal use or possible interest in making changes.

At intake, 64 per cent of participants met diagnostic criteria for cannabis dependence and of those who did not, 89.4 per cent met criteria for cannabis abuse (American Psychiatric Association 1994). Upon joining the study they were using marijuana on more than 80 per cent of days, were getting high two or more times per day, and fewer than a third had resolved to quit or cut back on their use. At a 7-week follow-up, only participants in the PF condition had made significant reductions in their marijuana use. At a 6-month follow-up, however, there was no difference in marijuana use by condition, but a significant condition by time effect indicated greater reductions in the number of dependence symptoms in the PF condition. At a 12-month follow-up, PF participants showed greater reductions in the proportion of days of marijuana use, number of dependence symptoms, and number of marijuana-related problems than MMF participants. No differences were found in measures of motivation. Taken together, these findings suggest that the PF condition was superior to no intervention and to a credible educational intervention in producing reductions in marijuana use in adults who were initially ambivalent about making changes.

The Teen Marijuana Check-Up

Roffman and Stephens completed a single group, pre-post study of a MET intervention with adolescent marijuana smokers. It was tailored to attract adolescents in the precontemplation (not yet considering behaviour change) or contemplation (conflicted feelings about use, weighing pros and cons of continuing use) stages of change (Prochaska and DiClemente 1983). The goal was to help adolescents evaluate their marijuana use in the context of peers' use patterns, their own daily life and their goals for the future. A MET intervention was used to engage adolescents in a candid and thoughtful discussion of their marijuana use, including options for the future. The ultimate objective was to enhance motivation for change and, for those expressing such motivation, to offer support in setting goals, selecting behaviour change strategies and seeking treatment (Roffman 2001).

As in the adult study, the Teen MCU (TMCU) involved two sessions: an assessment interview and a subsequent feedback session one week later. Participants were reassessed after three months.

Adolescents were recruited through counsellors, teachers, health education classes and flyers at school. Eligible participants, 14–18 years of age who smoked marijuana at least once in the past 30 days, were invited to two sessions in which they would be provided with information about marijuana and would be given an opportunity to talk about their use. They were informed that any information they shared would be kept confidential and the researchers obtained an IRB-approved waiver of parental consent.

In the baseline assessment interview, participants were asked about their marijuana use and its impact on their lives, life goals for the next few years, stage of change, depressive symptoms and immediate goals regarding marijuana use. In the personal feedback session one week later, a health educator reviewed with the participant a Personalised Feedback Report (PFR) regarding his or her use. The PFR presented summaries of the participant's responses at the assessment interview regarding positive and negative marijuana effects, frequency of marijuana, alcohol and other drug use, anticipated consequences of changing marijuana use, the attitudes of family and friends regarding the participant's marijuana use, and general life goals and marijuana-related goals. The substance use sections of the PFR utilised pie charts to compare the participant's level of substance use with other age and gender-matched adolescents. While presenting each piece of information, the health educator used motivational interviewing strategies to elicit the participant's reaction and to explore the meaning of the information. Any self-motivational statements were reinforced via reflective listening; resistance was minimised by reflecting indications of ambivalence. If participants expressed a desire to change their marijuana use, the health educator described various change options, including self-change or drug treatment. The health educator facilitated completion of a change plan worksheet and provided a pamphlet on coping strategies to reduce marijuana use. One additional session was offered to those interested, and half of the participants accepted the offer.

Fifty-four participants completed the assessment, feedback and 3-month follow-up sessions. At intake, participants reported smoking marijuana on an average of 10 of the last 30 days. However, there was considerable variability in the frequency of smoking, so the sample was divided into lighter (8 days or less; n=27) and heavier (9+ days; n=27) groups. Heavier smokers were slightly younger when they first smoked marijuana, were more determined to continue smoking, and anticipated more adverse consequences if they were to cut down or quit. While a majority of participants had attempted to reduce (56 per cent) or stop (80 per cent) their marijuana use, more than half of the heavier users were not currently committed to change.

At the 3-month follow-up 44 per cent of participants reported reducing their marijuana use, and almost 15 per cent reported abstinence from marijuana in the 30 days prior to the follow-up session. Non-whites and heavier marijuana smokers at baseline had larger reductions in use. Marginally significant increases in alcohol use among heavier users suggested that they may have increased drinking while reducing marijuana use.

The TMCU was able to recruit and retain non-treatment seeking adolescent marijuana smokers. The follow-up data indicated reductions in marijuana use following the intervention, particularly among the heavier smokers and persons of colour. These findings support the promise of this intervention with adolescents, although alcohol use may need to be addressed in future interventions to discourage substance substitution.

The Sex Check-Up

The Sex Check-Up (SCU) pilot study was conducted entirely by telephone. Eligible participants were males 18 years of age or older who engaged in unprotected anal or oral intercourse with a male partner on at least three occasions in the prior 6 weeks, and were not in a monogamous or negotiated safety relationship[2] with a male partner. Announcements of the SCU targeted men who have sex with men (MSM) who had concerns about their sexual behaviour or were interested in obtaining objective, non-judgemental and confidential information. Announcements emphasised that the services provided were not treatment, but rather an opportunity for the individual to assess his HIV risks (Picciano *et al.* 2001; Rutledge *et al.* 2001).

Eligible callers completed a baseline assessment and were randomly assigned to either immediate counselling ('immediates') or a delayed counselling control group. Immediates were scheduled for a telephone session to review their personal feedback report, identify goals and discuss strategies. Counsellors adopted a motivational interviewing style that allowed for a client-centred, non-threatening interaction with participants. A follow-up assessment was scheduled for 6 weeks later. Delay participants were asked to wait for 7 weeks, at which point they completed a follow-up assessment and were offered the counselling session to review their PFR.

2 Partners who agreed to always use condoms when having sex outside of their relationship.

At intake the majority (79.8 per cent) reported multiple partners, with a mean of 6.5 male sex partners in the prior six weeks. Over half (57.3 per cent) reported engaging in unprotected anal sex with a male partner. Nearly all (96.6 per cent) had been tested for HIV, and 20.2 per cent had tested positive.

Non-minority participants significantly reduced unsafe sexual behaviours over time, but there was not a differential effect of treatment. Among minority participants, those assigned to Immediate counselling reported significantly less unprotected anal intercourse at follow-up than those in the Delay group. Previous studies have revealed that some minority MSM feel less social support compared to white MSM (Stokes and Peterson 1998; Ryan *et al.* 1996), and may have less opportunity to explore their concerns and attitudes about their sexual behaviours. The investigators speculated that the present intervention may have provided for minority participants a unique and otherwise unavailable opportunity to discuss concerns about HIV in a way that was not judgemental or prescriptive, but rather empathic and client centred. At follow-up, Immediate condition participants reported significantly less ambivalence about adopting safer sex practices than Delay participants, and there was a trend toward greater intentions to use condoms.

This study demonstrated the feasibility of the check-up model for recruiting and retaining MSM who were at risk of HIV infection or transmission and were not committed to behaviour change. There was a significant effect of counselling on unprotected anal intercourse among minority participants. Non-minority participants reduced their risk regardless of condition.

Stand-alone and integrated MET: The Marijuana Treatment Project

In a multi-site trial evaluating brief interventions for marijuana-dependent adults, participants were randomised to either a wait-list control condition or one of two treatment conditions: a 2-session stand-alone MET condition or a 9-session integrated intervention incorporating MET, cognitive-behavioural skills training and case management (Marijuana Treatment Project Research Group 2004).

Stand-alone MET

Following a baseline assessment interview, the MET intervention consisted of two counselling sessions, spaced one month apart. During the first session, the counsellor and client systematically reviewed a PFR, in a reflective exploration of the client's experiences with marijuana. They reviewed the client's marijuana use, marijuana-related problems, reasons for wanting to change, and client perceptions of his/her capacity for changing. The counsellor used motivational interviewing strategies to elicit and reinforce client expressions of motivation for change, and to bolster self-efficacy. In the event that the client was prepared to change, the focus was shifted to goal setting and strategies to facilitate change.

The second session focused on debriefing client attempts at change, identifying successes and challenges, and re-evaluating treatment goals. The counsellor reinforced successful efforts at initiating change, helped the client brainstorm alternative change strategies, and discussed potential sources of social support. A supporter selected by the client (usually a spouse, family member or close friend) could participate in this session. If so, they reviewed a 'support agreement' listing suggested behaviours, selecting those they agreed would be helpful for the client and feasible for the supporter.

During both sessions, the counsellor adopted a non-judgemental stance, accepting of the client's stage of readiness for change. The counsellor reinforced client expressions of motivation and self-efficacy, without imposing goals or expectations that had not originated with the client.

Integrated MET

The 9-session condition incorporated several treatment elements: motivational enhancement therapy, case management and cognitive-behavioural therapy (Steinberg *et al.* 2002). Motivational enhancement therapy, as described above, came first, inaugurating a process of developing a collaborative working alliance that was maintained through the other treatment elements as well. Following the alliance building and goal setting of the first two sessions, the focus shifted for the next two sessions to a case management approach in which clients were coached to develop supportive connections with resources in the community for addressing other life problems (e.g. family, mental health, employment, education and legal).

For the final 5 sessions, the treatment protocol included core and elective CBT modules. Clients were taught a group of 'core' skills to aid them in reducing or stopping marijuana use, developing alternative means of coping with high-risk situations, and preventing relapse. The core sessions were:

1 *Understanding marijuana use patterns* – focused on clients' marijuana use patterns and their high-risk situations. This session also included training in relaxation, boredom management, and increasing pleasant activities.
2 *Coping with cravings and urges to use* – focused on triggers, strategies for coping with urges and cravings, with exercises on 'self-talk', 'urge surfing', and keeping a daily record of urges.
3 *Managing thoughts about resuming marijuana use* – reviewed thought processes and attitudes that may lead to relapse, and strategies for challenging and coping with those thoughts.

4 *Problem solving* – provided training in problem solving skills to help participants cope with a variety of challenging situations.
5 *Marijuana refusal skills* – offered training in effective refusal strategies.

If a client did not require either or both of the case management sessions, a selection could be made from among the following elective modules:

1 *Planning for emergencies/coping with a lapse* – prepared clients for coping with unforeseen circumstances. A plan was also developed for coping with a slip, to prevent it from turning into a full-blown relapse.
2 *Seemingly irrelevant decisions* – reviewed potential risks associated with choices clients make that could 'set up' an eventual slip, and the need to consider low-risk options.
3 *Managing negative moods and depression* – included strategies for increasing awareness of depression, negative thoughts and thinking errors, strategies for challenging negative thoughts, and suggestions for behaviour changes that would help improve negative moods.
4 *Assertiveness* – focused on developing assertiveness skills to cope effectively with interpersonal interactions that could otherwise undermine recovery.
5 *Anger management* – focused on recognising the antecedents of anger and techniques to manage anger.

Participants were 450 adult marijuana smokers with a DSM-IV diagnosis of cannabis dependence. Assessments were conducted at baseline, and at 4, 9, and 15 months post-randomisation. Follow-up data indicated that the 9-session integrated treatment reduced the number of days on which marijuana was used (59 per cent reduction) significantly more than 2-session stand-alone MET (36 per cent reduction), and both treatment groups decreased days of use more than the delayed treatment control group (16 per cent reduction). Reductions were also observed in marijuana-related problems and dependence symptoms among participants in the integrated treatment. The differences between treatments in days of marijuana use were maintained over a 12-month follow-up period.

Discussion

In this chapter we have presented examples of stand-alone and integrated MET interventions designed for treatment-seekers (Project MATCH, Marijuana Treatment Project). We have also discussed stand-alone MET interventions designed to function as catalysts for individuals who are at an early stage of readiness for change and not seeking treatment (Marijuana Check-Up, Teen Marijuana Check-Up and Sex Check-Up). The data from these trials stimulate several conclusions concerning the promise of MET interventions.

MET for treatment-seekers

Data from the MTP study indicated that two sessions of MET resulted in fewer days of marijuana use than a waiting-list control group and that the reduction in use was maintained for at least a year. However, the same study also found that combining two sessions of MET with seven additional sessions comprising case management and cognitive-behavioural interventions resulted in significantly improved outcomes over the MET-alone condition. Outcomes of the combined treatment were superior in terms of days on which marijuana was used, marijuana dependence symptoms and marijuana-related problems. These findings are consistent with literature cited at the beginning of this chapter in which it was noted that motivational interventions gained in efficacy when combined with other interventions. Nevertheless, the finding in the MTP study must be regarded with caution, because of the differences in number of sessions between the two conditions. A study designed specifically to test the difference between MET-alone and in combination with other interventions, including an attention control condition that would balance time spent with the counsellor across conditions, would be required to validate this finding.

The findings from Project MATCH indicate that although MET was less efficacious for outpatients than CBT or TSF during the period of active intervention, during the 1-year follow-up period all three treatments were equivalent, a finding that was maintained among those participants who were re-assessed after three years. When interpreting this general lack of differences following treatment with these three approaches, readers should be cautioned that the apparent variability in client exposure to staff among the different treatment conditions may not be as great as first appears. The extensive intake battery and repeated follow-up interviews tended to reduce differences in exposure to project staff among the various conditions (Project MATCH Research Group 1998a). What seems to be a safe conclusion is that, like many other studies (e.g. Emrick 1975), there were no differences in outcomes among different approaches to alcoholism treatment. This finding of few differences among treatments was also true for analyses of potential patient–treatment matching effects. In only one case was there a matching effect in which MET was superior to CBT and TSF: that was for outpatient clients who scored high on a measure of anger. It is speculated that the client-centred MET interactional style provoked less resistance or anger from angry clients (Waldron *et al.* 2001). Two questions that remain unexplained about that matching effect are why clients lower in anger had less favourable outcomes in MET than in the other two interventions, and why the matching effect to client anger occurred only in the outpatient arm of the Project MATCH trial and not in the aftercare arm. Further research on the anger matching effect seems warranted in light of the frequency at which anger is observed in clients with substance use disorders, and the robustness of the matching finding across both the quantity and frequency measures of drinking at the 1-year and 3-year follow-ups in Project MATCH (Project MATCH Research Group 1998b).

MET for non-treatment seekers

The data from three stand-alone MET interventions that were marketed as 'check-ups' for non-treatment-seekers (Marijuana Check-Up, Teen Marijuana Check-Up and Sex Check-Up) suggest that this modality may be useful for individuals at early stages of readiness for change. The check-up's attractiveness to participants may be a function of its brevity and the marketing theme emphasising that the intervention was intended to help participants to 'take stock' with no commitment to change being required.

Designing and delivering 'check-up' interventions present several challenges unique to this modality. One such challenge pertains to the training of clinicians. By virtue of their prior experience in working with treatment-seekers, counsellors may tend to evaluate their competence by the extent to which behaviour change occurs in the clients with whom they work. A check-up intervention, however, can be expected to attract a wide array of clientele in various stages of change, some of whom may not be at risk of adverse consequences. Their participation in the check-up may be motivated by a desire to become more fully educated, rather than by ambivalence about whether to change their behaviour. Therefore, clinicians who deliver this variety of MET may need to recalibrate their indicators of effectiveness. A counsellor who becomes discouraged by a client who neither acknowledges adverse consequences nor expresses motivation to change, may communicate an expectation to clients that they should change, thus losing sight of the check-up's purpose, and threaten the integrity of the modality's public presentation as a non-pressured opportunity to examine one's behaviours and one's options.

A second challenge, also focusing on clinician training, pertains to the perception of when a client is ready to have the focus shifted from motivational exploration to goal setting and strategising, and the therapist's skill in executing that shift. When MET is the first phase of an intervention designed for treatment-seekers, both client and counsellor expect that their work together will ultimately address behaviour change. The context of a check-up, however, is quite different insofar as some clients may not expect to discuss change. Using motivational interviewing skills to facilitate the client's exploration of attitudes when delivering a check-up requires clinicians to listen carefully for expressions of motivation for change, and sensitively offer a focus shift towards discussion of goals and strategies. A failure to execute these key elements with adequate, finely-tuned skill risks the clinician being perceived as attempting to entrap, or missing opportune moments when movement toward change might be optimally facilitated. Although this second challenge is critical to the success of the check-ups, it is also likely that the better these skills are implemented in all MET interventions, the more likely they are to be successful in moving clients towards the goal of behaviour change.

Future direction

Despite numerous studies of MET, one thing that remains unclear, regardless of whether MET is implemented as a stand-alone or integrated intervention, is its mechanism of action. Does it exert its effects through specific processes related to its rationale (resolving ambivalence, providing feedback regarding problem severity and risks, emphasising personal responsibility for change), or is it effective largely due to enhancement of non-specific aspects of treatment? The motivational interviewing approach prioritises the therapeutic relationship, promoting connection and attunement between counsellor and client (e.g. empathic listening, conveying respect and appreciation for the client's perspective and goal choices, reinforcing client self-esteem). Perhaps it works through this fostering of a strong therapeutic alliance. Delineating the mechanism(s) of action of MET seems especially pertinent as new hybrids of MET are continually evolving.

Acknowledgements

The projects reported here were supported by grant U10-AA08438 from the National Institute on Alcohol Abuse and Alcoholism, grant UR4 TI11310 from the Center for Substance Abuse Treatment, grants RO1 DA09425 and RO1 DA14296 from the National Institute on Drug Abuse, grant R18/CCR015252 from the Centers for Disease Control and Prevention, and by General Clinical Research Center grant M01-RR06192 from the National Institutes of Health.

References

American Psychiatric Association (1994) *Diagnostic and Statistical Manual of Mental Disorders* (4th edn, DSM-IV). Washington, DC: American Psychiatric Association.

Babor, T.F. and Del Boca, F. (eds) (2003) *Treatment matching in alcoholism*. Cambridge: Cambridge University Press.

Baer, J.S., Kivlahan, D.R. and Donovan, D.M. (1999) 'Integrating skills training and motivational therapies: Implications for the treatment of substance dependence', *Journal of Substance Abuse Treatment*, 17(1–2): 15–23.

Baker, A., Lewin, T., Reichler, H., Clancy, R., Carr, V., Garrett, R., Sly, K., Devir, H. and Terry, M. (2002) 'Evaluation of a motivational interview for substance use within psychiatric in-patient services', *Addiction*, 97: 1329–1337.

Barrowclough, C., Haddock, G., Tarrier, N., Lewis, S.W., Moring, J., O'Brien, R., Schofield, N. and McGovern, J. (2001) 'Randomized controlled trial of motivational interviewing, cognitive behaviour therapy, and family intervention for patients with comorbid schizophrenia and substance use disorders', *The American Journal of Psychiatry*, 158(10): 1706–1713.

Bien, T.H., Miller, W.R. and Boroughs, J.M. (1993) 'Motivational interviewing with alcohol outpatients', *Behavioural and Cognitive Psychotherapy*, 21: 347–356.

Brown, J.M. and Miller, W.R. (1993) 'Impact of motivational interviewing on participation and outcome in residential alcoholism treatment', *Psychology of Addictive Behaviours*, 7(4): 211–218.

Connors, G.J., Walitzer, K.S. and Dermen, K.H. (2002) 'Preparing clients for alcoholism treatment: Effects on treatment participation and outcomes', *Journal of Consulting and Clinical Psychology*, 70(5): 1161–1169.

Dench, S. and Bennett, G. (2000) 'The impact of brief motivational intervention at the start of an outpatient day programme for alcohol dependence', *Behavioural and Cognitive Psychotherapy*, 28(2): 121–130.

Donovan, D.M., Rosengren, D.B., Downey, L., Cox, G.B. and Sloan, K.L. (2001) 'Attrition prevention with individuals awaiting publicly funded drug treatment', *Addiction*, 96: 1149–1160.

Doyle, A., Swan, M., Roffman, R. and Stephens, R. (2003) 'The marijuana check-up: A brief intervention tailored for individuals in the contemplation stage', *Journal of Social Work Practice in the Addictions*, 3: 53–71.

Dunn, C., Deroo, L. and Rivara, F.P. (2001) 'The use of brief interventions adapted from motivational interviewing across behavioural domains: A systematic review', *Addiction*, 96: 1725–1742.

Emrick, C.D. (1975) 'A review of psychologically oriented treatment of alcoholism. II. The relative effectiveness of different treatment approaches and the effectiveness of treatment versus no treatment', *Journal of Studies on Alcohol*, 36: 88–108.

Marijuana Treatment Project Research Group (2004) 'Brief treatments for cannabis dependence: Findings from a randomized multi-site trial', *Journal of Consulting and Clinical Psychology*, 72: 455–466.

Miller, W.R. (2001) 'When is it motivational interviewing?' *Addiction*, 96: 1770–1771.

Miller, W.R. and Sovereign, R.G. (1989) 'The check-up: A model for early intervention in addictive behaviours', in T. Loberg, W.R. Miller, P.E. Nathan and G.A. Marlatt (eds), *Addictive behaviours: Prevention and early intervention*, Amsterdam: Swets and Zeitlinger.

Miller, W.R. and Rollnick, S. (1991) *Motivational interviewing: preparing people to change addictive behavior*. New York: The Guilford Press.

Miller, W.R., Benefield, R.G. and Tonigan, J.S. (1993) 'Enhancing motivation for change in problem drinking: A controlled comparison of two therapist styles', *Journal of Consulting and Clinical Psychology*, 61(3): 455–461.

Miller, W.R., Zweben, A., DiClemente, C.C. and Rychtarik, R.G. (1992) *Motivational enhancement therapy manual: a clinical research guide for therapists treating individuals with alcohol abuse and dependence*, Project MATCH Monograph 2, Rockville, Maryland: National Institute on Alcohol Abuse and Alcoholism.

Picciano, J.F., Roffman, R.A., Kalichman, S.C., Rutledge, S.E. and Berghuis, J.P. (2001) 'A telephone based brief intervention using motivational enhancement to facilitate HIV risk reduction among MSM: A pilot study', *AIDS and Behaviour*, 5: 251–262.

Prochaska, J.O. and DiClemente, C.C. (1983) 'Stages and processes of self-change of smoking: Toward an integrative model of change', *Journal of Consulting and Clinical Psychology*, 51(3): 390–395.

Project MATCH Research Group (1998a) 'Matching patients with alcohol disorders to treatments: Clinical implications from Project MATCH', *Journal of Mental Health*, 7(6): 589–602.

Project MATCH Research Group (1998b) 'Matching alcoholism treatments to client heterogeneity: Project MATCH three-year drinking outcomes', *Alcoholism: Clinical and Experimental Research*, 22(6): 1300–1311.

Resnicow, K., Dilorio, C., Soet, J.E., Borrelli, B., Hecht, J. and Ernst, D. (2002) 'Motivational interviewing in health promotion: It sounds like something is changing', *Health Psychology*, 21(5): 444–451.

Roffman, R.A. 'Motivating adolescent marijuana use cessation: Results of a pilot study', paper presented at the 5th annual conference of the Society for Social Work and Research, Atlanta, GA, January 2001.

Rutledge, S.E., Roffman, R.A., Mahoney, C., Picciano, J.F., Berghuis, J.P. and Kalichman, S.C. (2001) 'Motivational enhancement counselling strategies in delivering a telephone-based brief HIV prevention intervention', *Clinical Social Work Journal*, 29: 291–306.

Ryan, R., Longres, J.F. and Roffman, R.A. (1996) 'Sexual identity, social support and social networks among African-, Latino-, and European-American men in an HIV prevention program', *Journal of Gay and Lesbian Social Services*, 5: 1–24.

Saunders, B., Wilkinson, C. and Phillips, M. (1995) 'The impact of a brief motivational intervention with opiate users attending a methadone programme', *Addiction*, 90: 415–424.

Steinberg, K.L., Roffman, R.A., Carroll, K.M., Kabela, E., Kadden, R., Miller, M., Duresky, D. and The Marijuana Treatment Project Research Group (2002) 'Tailoring cannabis dependence treatment for a diverse population', *Addiction*, 97(S1): 135–142.

Stokes, J.P. and Peterson, J.L. (1998) 'Homophobia, self-esteem, and risk for HIV among African American men who have sex with men', *AIDS Education and Prevention*, 10: 278–292.

Waldron, H.B., Miller, W.R. and Tonigan, J.S. (2001) 'Client anger as a predictor of differential response to treatment', in R. Longabaugh and P.W. Wirtz (eds), *Project MATCH Hypotheses: Results and causal chain analyses*, Project MATCH Monograph 8, Bethesda, Maryland: National Institute on Alcohol Abuse and Alcoholism.

Zweben, A. and Zuckoff, A. (2002) 'Motivational interviewing and treatment adherence', in W.R. Miller and S. Rollnick, *Motivational interviewing: Preparing people for change* (2nd edn), New York: The Guilford Press.

Section III

Learning and practice

Chapter 6

Teaching, monitoring and evaluating motivational interviewing practice

Steve Martino, Kathleen M. Carroll and Samuel A. Ball

Introduction

The demand for professional training in Motivational Interviewing (MI) has been growing rapidly since the first edition of the MI textbook (Miller and Rollnick 1991) and the publication of its manualised version, Motivational Enhancement Therapy for Project MATCH (Miller *et al.* 1992). Several factors most likely have driven this demand. MI is recognised as an efficacious treatment for several substance use disorders (Burke *et al.* 2003; Dunn *et al.* 2001; Noonan and Moyers 1997). It is a relatively brief intervention typically delivered within one to four sessions (Burke *et al.* 2003; Miller and Rollnick 2002), making it compatible with a managed health care environment. MI also positively impacts addiction treatment engagement and retention (Dunn *et al.* 2001; Zweben and Zuckoff 2002), an area of great concern in the addictions treatment field where high dropout rates are common (Battjes *et al.* 1999; Simpson *et al.* 1997). As demonstrated in subsequent chapters of this book and in the second edition of Miller and Rollnick's (2002) textbook, MI has wide application to a variety of behavioural domains and patient populations. MI is also compatible with many different treatment approaches (Baer *et al.* 1999; COMBINE Study Research Group 2003; Steinberg *et al.* 2002), which permits its integration into many treatment-as-usual practices (Carroll *et al.* 2002). Furthermore, its widespread dissemination by the Center for Substance Abuse Treatment in its Treatment Improvement Series 35 (Miller 1999) has increased clinicians' familiarity with the approach and interest in receiving MI training. Finally, clinicians may find MI intuitively appealing in that they are likely to view themselves as highly empathic, reflective, and collaborative with clients (Ball *et al.* 2002a) even when direct observation of their work may contradict their own self-assessments (Carroll *et al.* 1998b; Miller *et al.* 2004). Thus, clinicians may seek MI training not only because of its clinical utility and the numerous available resources, but also because they view the basic MI tenets and strategies as consistent with how they work.

To address the demand for professional MI training and to promote real MI proficiency among community practitioners, systematic preparation of hundreds of trainers has occurred through the Motivational Interviewing Network of Trainers (MINT), developed and managed under the auspices of the Center on Alcoholism, Substance Abuse and Addictions at the University of New Mexico. These 'MINTed' trainers have been providing widespread MI training on an international basis (Miller and Rollnick 2002) and the number of training events provided overall has been escalating in the past several years (Miller 2003). Typically, MINT training involves two or more days of workshop training in which clinicians receive didactic instruction, demonstrations of MI skills and techniques, and direct skills practice (Miller and Rollnick 2002). While these types of workshops have been shown to produce some immediate gains in clinicians' MI proficiency (Baer *et al.* 2004; Miller and Mount 2001; Miller *et al.* 2004; Rubel *et al.* 2000), these gains have not been shown to endure over time and, hence, may have limited impact on client outcomes. In contrast, recent work by Miller and colleagues (Miller *et al.* 2004) has demonstrated that the provision of repeated and spaced feedback and/or coaching based on direct review of the clinicians' audio-taped work following intensive MI workshops maintains and further increases MI proficiency. This finding, paralleled in the cognitive behavioural therapy training literature (Sholomskas *et al.* 2005), has led to increasing interest in how to best provide rating-based post-workshop supervisory feedback and coaching to boost MI performance and to capture the clinicians' proficiency achievements. MI training systems used for this purpose have included the extensive Motivational Interviewing Skills Code (MISC) (Miller *et al.* 2003) from which clinicians receive feedback from MISC scores that summarise their performance, client session behaviours, and form the basis of coaching tips. In addition, a briefer tool adapted from the MISC, called the Motivational Interviewing Treatment Integrity Code (MITI) (Moyers *et al.* 2004) has been developed for use in non-research settings. More information about both systems may be obtained from the University of New Mexico Center on Alcoholism, Substance Abuse and Addictions website (http://casaa.unm.edu).

Additional efforts to disseminate proficient MI practice and to examine its effectiveness in non-university affiliated community treatment programmes (CTP) have been occurring within the United States through the National Institute on Drug Abuse (NIDA) Clinical Trials Network (CTN). In response to the Institute of Medicine's challenge to bridge the gap between empirical knowledge and clinical practice (Institute of Medicine 1998), NIDA initiated the CTN in 1999 to build partnerships between researchers and CTPs that previously had not been involved in academic research. The CTN's purpose is to conduct psychosocial, pharmacological, and combined treatment trials in community settings and to test their effectiveness under these real-world conditions. As of 2004, a network of 17 academic centres and more than 100 CTPs has been conducting over 20 studies. Twelve protocols evaluating psychosocial treatments have been implemented. All of the psychosocial treatment protocols have used CTP staff as the clinicians and implemented a variety of strategies for teaching, monitoring, and evaluating clinician performance to insure the integrity of the treatment being delivered within the protocol. Our centre at the CTN New England Node has been leading three protocols evaluating the effectiveness of MI or Motivational Enhancement Therapy (MET) in enhancing retention and substance use outcomes. One protocol involves the use of MI as part of the standard intake assessment process (CTN 0005: Motivational Interviewing to Improve Treatment Engagement and Outcome in Individuals Seeking Treatment for Substance Abuse). The other two protocols compare three sessions of MET with three sessions of standard counselling upon treatment entry for primary English-speaking (CTN 0004: Motivational Enhancement Treatment to Improve Treatment Engagement and Outcome in Individuals Seeking Treatment for Substance Abuse) and primary Spanish-speaking clients (CTN 0012: Motivational Enhancement Treatment to Improve Treatment Engagement and Outcome for Spanish-Speaking Individuals Seeking Treatment for Substance Abuse). In addition, our group supplied a fourth MET protocol for pregnant women (CTN 013: Motivational Enhancement Therapy to Improve Treatment Utilization and Outcome in Pregnant Substance Users) the training and supervision approach described in this chapter.

In each of these CTN protocols, we have implemented training plans that develop the clinicians' fidelity to MI treatment. The plans have involved MINT modelled 2-day skill-building workshops delivered by MI expert trainers on-site at the participating agencies (Carroll *et al.* 2002). We have also used a post-workshop clinician adherence and competence audiotape rating system implemented by agency supervisors to monitor the clinicians' actual MI performance within client sessions and to provide them with feedback and instruction for how to improve their MI skills, reach the protocols' MI certification criteria, and maintain ongoing proficiency standards (Carroll *et al.* 2002). We have used these training plans with a demographically, educationally, and professionally diverse group of clinicians drawn from community-based treatment programmes across the United States (Ball *et al.* 2002a). Through our experiences in implementing these CTN protocols, fine-tuning our training plans and clinician tape rating system, and building on the emerging MI training literature, we have gained extensive knowledge and experience in teaching, monitoring, and evaluating MI practice among real-world clinicians attempting to use it in addiction treatment programmes. In this chapter, we outline what we have learned in each of these training domains and provide the reader with recommendations of how to maximise training impact for clinicians trying to learn MI.

Teaching motivational interviewing

As described above, the most common format for teaching MI is through the use of intensive workshops wherein clinicians typically receive a MI textbook or treatment manual (e.g., Miller 1999; Miller and Rollnick 1991, 2002; Miller *et al.* 1992), review core concepts, view live and videotaped (Miller *et al.* 1998) demonstrations of MI strategies and techniques, and practise the approach with trainer input over two or more days (see for example Miller and Mount 2001). Detailed guidelines for the facilitation of workshop training are available in Miller and Rollnick (1991), on the www.motivationalinterviewing.org website, and in Chapter 14 of the second edition of the MI textbook (Miller and Rollnick 2002). We have applied these guidelines in our protocol workshop training. Typically, clinicians attend these workshops at an off-site location and then return to their agencies where they may or may not then attempt to use MI. Although this approach has the advantages of focused, uninterrupted skills training and the opportunity to network with others similarly invested in learning MI, it has several disadvantages, including: (1) limited appreciation of the unique administrative and clinical context within which MI practice will occur, (2) risk of information overload and training saturation by delivering a large amount of information within a concentrated timeframe, and (3) very little if any opportunity for ongoing practice and individualised performance feedback and coaching. All of these factors may undermine the clinicians' acquisition, utilisation, and retention of MI knowledge and skills.

In an attempt to address these disadvantages, we have adopted a decentralised model of training in which MI expert trainers, who have completed a centralised train-the-trainer programme modelled after the MINT approach, conduct MI workshop training on-site at the agencies only for the staff members who work there (Carroll *et al.* 2002). Participants include clinicians with active caseloads, supervisors, and occasionally clinical or medical directors who wish to become more familiar with and provide administrative support for the approach. Workshops, materials, activities, and discussions are tailored to the agency's needs and include role-play MI practice based on clinical scenarios that resemble the clientele and clinical presentations common to the agency. For example, training at agencies that provide services to large numbers of criminal justice system referred clients often require extra efforts to help clinicians reduce confrontational or other MI inconsistent clinical strategies and improve clinicians' skills for addressing the client's experience of coercion and psychological reactance (Miller and Mount 2001). Similarly, training provided to agencies working with large proportions of substance using patients with co-occurring psychiatric conditions may require modification of core MI skills (e.g. greater clarity and succinctness of open-ended questions and more frequent reflective statements and summaries to accommodate psychiatric and cognitive deficits) and increased use of strategies that address the interaction of the clients' psychiatric and addiction concerns (Martino *et al.* 2002). Our attempts to tailor training to the clinicians' work setting and identified needs is consistent with Rollnick, Kinnersley, and Butler's (2002) recommendation that MI trainers try to teach in a manner more finely tuned to clinical context and learner needs.

We also have adopted Miller's recommendation to promote a 'learning to learn' approach to workshop training (Miller *et al.* 2004). Rather than narrowly or exclusively emphasising specific techniques, this model focuses on helping the clinicians grasp the MI style or spirit of interacting with clients. MI spirit requires following the client's lead in the discussion by attending to change- and resistance-oriented client statements and blending the empathic and strategic MI elements. This 'learning to learn' training model primarily aims to solidify a MI consistent perspective on client change rather than only being technically correct in their use of MI skills. We find that clinicians often encounter this problem as illustrated in the transaction below:

Clinician: Tell me about your drinking. (*open-ended question*)
Client: What do you want to know? There is not much to say.
Clinician: There is not much to say about your drinking. (*repeating reflection*)
Client: Yeah. I'm not sure what information you need.
Clinician: Tell me what you would like to tell me. (*open-ended question*)
Client: Well, I was arrested for drunk driving, and I was told I had to come here for treatment.
Clinician: So drinking has caused you problems like getting arrested, and now you find you may need treatment. (*paraphrasing reflection*)
Client: I don't think my drinking is that bad.
Clinician: What do other people think? (*open ended question*)
Client: People who know me would agree with me.

This example demonstrates how, at an item level, the clinician uses technically correct MI strategies (i.e. open-ended questions and reflective statements) but fails to embrace the collaborative communication spirit of MI. The clinician initially could have provided the client with an early structuring statement to orient the client to the first session or offer this information after the client had solicited it. Instead, the clinician asks several questions at the beginning of the session that risk directing the client into a passive, question-answering role if it were to continue even though the questions were open ones (Miller and Rollnick 2002). Moreover, the clinician's reflections do not tag important meaning in the client's statements and move beyond what the client said in a non-empathic manner rather than reflecting the client's resistant perspective and encouraging him to elaborate further before attempting to evoke change-related statements. When we teach clinicians MI in our protocols, workshops become the clinicians' first step for them to grasp these important concepts rather than the endpoint of their training. After the workshop, the development of MI proficiency takes repeated practice with follow-up supervision based upon direct observation of the clinicians' work (Miller *et al.* 2004).

Consistent with a decentralised 'learning to learn' teaching philosophy, we have trained site-based MI supervisors to provide ongoing feedback and coaching to recently trained clinicians. Developing site-based supervisors has the additional advantages of helping clinicians better integrate MI into the agencies' clinical and administrative realities and providing durable, continuing MI training resources at each participating programme (Carroll *et al.* 2002). We first work with the clinical administrative leadership to identify a staff member(s) who has an interest, apparent aptitude, credibility with staff, and role supporting their supervising clinicians in MI. The supervisor previously must have received MI workshop training or attended a workshop with their clinicians. The supervisor also receives additional training in how to use a model of supervision organised around our audiotape MI adherence and competence monitoring system (described in the next section). This training concentrates on developing the supervisor's skills in rating the clinician's audiotaped MI sessions and teaching him or her how to supervise in a MI consistent fashion. This means we teach the supervisor how to evaluate the extent to which the clinician uses several MI consistent, MI inconsistent, and MI neutral drug counselling strategies during the session (i.e. adherence dimension) and how skilled the clinician is implementing these strategies (i.e. competence dimension). The supervisor records his/her detailed assessments of the clinician's performance on the rating form and uses these ratings to provide the clinician feedback. During the supervisory meeting, the supervisor presents the feedback in a style that resembles the personalised feedback provided to clients in MET (Miller *et al.* 1992). The feedback is organised around affirming the clinicians' successful efforts to use MI and collaboratively problem-solve and develop coaching tips for improving their practice. The supervisor may meet individually with clinicians, use a group supervision model in which clinicians rotate presentation of their work, or incorporate both means of reviewing MI performance. A detailed format for such supervision is outlined in Box 6.1.

Similar to the recommendation for trainers to adopt a style of training that models the approach (Miller and Rollnick 2002), we underscore the importance of conducting MI supervision in a manner consistent with MI. MI supervision is fundamentally clinician-centred, and approaches the development of a clinician's MI proficiency as a collaborative work in progress. This means supervisors avoid presenting themselves as experts fully armed with tape ratings and helpful feedback, even if well intentioned.

Box 6.1 A format for motivational interviewing supervision

1. Begin supervision by asking the clinician about his or her view of the session using an open-ended question. *What do you think went well in the session?* then *What about the session presented challenges for your use of MI?*
2. Reflect the clinician's main points. *You felt you were able to understand the client's reasons for drinking. At the same time, you found it difficult to draw out the client's reasons for changing his drinking pattern.*
3. Look for opportunities to support the clinician's efforts to use MI in the session. *You did a nice job in questioning less and reflecting more in this session.*
4. Acknowledge the challenges the clinician may have had in practising MI. *When the client became more resistant as you were both developing a change plan, you seemed unsure how to proceed.*
5. Provide the clinician with feedback from the MI Tape Rating Form.
   a. Begin by focusing on areas in which the clinician performed well. *You used a lot of nice reflections and the majority of them were accurate and empathic paraphrases that really got at what the client meant.*
   b. Next, note areas in which the clinician struggled and provide some ideas in collaboration with the clinician about what might have contributed to these difficulties. *You seemed to lose some of the collaborative spirit when you conducted the decisional balance activity. Although you were trying to be helpful, sometimes you gave unsolicited suggestions to the client about potential drawbacks to using cocaine. It wasn't clear if the negative consequences you noted were really true from the client's point of view.*
   c. Discuss ways to promote the clinician's abilities in these areas. *One way to improve in the impact of the decisional balance might be to bring in your reflective listening strength and simply paraphrase what the client has said about the negative consequences. This might help the client elaborate further and potentially generate more disadvantages of using while maintaining your good MI spirit.*
6. As time permits, enhance the supervision with specific coaching activities that focus on a training area.
   a. Use of role-plays constructed to target the development of specific skills or that simulate challenging client scenarios that lead to reduced MI proficiency.
   b. With permission or at the clinician's request, listen to a segment of the audiotape together and consider retrospectively what else the clinician might have said or done. The tape may be cued to segments that carry maximal teaching opportunities.
7. Summarise the supervision session with a succinct review of the clinician's strengths and ongoing learning objectives.

Instead, supervisors ask about the clinicians' view of their MI performance before commenting on the session. Supervisors elicit clinician descriptions of what went well, what challenges occurred, what other ideas or options were available, and what the client communicated and how this guided the clinician in the session. Next, the supervisor presents the tape rating results to the clinician and asks for the clinician's reactions. Based on these discussions, the supervisor helps the clinician identify areas for performance improvement, mirroring the change planning process used in MET (Miller *et al.* 1992) as illustrated in Chapter 7 of this book.

Although most clinicians find the degree of specific feedback and targeted coaching generated from our supervisory tape rating system very helpful and benefit from it (see Miller *et al.* 2004; Sholomskas *et al.* 2005), we often encounter clinicians who find that MI is harder to conduct than they expected. They often have mistakenly assumed after completing training that the use of core MI skills is straightforward, elementary, or consistent with what they already do and that they can perform these strategies fairly well with little practice or concentrated effort. Close monitoring of their work, however, reveals problems in their implementation of MI, including: (1) establishing a highly empathic, client-centred MI spirit; (2) reflecting with increasing depth and accuracy; (3) understanding the relationship between client change talk and resistance and how to attend to both discourses within the session; and (4) knowing how to follow a client's lead in a conversation and when to proceed strategically with directive methods for eliciting change talk and handling resistance skilfully. For some clinicians, recognising overuse of closed-ended questions and incorporating more open-ended ones into the interview may be challenging. For others, even reducing the amount of time they spend talking during the session is an early challenge.

These types of training challenges present a dilemma to the MI supervisor. If the supervisor conveys to clinicians that they are less skilled than they imagine themselves to be, the supervisor and clinician may find themselves in what MI might call a 'communication roadblock' or 'confrontational trap' in which the supervisor becomes excessively corrective or authoritative in pointing out what a clinician has done wrong (Miller and Rollnick 2002). The supervisor also might fail to address the clinician's understandable ambivalence about learning a new counselling approach. At the same time, the supervisor's responsibility is to promote the clinician's best MI practice and to enhance an appreciation for the deceptive complexity and challenges of conducting MI. These supervisory conflicts often parallel the conflicts (e.g. between advice/direction giving and exploring ambivalence) the clinician faces when using MI with clients and can be grist for the mill of supervisory discussion. The supervisor navigates these dilemmas by always acknowledging any familiarity the clinician has with MI techniques and inquiring about the clinician's experience using these skills. The supervisor attempts to meet the clinicians at their current skill and interest in learning MI just as the clinician should be meeting his/her client at his/her current stage of readiness regarding behaviour change. The supervisor then asks the clinician in what ways he or she might hope to develop further. In this way, the supervisor manages resistance to the potential challenges encountered in training and supervision, fosters a collaborative learning environment, and sets the stage for the clinician to discover and develop his or her essential MI skills. Again the parallel to practice with clients should be obvious. As the supervisor provides the clinician with objective feedback from the audiotape ratings, the clinician may become more mindful of his or her strengths and weaknesses and appreciative of the subtleties and challenges posed by using MI without this process excessively raising resistance to ongoing learning.

Nonetheless, sometimes a clinician may experience resistance to learning MI upon discovering through feedback that some of his or her counselling behaviours may be inconsistent with a MI approach. The supervisor avoids conveying that MI is the 'best' or 'preferred' counselling approach. In fact, clinical research does not support the superiority of any one major addiction counselling approach over all others, provided that they are conducted with a high level of competence and have been empirically validated (Project MATCH Research Group 1997; 1998). Instead, the supervisor presents MI on its own merits and encourages the clinician to consider the possibility of practising the approach in its purest form before drawing a final conclusion about its merit. The clinician's freedom to choose how to counsel clients in the end may seem obvious, but often is worth underscoring in supervision. The key is that the supervisor avoids the trap of knowing better than the clinician and affirms his or her respect for the multitude of ways in which the clinician may counsel others. However, the supervisor does highlight that the development of MI skills often involves curtailing or eliminating counselling approaches or styles that are not obviously consistent with MI. Once MI is mastered, then the sequencing or integration of other approaches with MI (e.g. relapse prevention skills training after enhancing a client's motivation) may become the focus of supervision.

We have found also that in some cases, clinician resistance to MI training may arise simply in reaction to the supervisor's use of detailed tape rating information for feedback. Clinicians are often unfamiliar with the approach of providing supervision based on detailed review of session tapes and may be surprised by their supervisor being consistently vigilant to their actual performance of MI instead of relying solely on (i.e. trusting) the clinicians' self-report. Some clinicians become anxious about the close focus on their work and uncomfortable with the process. When clinicians react in this manner, the supervisor reinforces the expectation that learning MI takes practice and becoming comfortable with direct evaluation occurs gradually, that clinicians commonly experience some difficulties initially implementing the approach with fidelity and that close monitoring and coaching is the most effective method for developing proficiency. Any feedback provided by the supervisor is used collaboratively primarily to identify potentially beneficial MI training supports and activities, not to point out their shortcomings per se. By recognising and affirming the clinicians' MI performance strengths and training efforts, the supervisor further helps alleviate clinician performance anxiety and supports their self-efficacy in conducting MI. Again, the parallels to the goals of conducting MI with clients are obvious.

Finally, as in practice where resistance is seen as a meaningful signal of dissonance in the counselling relationship (Miller and Rollnick 2002), supervisors view resistance to learning MI as an opportunity to understand what makes using it in clinical practice difficult for the clinician, instead of blaming the clinician for not wanting to learn and practise MI. We have found that clinicians commonly confront real implementation dilemmas involving agency practices that hinder proficient use of MI. Rather than ideal clinical conditions, clinicians in community-based settings typically must deal with heavy information gathering demands within narrow time constraints at intake combined with contrasting treatment philosophies (e.g. total abstinence, disease concept, even relapse prevention) that make using MI more challenging. In addition, clients may present with complicated poly-drug, psychosocial, psychiatric, and medical problems and symptoms and often have significant case management needs that may seem to conflict with the less direction and advice giving approach of MI. Listening carefully to and understanding this 'resistance' is an important part of supervision and helps the supervisor assist the clinician in resolving problems applying MI.

We encountered this type of dilemma early in our MI protocol development. Clinicians noted how it was difficult for them to maintain a MI style when they had important administrative functions to fulfil (e.g. completion of agency forms or structured assessments) during the intake session. To address this dilemma, we conceptualised the integration of MI in the intake session as akin to a 'big MI sandwich'. By this we mean that clinicians spend the first 20 minutes of the session conducting the intake in a manner consistent with MI collaboratively and accurately to understand the client's perspective. Clinicians next move to the middle portion of the intake to collect information necessary for intake form completion, sometimes including a formal administration of the Addiction Severity Index (McLellan *et al.* 1992) or other intake assessment tools. Clinicians conclude the last 20 minutes of the session by summarising the client's statements and returning to MI interventions matched to the client's stage of change. The supervisor's ability to remain flexible about the various ways that MI can be incorporated into real-world clinical contexts where real-world clinicians treat real-world clients will facilitate the clinician's motivation to incorporate MI whenever possible. Through this open, flexible stance, the supervisor models for the clinician a style of interaction essential to performing MI and that may dually enhance the clinician's intrinsic motivation to learn the approach.

Monitoring motivational interviewing practice

A system for monitoring MI performance after workshop training provides an essential foundation for the ongoing supervisory feedback and coaching necessary for skill development. To this end, we have developed a supervisor tape rating system based on an adaptation of the Yale Adherence and Competence Scale (YACS; Carroll *et al.* 2000). In brief, YACS is a general system for evaluating clinician adherence and competence across several types of substance abuse treatments. Versions of it have been used in several prior clinical trial studies, including Project MATCH in which MET was evaluated (Carroll *et al.* 1998a). Most recently, we have used it successfully to evaluate acquisition of clinician skills in a study examining strategies to train clinicians in cognitive behaviour therapy (Sholomskas *et al.* 2005). The YACS has shown high internal consistency for the treatment scales (coefficient alphas in the .80–.95 range), good inter-rater reliability across studies (ICCs of .75 to .90), and an ability to discriminate MET from other treatments (Carroll *et al.* 1998a; 2000).

The version we have been using for supervisory purposes in our CTN MI and MET protocols contains 30 items that address specific therapeutic strategies involving MI consistent, MI inconsistent, and MI neutral drug abuse counselling interventions (Ball *et al.* 2002b). These categories parallel the types of items typically recommended for inclusion in behavioural therapy adherence and competence monitoring systems (Waltz *et al.* 1993). For each item within these categories, supervisors rate the clinicians using a 7-point Likert scale for both adherence (1 = not done at all, to 7 = extensively) and competence (1 = very poor, to 7 = excellent). Ten MI consistent items include core skills that underpin the overall approach (e.g. open-ended questions, affirmations, reflective statements, MI style or spirit) as well as more directive methods for eliciting change talk and handling resistance (e.g. motivation for change techniques such as importance and confidence rulers or evocative questions; ways to elicit or resolve ambivalence like decisional balance, double-sided reflections, or client-centred feedback and heightening discrepancy methods such as exploring goals and values or looking forward or back to elicit dissonance with current behaviour). Ten MI inconsistent items include clinician behaviours that undermine and are antithetical to MI (e.g. asserting therapeutic authority, directly confronting the client, emphasising total abstinence and the concepts of powerlessness and loss of control, providing unsolicited advice, direction, or feedback) or that involve a broad range of counselling strategies common to alternative substance use

Table 6.1 Motivational interviewing monitoring system items per category

MI consistent items	*MI inconsistent items*	*MI neutral counselling items*
1. Motivational interviewing style or spirit	1. Emphasis on abstinence	1. Assessing/monitoring substance use
2. Open-ended questions	2. Direct confrontation	2. Assessing psychosocial functioning and factors
3. Affirmations of strengths and self-efficacy	3. Powerlessness and loss of control	3. Addressing spirituality
4. Reflective statements	4. Unsolicited advice, direction giving, and feedback	4. Assessing psychopathology
5. Fostering a collaborative atmosphere/ emphasising freedom of choice	5. Asserting authority	5. Assessing risk behaviours and reduction
6. Motivation for change strategies	6. Promoting self-help group involvement	6. Assessing medical and medication issues
7. Client-centred problem discussion and feedback	7. Reality therapy principles	7. Psycho-education about substances
8. Heightening discrepancies	8. Skills training	8. Programme orientation
9. Pros, cons, and ambivalence	9. Cognitions	9. Case management
10. Change planning	10. Psychodynamic interventions	10. Treatment planning

treatment approaches (e.g. reality therapy, skills training, cognitive therapy, psychodynamic interventions) that often are delivered in a manner unlike MI. Ten MI neutral items describe common drug abuse counselling interventions that clinicians may deliver in either a MI consistent or inconsistent manner but which do not necessarily impede or promote MI proficiency (e.g. assessing substance use, evaluating psychosocial factors related to the client's substance use, conducting case management, orienting the client to the treatment programme). All items under each category are listed in Table 6.1. Box 6.2 provides a sample MI consistent item description to illustrate the format of items in our monitoring system.

Distinguishing between clinician adherence and competence across these strategies is essential for training clinicians in MI. Adherence refers to how often (i.e. the extent and frequency with which) clinicians implement specific treatment strategies. Competence refers to how well (i.e. the skilfulness with which) clinicians use these strategies. These dimensions are not necessarily related (Carroll *et al.* 2000; Rounsaville *et al.* 1988), and they may have different implications for feedback and coaching purposes. For example, one clinician may use many more MI inconsistent than MI consistent strategies. The target for supervision may be first to decrease MI

Box 6.2 Sample MI Consistent Item Description

REFLECTIVE STATEMENTS: *To what extent did the clinician repeat (exact words), rephrase (slight rewording), paraphrase (e.g. amplifying the thought or feeling, use of analogy, making inferences) or make reflective summary statements of what the client said?*

Adherence rating guidelines
Reflective statements made by the clinician restate the client's comments using language that *accurately clarifies and captures the meaning* of the client's communications and conveys to the client the clinician's effort to understand the client's point of view. The clinician uses this technique *to encourage the client to explore or elaborate* on a topic. These techniques include *repeating* exactly what the client just stated, *rephrasing* (slight rewording), *paraphrasing* (e.g. amplifying thoughts or feelings, use of analogy, making inferences) or making *reflective summary* statements of what the client said. Reflective summary statements are a special form of reflection in which the clinician selects several pieces of client information and combines them in a summary with the goal of inviting more exploration of material, to highlight ambivalence, or to make a transition to another topic.

Examples
Client: 'Right now, using drugs doesn't take care of how bad I feel like it used to. If anything, I feel worse now.'

Simple reflection
- Using drugs makes you feel worse now.

Rephrasing
- You have found that using drugs to deal with how badly you feel is not working well for you anymore.

Paraphrasing using a double-sided reflection
- In the past using drugs helped you feel better when you were having a hard time or feeling badly. Now, it is only making matters worse for you.

Introduction to a reflective summary
- Here is what I've heard you say so far . . .

inconsistent actions and increase MI consistent strategies. Competency development would then follow the establishment of basic MI adherence. Although speculative, our experience is that intensive MI workshop training primarily boosts adherence and motivates clinicians to adopt these skills in their practice. Some clinicians may learn the technical application of MI skill, but implement it with marginal quality. These clinicians may benefit most from supervisory efforts to develop their sophistication in using the identified MI techniques and to enhance MI spirit and strategic direction. In this situation, competence building becomes the more focal point of MI supervision.

This latter point dovetails with the MI 'learning to learn' training philosophy by conceptualising supervision as the means to move beyond basic skill learning to advanced proficiency. For this reason, we have incorporated detailed guidelines for rating competence for all items in our monitoring system to help the supervisor provide individualised feedback and coaching. As supervisors listen to taped sessions, they consider the guidelines to determine if the clinicians are performing with more than or less than adequate proficiency for each of the items (see Box 6.3 for sample competency guidelines). They are careful to write down examples to support their evaluation of the clinicians' implementation skills, in addition to some examples that deviate from the clinicians' typical or desired style. The supervisors and clinicians discuss the competency ratings and examples and then meld these discussions into supervision learning activities to promote the clinicians' best MI practice.

One commonly occurring example of MI competency that clinicians find difficult to master is the skill of reflecting client statements with depth instead of merely echoing the client without helping the client move forward motivationally. In the first example, the clinician is ineffective in articulating the intended meaning of what the client has said.

Client:	I don't know what to say. I really don't know where to begin. There's been so much going on.
Clinician:	There's a lot going on. (*repeating reflection*)
Client:	Yeah, I don't know where to begin.
Clinician:	It's hard to know where to start. (*rephrasing reflection*)
Client:	Well, with everything that has been happening, it really is difficult for me.
Clinician:	It's difficult to know where to start with everything going on. (*rephrasing reflection*)
Client:	Yes, it's just overwhelming to me.
Clinician:	Overwhelming. (*repeating reflection*)
Client:	[remains silent]

These reflections would receive low competency ratings and the supervisor would coach the clinician to improve reflective quality, perhaps by cueing the audiotape to this section and discussing alternative reflective statements the clinician might have made (as detailed in the next example).

Beginning with the same client statement, the next example illustrates how a clinician reflects with increasing depth by 'moving past what the client has said without jumping too far ahead' (Miller and Rollnick 2002, p. 7).

Box 6.3 Sample competency guidelines

Open-ended questions

Higher: High quality open-ended questions are relevant to the clinician–client conversation and pull for greater client exploration and recognition of problem areas and motivation for change, without appearing to be judgemental or leading to the client. They are simple and direct, thereby increasing the chance that the client clearly understands what the clinician is asking. Usually, several open-ended questions do not occur in close succession. Rather, high quality open-ended questions typically are interspersed with reflections and ample client conversation to avoid the creation of a question–answer trap between the clinician and client. The clinician pauses after each question to give the client time to respond to each query.

Lower: Low quality open-ended questions are poorly worded or timed or target an area not immediately relevant to the conversation and client concerns. They often will occur in close succession, giving the conversation a halting or mechanical tone rather than one that flows naturally between the clinician and client. Lower quality open-ended questions also may compound several questions into one query (e.g. 'Tell me about how you felt before and after you got high and how that all affects your future risk for using cocaine'), making them harder to understand and respond to by the client. Further reductions in Skill Level ratings may occur if the clinician seems to be leading or steering the client, uses a judgemental or sarcastic tone when asking open-ended questions, or does not pause sufficiently after each question to give the client time to contemplate and respond.

Affirmations

Higher: Higher quality affirmations occur when the clinician affirms qualities or efforts made by the client that promote productive change or that the client might harness in future change efforts rather than being general compliments. The clinician derives these affirmations directly from the conversation. As a consequence, high quality affirmations are meaningful to the client rather than being too global or trite. A key ingredient in a high quality affirmation is the appearance of genuineness rather than the clinician merely saying something generally affirming in a knee-jerk or mechanical fashion.

Lower: Low quality affirmations are not sufficiently rooted in the conversation between the client and clinician. The affirmations are not unique to the client's description of him/herself and life circumstances or history. The clinician may appear to affirm simply to buoy a client in despair or encourage a client to try to change when he/she has expressed doubt about his/her capacity to do so. In short, poor quality affirmations sound trite, hollow, insincere, or even condescending.

Client: I don't know what to say. I really don't know where to begin. There's been so much going on.

Clinician: There has been a lot going on. (*amplified reflection*)

Client: Yeah . . . an awful lot. My drug use, my legal problems, my messed up family, my . . . [pause – client becomes tearful] .

Clinician: And even other difficult problems making it that much harder to discuss or know where to begin. (*paraphrasing by finishing the paragraph*)

Client: [pause – as client collects herself] My father died last year and that has been very difficult for me. I was very close to my father. He was sick for a while with cancer. When he started to get worse, I started to use again after two years of being clean and sober. He was very proud of me for getting into recovery, and I feel terribly guilty for not being clean when he died.

Clinician: You found it very hard not to use drugs as your father became sicker and you became upset by what was happening, even though you wanted to stay clean and sober. (*paraphrasing using a double-sided reflection with reflection of feeling*)

Client: I really did want to stay clean, but I was so upset about my father dying and seeing him so uncomfortable that I couldn't handle it. Now I feel even more terrible that I used and that he knew I relapsed before he died. Now, my brother and sister are very angry with me and haven't talked with me since his funeral. [client becomes tearful again].

Clinician: Thinking about what you have been going through with your family is truly upsetting and hard to talk about. I appreciate your willingness and effort to share this with me. You also mentioned legal problems. (*paraphrasing with reflection of feeling and affirmation*)

Client: After my father died and my brother and sister refused to talk with me, I started using more and more cocaine. I kind of turned to it and my old friends who use, especially when I felt my family had turned away from me. I . . .

These reflective statements would receive higher (i.e. above average) skill level ratings, and the supervisor would underscore them to support the clinician's continued competent performance and confidence in using MI.

As an additional supervision technique, clinicians also have the option of completing a Clinician Session Report (see Box 6.4 for sample items) to help them monitor their behaviour during the session and hone their MI skills. We have used this supervision technique as part of clinician training and monitoring plans in several past psychosocial substance abuse treatment trials (Carroll *et al.* 1998a). Specifically, at the end of each session clinicians rate how often they believe they used each of the three types of

Box 6.4 Clinician Session Report sample items

MOTIVATIONAL INTERVIEWING CONSISTENT ITEM

MOTIVATIONAL INTERVIEWING STYLE OR SPIRIT: To what extent did you provide low-key feedback, roll with resistance (e.g. avoiding arguments, shifting focus), and use a supportive, warm, non-judgemental, collaborative approach? To what extent did you convey empathic sensitivity through words and tone of voice, demonstrate genuine concern and an awareness of the client's experiences? To what extent did you follow the client's lead in discussions instead of structuring the discussion according to your agenda?

1 . . . . . . 2 . . . . . . 3 . . . . . . 4 . . . . . . 5 . . . . . . 6 7

not at all | a little | infrequently | somewhat | quite a bit | considerably | extensively

Comments:____

MOTIVATIONAL INTERVIEWING INCONSISTENT ITEM

ASSERTING AUTHORITY: To what extent did you verbalise clear conclusions or decisions about what course of counselling would be best for the client? How much did you warn the client that recovery would be impeded unless the client followed certain steps or guidelines in treatment? To what extent did you tell the client about 'what works' best in treatment or the likelihood of poor outcome if the client tried to do his/her own treatment? To what extent did you refer to your own experiences, knowledge, and expertise to highlight the points you made to the client?

1 . . . . . . 2 . . . . . . 3 . . . . . . 4 . . . . . . 5 . . . . . . 6 7

not at all | a little | infrequently | somewhat | quite a bit | considerably | extensively

Comments:____

MOTIVATIONAL INTERVIEWING NEUTRAL COUNSELLING ITEM

ASSESSSING/MONITORING SUBSTANCE USE: To what extent did the clinician maintain focus during the session on the client's past or recent use of drugs and alcohol, including the pattern of use, extent of urges/thoughts, extent of reduction in use, results of recent urine/breath tests?

1 . . . . . . 2 . . . . . . 3 . . . . . . 4 . . . . . . 5 . . . . . . 6 7

not at all | a little | infrequently | somewhat | quite a bit | considerably | extensively

Comments:____

items (e.g. MI consistent, inconsistent, and neutral drug counselling strategies). They also may listen to their taped sessions prior to rating their performance as an additional mechanism for self-evaluation and learning. They then compare their self-ratings with the supervisor's tape ratings and discuss the similarities and differences. Clinicians in our protocols tended to view their work as highly empathic or attuned to their clients' needs (Ball *et al.* 2002a) and often rate themselves as having used more targeted skills than actually observed in practice (Carroll *et al.* 1998b; Miller *et al.* 2004). Tape rating comparisons sometimes surprise clinicians, but when provided by a skilled MI supervisor can pique clinician interest in getting more feedback about their performance and how to become more proficient in using MI. For example, a clinician may see him/herself as highly reflective and unlikely to give unsolicited advice and direction, but may not be aware of a tendency to offer reflections as a set-up for unsolicited advice. In this case, the clinician would rate him/herself has having used reflective statements and consider the advice as simply an extension of the reflection. The supervisor would rate a similar number of reflections (albeit with lower competency ratings) and also indicate the clinician's frequent use of unsolicited advising as illustrated in this brief excerpt below:

Client: No matter how hard I try, I always seem to relapse. I must be doing something wrong.

Clinician: You are trying but may be going about it the wrong way. (*reflection*) There are other things you haven't tried that may be more helpful to you. Let's talk about them. (*unsolicited advising*)

In this case, the supervisor would support the clinician's use of reflective statements and coach the clinician how to reflect more effectively by removing the advice-giving tailgate. In addition, the supervisor might discuss with the clinician how to provide advice only when the client asks for it or when the clinician solicits the client's permission first.

Evaluating motivational interviewing proficiency

The effective teaching and monitoring of MI practice and using feedback and coaching based on direct observation of the clinicians' work requires proficiency standards for skill development and evaluation. Miller and Mount (2001) have proposed six preliminary proficiency standards based on MISC coding of four experts using MI with role-played clients. The standards include:

1. greater than a 5 on a 7-point Likert global rating of MI spirit,
2. percentage of MI-consistent responses relative to all clinician responses > 80 per cent,

3. ratio of reflections to questions > 2,
4. percentage of questions that are open-ended questions > 50 per cent,
5. percentage of reflections that are complex reflections > 50 per cent, and
6. clinician's percentage of in-session talk time < 50 per cent (Moyers *et al.* 2003).

Recent work by Miller and colleagues (Miller *et al.* 2004) has shown that individualised post-workshop feedback and coaching increased clinician MI proficiency relative to control and workshop-only training conditions, with the greatest gains in global ratings of MI spirit and reduction in clinicians' MI inconsistent responding. Other MI workshop-only training studies have shown greater impact on increasing MI consistent responses rather than on decreasing MI inconsistent behaviours among parole officers (Miller and Mount 2001) and improving the reflection to question ratio by suppressing the use of questions among addiction and mental health counsellors (Baer *et al.* 2004). These results are encouraging and demonstrate that MI training efforts can produce observable effects that supervisors can evaluate. Moreover, clinicians who continue to practise MI with supervisory guidance can further develop their proficiency along specific dimensions deemed critical to the treatment approach.

We have taken a slightly different approach to establishing proficiency standards in our protocols. Our efforts to teach clinicians MI have occurred in previously non-academically affiliated community treatment programmes where clinicians vary greatly in experience, education, training background, and prior MI knowledge. They are not a highly selected group with substantial pre-training commitment to MI or a head start in MI skills (Ball *et al.* 2002a; Carroll *et al.* 2002). As a result, we did not want to set the MI proficiency bar too high initially by basing our standards on expert MI clinicians used in clinical trials conducted in research clinics. We also felt that an overly challenging initial standard might be inconsistent with a 'learning to learn' philosophy and be insufficiently reinforcing of clinician self-efficacy in learning MI and changing their behaviour. Instead, we initially set reasonable proficiency standards to help clinicians reach an important milestone toward the longer-term goal of becoming an MI expert. Operationally, clinicians have to demonstrate the use of half of the MI consistent items at least three to four times and, for these items, achieve an above average competency rating (4 on the 7-point scale). It should be noted that our standards were derived consensually by our CTN protocol team members who had extensive knowledge and experience with MI. The relationship of our proficiency standards to client outcomes and determination if we set the bar just right or too high or low await completion of our protocols and subsequent data analyses.

In our experience, most clinicians in our protocols are able to achieve these proficiency standards within three to six sessions over a period of one to three months. During this credentialing period, they meet individually with their supervisors who provide rating feedback about the practice sessions and coach the clinicians to improve in areas necessary to perform MI well. Thus, early in the training process, supervisors are training clinicians to objective criteria. We find that this process motivates the clinicians to keep practising MI in order for them to reach the performance benchmarks and helps them become more confident in using MI as they gain more and more experience with it. After achieving the proficiency criteria, clinicians receive supervision on a biweekly basis. This post-credentialing supervision often occurs in a group rather than an individual format to make the provision of ongoing MI supervision feasible. We have found that this two-tiered approach has been effective in getting clinicians to reasonable levels of MI performance and maintaining and boosting their MI skills. We also have set standards that flag clinicians who fall below adequate levels of MI performance. If three successive sessions occur in which a clinician falls below proficiency standards, the clinician receives additional training, feedback, and coaching on an individual basis until he or she demonstrates again sufficient MI skills.

Miller *et al.* (2004) have advocated the use of an additional method to discern clinicians' MI proficiency. Namely, they recommend tracking changes in client change talk and resistance via the MISC since the frequency of these types of client statements in a session is prognostic of behavioural outcomes (Amrhein *et al.* 2003) and the relative balance of each supplies an inroad to the level of motivation or commitment a client has toward change. Clients who are more motivated or committed to change would be expected to use more change talk than resistance (and vice versa for clients with less motivation or commitment to change). If clinicians conduct MI proficiently, supervisors would be expected to hear the balance of change talk versus resistance tip in the expected direction as the session proceeds. Miller found this to be true when clinicians received a combination of supervisory feedback and coaching following workshop training. Overall, as clinician MI proficiency improved along the MISC standards, simultaneously the clinicians' clients demonstrated more change talk and less resistance in their follow-up sessions (Miller *et al.* 2004). This finding points to the importance of attending not only to what clinicians are doing, but also to what the clients are saying for evaluating MI proficiency and getting at the transactional nature between clinicians and clients during the motivational enhancement process.

We created a 7-point global rating scale (see Box 6.5) of a client's motivation for change at the beginning and end of the session (first and last 5 minutes, respectively) to attend to the dynamic nature of client change talk and resistance. We have defined each scale point to reflect the relative balance of client change talk and resistant statements, such that 1 represents no motivation for changing a specific behaviour (very little change

Box 6.5 Motivation for change scale

MOTIVATION – BEGINNING: *How would you rate the client's stage of change or motivation at the beginning of this session?*

MOTIVATION – END: *How would you rate the client's stage of change or motivation at the end of this session?*

Motivation is the readiness and commitment the client demonstrates to change his or her substance use behaviors.

Rating	*Definition*
1. *Not at all.*	The client does not believe he/she has a substance use problem. The client resists the clinician's efforts to identify substance use as problematic or concerning. The client believes no changes are necessary and shows no initiative to change his/her behaviour
2. *Very weak.*	The client acknowledges a few problematic aspects of his/her substance use and considers the clinician's questions and comments. However, the client concludes substance use is relatively non-problematic and no changes are necessary. If the client has initiated any changes in substance use or related behaviours, the client made these changes under coercion or as a temporary measure to reduce the pressure from others to change.
3. *Weak.*	The client is highly ambivalent about the problematic aspects of his/her substance use. The client engages with the clinician during the session, but vacillates in his/her position that substance use is a problem. If a client states a desire to change, this desire is counterbalanced with scepticism about his/her capacity to change and the options available to produce it. The client approaches any initial change efforts with only slight commitment and fluctuating willingness to follow-through.
4. *Adequate.*	The client believes he/she has a substance use problem but continues to acknowledge some significant benefits to use and anticipated difficulties in cessation. The client wants to make changes in his/her substance use patterns (abstinence or reduced consumption) and commits to an initial plan for change. While not sceptical, the client is uncertain about his/her capacity to sustain change and the outcomes of these efforts.

5. *Strong.*	The client believes he/she has a substance use problem. The client responds well to the clinician's efforts to manage any client resistance that arises during the session. The client cooperatively discusses both positive and negative aspects of substance use and firmly anticipates significantly greater benefits than costs through cessation or reduction. The client makes a commitment to a change plan, expresses some optimism about his/her capacity to change, and may have begun to self-initiate specific change efforts.
6. *Very strong.*	The client firmly believes he/she has a substance use problem. The client shows little resistance to change and very openly and collaboratively talks with the clinician. The client sees the relative benefits of changing his/her substance use as much greater than any benefits that might accrue from continued status quo patterns of use. The client makes the argument for change with little assistance from the clinician. The client most likely has begun to change substance use behaviours and speaks positively about these initial experiences. The client is clearly hopeful and optimistic about his/her capacity to sustain a change plan.
7. *Extremely strong.*	The client emphatically believes he/she has a substance use problem. The client shows no resistance to change and works very openly and collaboratively with the clinician. The client is very thoughtful and earnest in his/her assessment of prior substance use and very clear and convincing about how these experiences underpin his/her current reasons for change. The client expresses determination to change his/her behaviour and has begun to initiate his/her change plans.

talk and very strong resistance), and 7 represents extremely strong motivation for change (almost all change talk and very little resistance). Since the aim of an MI session is for the clinician to build and strengthen the client's motivation for change, we consider any movement upward on the scale a potential indicator of good MI proficiency. The supervisor uses this scale to help the clinician consider how motivation for change shifted (or not) during the session, what the clinician said that affected this process, and how to use these shifts in relative change talk and resistance as signals that guide the clinician's interventions in real-time. As needed, the clinician reviews and practises with his or her supervisor how to use core MI consistent skills (open-ended questions, affirmations, reflections, and summaries) and directive methods for eliciting change talk or for handling resistance skilfully to facilitate greater motivation for and commitment to change.

Conclusion

In the past two decades, interest in MI has grown rapidly and has increased the demand for training clinicians and establishing proficient application. This trend has paralleled the general challenge to the addictions treatment field to find means of transferring into clinicians' everyday practices substance abuse treatments that have shown the capacity to improve client outcomes (Institute of Medicine 1998). The psychotherapy field as a whole also has emphasised the importance of determining how specific clinician training efforts impact the acquisition of specific clinical skills (Beutler and Kendall 1995). Given the extensive literature supporting MI's efficacy across multiple studies in a range of situations and heterogeneous samples (Burke *et al.* 2003), it makes sense that interest is growing in developing and evaluating effective strategies for teaching, monitoring, and evaluating MI practice among community clinicians beyond the initial skill/style training period. We have presented our experiences in each of these areas based on our efforts to train and work collaboratively with supervisors and clinicians in our CTN protocols.

Although we believe that our teaching, supervision, and monitoring model has merits, it has shortcomings that require ongoing work so that it can mesh better with the complex and varied administrative realities of any agency where MI might be implemented. Potential shortcomings, particularly in smaller agencies, include the administrative burdens entailed in arranging intensive workshop training for a large number of clinicians, even when delivered on-site, as this may dramatically decrease the availability of clinicians in the agency. Some agencies prefer to have initial MI workshop training spread out over more than two days in order to stagger staffing patterns and meet training needs without significantly disrupting clinical operations. Other agencies elect to have repeated brief MI training sessions over several weeks or months to fit into existing staff meeting and training structures. Such tailored training formats may promote MI learning in a way that is more consistent with worksite responsibilities and practices rather than trying to replace clinician habits with an entirely new set of skills. In this manner, trainers try to integrate MI into clinicians' established clinical patterns rather than replacing them outright. Another issue is the additional training required of supervisors learning the tape rating monitoring and evaluation system. Much like the clinicians, supervisors need their own feedback and coaching over time as they learn and develop proficiency in using the monitoring system and in providing accurate, properly targeted, and MI consistent guidance to their supervisees. Although we have supplied MI expert consultants to all supervisors in our protocols for these purposes, how this would occur in broader community practice settings is an open question and might require the development of continuing education requirements for MI training and supervision currently lacking in the field.

We have not discussed in great detail what trainer qualities are most effective in teaching and supervising MI. At this point, little information exists about potentially important characteristics of MI trainers such as their own level of MI knowledge and expertise, general group and role-play facilitation abilities, and communication skills, including the capacity to empathise with the learners, actively engage them in the training, and offer clear and precise information, feedback, and coaching about MI. Although there are emerging MI proficiency standards for MI clinicians, there are no equivalent proficiency standards proposed for MI trainers. Talent in conducting MI and talent in training MI does not necessarily involve the exact same skill sets any more than being an elite athlete makes for an outstanding coach. The area of specifying trainer competencies and how to train them to these standards clearly requires future development.

Regarding our monitoring system, we have presented it as an option that CTN MI and MET protocol supervisors and clinicians have found very useful for continuing to develop MI skills. MI trainers also have the option of using the MISC or MITI for the same purposes. Since published work in the area of developing and evaluating effective strategies to train clinicians in scientifically validated addiction treatments has only emerged in the past five years and few practitioners have familiarity and experience using carefully crafted monitoring systems as part of the MI training process, the relative benefits and drawbacks of the systems remain to be determined. For now, each system has the merits of providing global clinician ratings, detailed item descriptions for capturing MI adherence, and mechanisms for determining clinician competency (in our system) or proficiency (in the MISC). Initial data on MISC's reliability also suggests that it is good to excellent for measuring several global clinician characteristics (e.g. MI spirit), although reliability falls when tallying specific clinician behaviours (Moyers *et al.* 2003). Published accounts of our monitoring system's psychometric properties will be the subject of future reports, but they appear very promising. Nonetheless, as Moyers and colleagues have pointed out, the greatest drawback to all existing MI monitoring systems is their inability to measure sequential information in clinician and client interactions. The ability empathically and strategically to judge how to respond to a client based upon the client's use of change-oriented or resistant language appears to be a critical skill for MI clinicians. A monitoring measure that reliably captures this dynamic interchange would be a significant advancement for the MI training field.

Despite these open-ended challenges to those committed to training MI clinicians, the strength of commitment shown to the MI training endeavour via the MINT system, burgeoning research to establish effective training strategies for clinicians to become proficient in MI, the MI monitoring and evaluation systems being developed to capture the training process, and CTN efforts to study how to disseminate MI and evaluate its effectiveness in the real world are impressive. As we learn more from all of these initiatives, advancements in teaching, monitoring, and evaluating MI will likely occur that improve client outcomes.

Acknowledgements

Support for this work was provided by NIDA grants R01 DA16970 and U10 DA13038.

References

Amrhein, P.C., Miller, W.R., Yahne, C.E., Palmer, M., and Fulcher, L. (2003) 'Client commitment language during motivational interviewing predicts drug use outcomes', *Journal of Consulting and Clinical Psychology*, 71: 862–878.

Baer, J.S., Kivlahan, D.R., and Donovan, D.M. (1999) 'Integrating skills training and motivational therapies: Implications for the treatment of substance dependence', *Journal of Substance Abuse Treatment*, 17: 15–23.

Baer, J.S., Rosengren, D.B., Dunn, C.W., Wells, E.A., Ogle, R.L., and Hartzler, B. (2004) 'An evaluation of workshop training in motivational interviewing for addiction and mental health clinicians', *Drug and Alcohol Dependence*, 73: 99–106.

Ball, S.A., Bachrach, K., DeCarlo, J., Farentinos, C., Keen, M., McSherry, T., Polcin, D., Snead, N., Sockriter, R., Wrigley, P., Zammarelli, L., and Carroll, K.M. (2002a) 'Characteristics of community clinicians trained to provide manual-guided therapy for substance abusers', *Journal of Substance Abuse Treatment*, 23: 309–318.

Ball, S.A., Martino, S., Corvino, J., Morganstern, J., and Carroll, K.M. (2002b) 'Independent tape rater guide', unpublished tape rating manual.

Battjes, R.J., Onken, L.S., and Delany, P.J. (1999) 'Drug abuse treatment entry and engagement: Report of a meeting on treatment readiness', *Journal of Clinical Psychology*, 55: 643–657.

Beutler, L. and Kendall, P. (1995) 'The case for training in the provision of psychological therapy [Special issue]', *Journal of Consulting and Clinical Psychology*, 63: 179–181.

Burke, B.L., Arkowitz, H., and Menchola, M. (2003) 'The efficacy motivational interviewing: A meta-analysis of controlled trials', *Journal of Consulting and Clinical Psychology*, 71: 843–861.

Carroll, K.M., Nich, C., and Rounsaville, B.J. (1998b) 'Use of observer and clinician ratings to monitor delivery of coping skills treatment for cocaine abusers: Utility of clinician session checklists', *Psychotherapy Research*, 8: 307–320.

Carroll, K.M., Nich, C., Sifry, R., Frankforter, T., Nuro, K.F., Ball, S.A., Fenton, L.R., and Rounsaville, B.J. (2000) 'A general system for evaluating clinician adherence and competence in psychotherapy research in the addictions', *Drug and Alcohol Dependence*, 57: 225–238.

Carroll, K.M., Farentinos, C., Ball, S.A., Crits-Christoph, P., Libby, B., Morgenstern, J., Obert, J.L., Polcin, D. and Woody, G.E., for the Clinical Trials Network (2002) 'MET meets the real world: Design issues and clinical strategies in the Clinical Trials Network', *Journal of Substance Abuse Treatment*, 23: 73–80.

Carroll, K.M., Connors, G.J., Cooney, N.L., DiClemente, C.C., Donovan, D.M., Longabaugh, R.L., Kadden, R.M., Rounsaville, B.J., Wirtz, P.W., and Zweben, A. (1998a) 'Internal validity of Project MATCH treatments: Discriminability and integrity', *Journal of Consulting and Clinical Psychology*, 66: 290–303.

COMBINE Study Research Group (2003) 'Testing combined psychotherapies and behavioral interventions in alcohol dependence: Rationale and methods', *Alcoholism: Clinical and Experimental Research*, 27: 1107–1122.

Dunn, C., Deroo, L., and Rivara, F.P. (2001) 'The use of brief interventions adapted from motivational interviewing across behavioural domains: A systematic review', *Addiction*, 96: 1725–1742.

Institute of Medicine (1998) *Bridging the Gap Between Practice and Research: Forging Partnerships with Community-Based Drug and Alcohol Treatment*. Washington, DC: National Academy Press.

McLellan, T.A., Kushner, H., Metzger, D., Peters, R., Smith, I., Grissom, G., Pettinati, H., and Argeriou, M. (1992) 'The 5th edition of the Addiction Severity Index', *Journal of Substance Abuse Treatment*, 9: 199–213.

Martino, S., Carroll, K., Kostas, D., Perkins, J., and Rounsaville, B. (2002) 'Dual diagnosis motivational interviewing: A modification of motivational interviewing for substance-abusing patients with psychotic disorders', *Journal of Substance Abuse Treatment*, 23: 297–308.

Miller, W.R. (1999) *Enhancing Motivation for Change in Substance Abuse Treatment*, TIP Series 35. Rockville, MD: U.S. Department of Health and Human Services Publication No. (SMA) 02–3693.

Miller, W.R. (2003) 'Disseminating motivational interviewing into clinical practice', paper presented in W.R. Miller (chair), Motivational Interviewing. Symposium presented for the College of Problems on Drug Dependence. Miami, Florida, 15 June 2003.

Miller, W.R. and Rollnick, S. (1991) *Motivational Interviewing: Preparing People to Change Addictive Behavior*. New York: The Guilford Press.

Miller, W.R. and Mount, K.A. (2001) 'A small study of training in motivational interviewing: Does one workshop change clinician and client behavior?', *Behavioural and Cognitive Psychotherapy*, 29: 457–471.

Miller, W.R. and Rollnick, S. (2002) *Motivational Interviewing: Preparing People for Change* (2nd edn), New York: The Guilford Press.

Miller, W.R., Rollnick, S., and Moyers, T.B. (1998) *Motivational Interviewing* (6-tape series), University of New Mexico.

Miller, W.R., Zweben, A., DiClemente, C.C. and Rychtarik, R.G. (1992) *Motivational Enhancement Therapy Manual: A Clinical Research Guide for Therapists Treating Individuals with Alcohol Abuse and Dependence*. Project MATCH Monograph 2, Rockville, Maryland: National Institute on Alcohol Abuse and Alcoholism.

Miller, W.R., Moyers, T.B., Ernst, D., and Amrhein, P. (2003) *Manual for the motivational interviewing skill code (MISC)*. University of New Mexico.

Miller, W.R., Yahne, C.E., Moyers, T.B., Martinez, J., and Pirritano, M. (2004) 'A randomized trial of methods to help clinicians learn motivational interviewing', *Journal of Consulting and Clinical Psychology*, 72: 1052–1062.

Moyers, T.B., Martin, T., Manuel, J.K., and Miller, W.R. (2004) *The Motivational Interviewing Treatment Integrity (MITI) Code: Version 2.0*, University of New Mexico.

Moyers, T., Martin, T., Catley, D., Harris, K.J., and Ahluwalia, J.S. (2003) 'Assessing the integrity of motivational interviewing interventions: Reliability of the motivational interviewing skills code', *Behavioural and Cognitive Psychotherapy*, 31: 177–184.

Noonan, W.C. and Moyers, T.B. (1997) 'Motivational interviewing: A review', *Journal of Substance Misuse*, 2: 8–16.

Project MATCH Research Group (1997) 'Matching alcoholism treatment to client heterogeneity: Project MATCH post treatment drinking outcomes', *Journal of Studies on Alcohol*, 58: 7–29.

Project MATCH Research Group (1998) 'Clinician effects in three treatments for alcohol problems', *Psychotherapy Research*, 8: 455–474.

Rollnick, S., Kinnersley, P., and Butler, C. (2002) 'Context-bound communication skills training: Development of a new method', *Medical Education*, 36: 377–383.

Rounsaville, B.J., O'Malley, S., Foley, S., and Weissman, M.M. (1988) 'Role of manual-guided training in the conduct and efficacy of interpersonal psychotherapy for depression', *Journal of Consulting and Clinical Psychology*, 56: 681–688.

Rubel, E.C., Shepell, W., Sobell, L.C., and Miller, W.R. (2000) 'Do continuing workshops improve participants' skills? Effects of a motivational interviewing workshop on substance-abuse counselors' skills and knowledge', *The Behavior Clinician*, 23: 73–77.

Sholomskas, D., Syracuse, G., Rounsaville, B.J., Ball, S.A., Nuro, K.F., and Carroll, K.M. (2005) 'We don't train in vain: A randomized trial of three strategies for training clinicians in CBT', *Journal of Consulting and Clinical Psychology*, 73(1): 106–115.

Simpson, D.D., Joe, G.W., and Brown, B.S. (1997) 'Treatment retention and follow-up outcomes in the Drug Abuse Treatment Outcome Study (DATOS)', *Psychology of Addictive Behaviors*, 11: 294–307.

Steinberg, K.L., Roffman, R.A., Carroll, K.M., Kabela, E., Kadden, R., Miller, M., and Duresky, D. (2002) 'Tailoring cannabis dependence treatment for a diverse population', *Addiction*, 97: 135–142.

Waltz, J., Addis, M.E., Koerner, K., and Jacobson, N.S. (1993) 'Testing the integrity of a psychotherapy protocol: Assessment of adherence and competence', *Journal of Consulting and Clinical Psychology*, 61: 620–630.

Zweben, A. and Zuckoff, A. (2002) 'Motivational interviewing and treatment adherence', in W.R. Miller and S. Rollnick (eds), *Motivational Interviewing: Preparing People for Change* (2nd edn), New York: The Guilford Press.

Chapter 7

Supervision in the style of motivational dialogue

Rob Kenyon

Introduction

Clinical governance requires professionals to demonstrate that interventions are delivered in a structured manner that is consistent with best practice protocols. The challenge is to enable practitioners to achieve and maintain competence to practise consistently over time. In the UK Alcohol Treatment Trial (UKATT Research Team 2001) supervision of Motivational Enhancement Therapy (described in Chapter 10 of this book) was offered in the style of motivational interviewing, which appeared to facilitate learning. This chapter outlines a method of supervising in this way and documents a specific case for illustration.

Understanding the approach

Experience of conducting supervision in the United Kingdom Alcohol Treatment Trial (Tober *et al.* 2005), in higher education and in routine clinical settings would suggest that a practitioner's motivation to adhere to a treatment protocol is an important factor in their ability to do so. It is likely that practitioners' motivation will fluctuate over time and will be a function of confidence and belief in the effectiveness of the treatment they are delivering. Motivation to practise may also be influenced by the depth of the practitioner's understanding and knowledge of the treatment. Practitioners may be resistant to learning new skills and ambivalent about practising them. It is the premise of this chapter that supervision delivered in the style of motivational interviewing might best address these challenges, whether it is motivational enhancement therapy or another approach that is being developed. In the case of the development of motivational interviewing core skills, a dual purpose may be achieved: that of addressing resistance and motivation to learn as well as modelling the new skills themselves.

Resistance to the acquisition of motivational interviewing skills

Resistance to learning new skills might be greatest when new practices are adopted at the institutional level, imposed through organisational changes or through participation in clinical trials. Examples of statements suggesting resistance and possible remedial approaches are:

'This is no different from what I usually do.'

This commonly heard statement might denote a need for greater understanding of the unique features of a motivational interviewing approach, but might also best be addressed with a recognition on the part of the supervisor that the supervisee has knowledge and skills that she or he wishes to be recognised.

'It's OK but I've got lots of other things to do in the session.'

This sort of statement might well be met with the suggestion that it is not always clear how some things can be addressed in this style.

'I think this technique is good, but this client is too resistant.'

Claims that a client is too resistant for the approach (rather than for the purpose of eliciting intention to change) probably denotes a lack of competence or confidence in dealing with resistant clients, rather than in the approach itself (a case of blaming the tools).

'Asking open questions is fine most of the time, but sometimes you just need to get a specific piece of information.'

This sort of resistance may allude to a lack of confidence in the skill of asking open questions, however, there may be a real difficulty that was addressed in Chapter 6.

The delivery of supervision in a motivational interviewing style is much like the delivery of a motivational interviewing session with a client. The focus is on exploration and resolution of a practitioner's ambivalence about practising this method, before and during supervision of the method. It is practitioner centred, directive, empathic, agenda driven and seeks to address problems of a practitioner's motivation as a way of unlocking their ability to practise more effectively.

Assessing supervisee motivation

Different strategies can be employed by the supervisor to match the supervisee's level of motivation for practising the approach. The Stages of

Change model (Prochaska and DiClemente 1984) which is a popular tool for understanding client motivation, can equally be used as a framework for understanding a therapist's readiness to practise a new treatment or deliver it in a new way. Again some examples of stage related supervisee comments followed by actions the supervisor might take are given.

Precontemplation

Therapist: 'I don't want to do it.' 'I can't do it.' 'There's no point in doing it.' 'It doesn't work.' 'I don't practise this way.' 'My clients are not suitable for this approach.'

Supervisor: Reflects resistance, explores reluctance, reinforces therapist responsibility, elicits therapist's concerns about suitability, provides information about motivational interviewing.

Contemplation

Therapist: 'It's such hard work.' 'It's making me question how I've been practising until now.' 'I'd like to be able to do it.' 'I don't understand it properly.'

Supervisor: Reframes concerns into aspirations, develops discrepancy between where the practitioner is currently and where they want to be, highlights positive thoughts or experiences.

Determination

Therapist: 'I think it will be good way of working.' 'I want to do it like that.' 'I'm going to have a go.' 'I think I can see the benefits of working this way.'

Supervisor: Elicits commitment to practise, reinforces positive perceptions of practice, de-emphasises concerns and skill deficits.

Action

Therapist: 'How do I ask this in a motivational interviewing style?' 'I think this was OK, am I doing it right?' 'I can see how it works.' 'The clients seem to like it.' 'I didn't do this bit well.'

Supervisor: Provides objective information about therapist's practice, affirms progress, elicits positive outcome expectations and explores solutions to difficulties with the aim of enhancing self-efficacy.

Maintenance

Therapist: 'It's a great way of working.' 'I'm fairly confident about doing it in this setting, so I'd like to try it with more difficult clients.' 'I've tried everything I know, but this client didn't change. What else can I do?' 'Clients really like it.'

Supervisor: Encourages regular practice and monitoring of practice as a method of improving through reflection and supervision; focuses on future opportunities.

In addition to the therapist's level of motivation, the supervisor will also need to pay attention to their skill level. If the supervisee is at the early stages of acquiring competence, even if they are highly motivated to practise motivational interviewing, it is unlikely that concentrating on complex issues or a multitude of areas will enable them to develop their practice. In fact it may even be counter-productive resulting in a lowering of self-esteem and self-efficacy. One of the challenges of training and supervision is the need to ensure early practice with more straightforward cases. The principle of taking on the challenges one by one is similar to the principle of learning to drive a car on a disused airfield rather than a busy motorway. A competent therapist may lose motivation if supervision is not tailored to their needs.

A protocol for supervising in a motivational interviewing style

The aims of this approach to supervision have much in common with those of other approaches. Broadly these can be stated as:

- Increase the therapist's understanding of what they are trying to achieve
- Increase the therapist's confidence in the approach and commitment to use it.

It may be that the supervisor adheres to a purely motivational approach, or adds some behavioural components by providing an opportunity for therapists to rehearse their skills and to learn by the method of modelling from observation of the supervisor's behaviour. Objective feedback will enable the supervisee to gauge their own level of knowledge and understanding as well as their current skill level.

Modelling is best achieved through supervisor adherence to the general principles, skills and strategies of the approach. There should be a clear structure and agenda which is directed by the purpose of the session (to acquire and maintain competence). Supervision should be conducted in an empathic manner, and in a way that is able to give attention to serious issues. It should be objective, focusing on what actually occurred rather than on what the therapist thought may have happened. Therefore the gold standard should be an appropriately consented video or audio recording. The following agenda is proposed:

1 Introduce and elicit consent for agenda as proposed.
2 Watch section of video with supervisee
   - Elicit specific good and less good aspects of practice to focus on
   - Use coding sheet to provide objective feedback (see Box 7.1).
3 Explore practice confidence and competence using decisional balance focused on current practice
   - Elicit self-esteem building statements
   - Elicit statements regarding areas of concern.
4 Develop discrepancy regarding competent and less good practice
   - Elicit positive effects on session when practice was good
   - Elicit downsides when practice was less good.
5 Elicit optimism for future
   - Identify key learning points – things to do differently
   - Link improved practice to implementation of changes.
6 Resolve ambivalence to practise
   - Ask key question to renew commitment
   - Link change in practice to review at future sessions.
7 Arrange next session.

Case Study: Melanie

The following case study focuses on a 30-year-old female undergraduate, undertaking a module on Motivational Interviewing, which forms a component of her bachelor degree in Addiction Studies. She is highly motivated to achieve competence in the approach in order to complete her studies successfully. This is Melanie's first supervision session and focuses on a video in which she demonstrates motivational interviewing with a young male heroin user in a criminal justice setting. It demonstrates the practical application of the supervision template described above. S refers to the supervisor and M to Melanie.

S: (smile) Let's talk about what we're going to do together. The purpose is to help you develop your motivational interviewing skills. We've got half an hour in total, so, first, I would be interested in how you think it best to use the time if that's OK with you.

M: I presumed we would look at the video.

S: Can I suggest that we look at about 10 minutes of video and that either of us can stop the recording if there's something that we want to

Box 7.1 The Supervision Coding Sheet

CODE	TEXT

Code Key
r = simple reflection
r+ = reflection reinforcing change
r– = reflection reinforcing current behaviour
dr = double sided reflection
o = open questions
c = closed questions
a = advise
i = information
x = verbal utterances (umm, yup, ehem, aha, okay, right)
s = summary
b = arguments, persuasion

comment on? It is preferable not to talk about it while we're watching it so we don't miss anything.

Therapists may feel compelled to discuss any perceived errors as they see them or want feedback from the supervisor throughout the video. This is not inconsistent with the function of reflection in the encouragement of the recipient to continue in a particular line of dialogue. It highlights the importance of feedback and its use in eliciting and addressing concerns and creating optimism for change.

S: The idea of these supervision sessions is to help you to develop your skills and knowledge about motivational interviewing, so after we've viewed your video together I'm going to ask you to make some comments so that I can understand more about how you're thinking. We can then discuss your thoughts about your work.

Therapists may expect the supervisor to castigate them for their practice and may make all sorts of defensive comments. If the supervisor were to tell the therapist what they think, they would not be demonstrating the skill of eliciting concerns rather than telling people what they should be concerned about. Instead the supervisor can encourage confidence in critical self-appraisal by eliciting comments of concern, reinforcing these and eliciting suggestions of alternative courses of action.

S: My job is to help you to develop your skills and to keep us focused on talking about motivational interviewing. How do you see your role here?
M: To try to learn something to improve my motivational interviewing skills.
S: It would be helpful to me if you were to tell me what you think about what you've done and describe the rationale for what you've done. I would really like you to highlight your new skills and things you are particularly pleased with. At the end of the session we can agree what you might want to concentrate on in order to improve or maintain your practice. As this is the first time we've met like this, I should also explain that the focus is very much on what we say and do as therapists, as well as what the client is like so I'm going to take some notes about the interaction. What do you think about this?

This establishes a consensus about relative roles, the purpose of the session and the way it is to be conducted. From the outset, the task is negotiated in a motivational interviewing style using open questions and seeking consensus. Resistance is reflected from the outset, encouraging the practitioner to feel comfortable exploring practice without needing to be defensive.

M: I've had some thoughts already. (heavy sigh, sounds critical) Yes that's fine.

S: OK. You're feeling a bit hesitant but resolved to get started. Let's make a start then.
Supervisor gives control over watching the video, in both a symbolic and literal sense, by handing over the remote control, once consent established.

M: OK. (presses play)
S Takes notes on coding sheet. When the therapist makes verbal utterances of discomfort with the session being observed the supervisor does not attend to these.

S: Let's stop there. (after 10 minutes)

M: Have you had enough? (arms folded, leaning back, legs outstretched) It goes on and on. (nervous laughter)

S: You are worried that I might have seen enough already to form an opinion. It's useful to watch people's practice and I'm grateful that we are able to watch this video. (affirming) This is always a difficult process at first and it sounds like you'd like me to make some comments straight away. I would prefer to get a feel for what you think about it first and then we can have a look at some of my notes together. How would you like to proceed?

M: Mm. Yeah. I bet you've got a lot to say. (arms folded, leaning back, legs outstretched)

The therapist's comments and body language so far suggest that she is unhappy with her practice and uncomfortable watching it together. Having seen the video and coded the therapist's skills, the supervisor is able to determine the therapist's level of competence and is assured that there is good practice in the session, with a number of things that could be done differently. It is clear that the therapist is attending mainly to those parts with which she is less pleased. The discrepancy between quality of practice and negative comment could be attributed to her lack of confidence in her practice and about viewing the video in this way.

The supervisor avoids saying 'and then I'll tell you what I think' but obtains consent for making comments in an objective manner from a coding sheet. The supervisor acknowledges the negative comments without reinforcing them. The next task is to identify areas to focus upon to improve practice.

S: Perhaps you could start off by telling me some of your general thoughts and to what extent you think you achieved what you set out to achieve? (open question – seeking to understand therapist's knowledge)

M: I think I did stick to my agenda although I then went back to look at some of the good things about changing and what he thought was not good about continuing, so I sort of did it but in the wrong order. (expression of concern)

S: You think you might have planned your questions to follow a different order. (reflection)

M: Yeah. That was a problem in terms of the overall agenda. I think the decision bit should have come afterwards. (accurately recognises the principle of working towards positive reasons for change)

S: You think that asking him a key question about change should have come at the end. (reinforces therapists view by reflection)

M: Yeah. (arms relaxing) So I sort of went off the agenda although I did get through what I wanted to get through . . . (expression of optimism)

S: You achieved what you set out to do. (reinforces recognition of competent practice)

M: Yeah just not in the right order. (disappointed sigh). So I'm not sure, will it do? Is it good enough? Does the order matter? (ambivalence – seeking reassurance and possibly a view from the supervisor)

S: You think it could have been more effective to reflect those statements in a different order (reframe), though you got to where you wanted to be. (double-sided selective reflection)

Supervision conducted in a motivational interviewing style takes on a discursive, as opposed to a didactic, style. This emphasises the way that there is not so much a right or wrong way of doing things, but that there are more and less effective ways of doing things, ways that are less likely to elicit resistance. Rather than telling the supervisee what the supervisor thinks, he uses reflections to reframe and reinforce recognition of these differences.

M: Yeah. (nods, smiles, legs and arms more relaxed, still leaning back) It just made it a bit harder I suppose.

S: It was more difficult, but you elicited a clear decision to change. (reflection emphasising the achievement by changing the order)

M: Yeah. I did. Another thing I wasn't happy with was that I don't think my reflections are very good. I use a lot of 'kind ofs' and they're a bit woolly. I don't think I'm very clear or sharp. (gains confidence in expressing concerns)

S: You'd like to be more accurate. (reframing reflection designed to emphasise intention to change)

M: Yeah I've noticed that that's a problem so I'm trying to think about what to do with it but I'm having difficulty, I remain woolly. (laughs, expresses desire to change)

S: You want to be less woolly, more accurate, sharp, more precise and less vague. (reframing reflection emphasising intention to change)

M: Yeah I think I am always quite vague.

S: OK we can come back to that later. What else? (acknowledges concern and moves on)

M: Well I think my questions sound boring. (expression of concern)

S: You think your questions could be better. (reframing reflection)

M: Yeah. I ask a lot of open questions, but they sound boring, I just seem to ask the same things. (resigned look, crossed arms and outstretched legs) I just seem to ask the same questions and say a lot of 'tell me more about that'. (concern about repetitive questioning)

S: You'd like to use more variety; use different questions. (reframe to elicit intention to change)

M: Yeah.

S: You're aware that you're using mainly open questions and using reflection a lot, at the same time you feel you could be doing better. You'd like to improve the variety of your questions and be more punchy and accurate in your reflections. (reinforce competence and intention to change)

M: Yeah.

During the session so far the therapist has been quick to follow any reflection of her acknowledgement of competent practice with comments like: 'yes – but I did this badly'. The supervisor meets this resistance with reflection, focusing both on what she had done well and what she would like to do in the future. After several exchanges, the supervisor's summary is met with an agreement without further resistance, signalling an opportunity to continue with the agenda.

S: OK let's look at things a bit more specifically. What are the things you're doing well? What are you pleased with when you look back at the video? (open question)

M: I think I'm trying to maintain a certain amount of control rather than letting it go off completely. (acknowledges need to set the agenda and maintain focus and identifies achievement)

S: You feel better about the way you control the agenda. (reflection emphasising optimism)

M: Yeah. (looks more relaxed) I'm trying to keep on top of that so it's not going too badly. (cautious optimism)

S: It's going quite well. (reframing reflection reinforcing positive thought)

M: Yeah. (more relaxed again), although I notice that when I'm reflecting back selectively that I'm nodding all the time so I'm reinforcing things I shouldn't be. (understands the need to reflect selectively and that body language can undermine this)

S: Your nodding is having a different effect to what you're trying to achieve and yet your verbal reflections are selective. (double sided reflection reinforcing accurate self-appraisal)
M: Yeah. (agreement)
S: Your verbal reflections are selective which is what you're trying to do. (amplified reflection)
M: Yeah it's just that I'm not doing the right things all the time. I'm just trying to take in so much. (laughs folds arms) I don't know what to do. ('yes – but' resistance)
S: It's a lot to concentrate on. There's a lot to do. (affirming – acknowledges learning new skill is difficult)
M: Mmm. Yeah. (agrees – feels understood)
S: What other things are you doing well, what else are you pleased with? (open question to continue agenda)
M: Well I am asking open questions; it's just that they're always the same one. (expression of concern)
S: Your questions are not as varied as you want them to be. You're going to try to make them more varied. (reinforce intention to change)
M: Yeah so I'm trying to do that. (sounds more optimistic) I'm trying to amplify a bit as well. (optimism)
S: As well as reinforcing selectively you're using amplification. (reflection)
M: A bit.
S: You're doing some of it. (amplifying)
M: Yeah I think that's it. (agreement)

The supervisor deals with the therapist's 'I can't do it!' resistance by listening to and affirming the real concern – 'It's very difficult and a lot to remember'. Answering objections will rarely stop further resistance. Instead resistance is met with affirming, reflective statements. This acknowledgement leads to the therapist being able to discuss things she is trying to do in a more optimistic light rather than in a self-deprecating manner. Hints at optimism are met with amplified reflection by the supervisor in order both to boost the therapist's self-esteem and to model the very thing that the therapist is identifying. As a result her body language becomes more relaxed; she begins to smile and leans toward the supervisor. The supervisor seizes this opportunity to elicit additional self-motivational statements.

S: From a skills point of view you're pleased with asking open questions, reflecting selectively and using some amplification. (reinforcing summary) How about from the techniques point of view, how do you think you're doing with the techniques you are using? The decisional balance, looking forward and trying to create some dissonance? (open question to shift focus)

M: Not too bad, those methods seem to have generated the right sort of things. (tentative optimism for change)
S: The right things. (simple reflection seeking elaboration)
M: Yeah, well maybe I'm not . . . I don't know. (hesitant) There seems to be a lot of self-motivational statements but I find it difficult to keep track of them during the session. (ambivalent about ability to change)
S: It's a bit tricky keeping track of them at the time, yet you are eliciting change statements. (double sided reflection, acknowledging but minimising difficulty and reinforcing therapist skilfulness at eliciting self motivational statements)
M: Yeah. (agreement)
S: What other things are you doing well? How do you think you are using the different techniques? (reinforcing personal responsibility for self-appraisal)
M: I think I am doing OK following my agenda. Using a decisional balance helped him to identify what the problems are and what the concerns are. (demonstrating confidence in effectiveness of the method)
S: You got him to tell you his concerns and the problems he is having, which is what you intended to do. That was part of your agenda.
M: Yes, I thought it would be useful for him to hear himself say these things in order to move towards change.
S: They are the things you'd expect to elicit from a decisional balance to help move your client towards change. (summary) How do you think this worked? (open question to explore understanding)
M: Well after this passage that we've looked at I used a different kind of decisional balance, sort of looking forward and that seemed to elicit some optimism and some hints about change. (demonstrates understanding of how therapist might elicit optimism)
S: Looking forward can elicit statements of optimism about change. (amplified reflection)
M: Yes. I need to get more concrete statements. How do I do that? (seeking advice)
S: You're not sure how to do this. What do you think might have helped to get more statements of optimism from this decisional balance? (reflection and open question)
M: I did not ask the client to focus on change, I asked about his problems and his concerns.
S: The questions that you asked elicited the answers you were aiming for. (amplified reflection reinforcing personal responsibility for outcome)
M: Yeeaah. (hesitant agreement)
S: You decided to use a decisional balance, you asked questions that elicited concerns, the sort of statements you were directing the client towards. You reinforced the statements selectively in the direction of

change and amplified some of them. Is that an accurate summary? (summary seeking clarification)

M: Yes. (agrees)

The supervisor has led the therapist to being able to identify what she has done well and what she might have done differently. She has identified that the outcome that she wanted to obtain was achieved by pursuing her plan. In other words the therapist has linked the client's responses to her practice. This has helped to shape the therapist's perception that her behaviour influences what happens. This has not been achieved by the supervisor telling her that she has done well, but by the therapist telling herself that this is what she has achieved. So far the supervisor has helped the therapist to identify what she has done. In order to boost her motivation to practise in this way, the supervisor plans to elicit some values from the therapist associated with her practice.

S: Tell me what you think about that. (seeking further optimism)

M: (Smiles, moves forward and sits upright) It's what I'm meant to be doing isn't it? (optimism)

S: You're pleased. (paraphrase)

M: I think so. (reluctant agreement)

S: You think you are pleased. (amplified reflection)

M: Yeaaaahh. (agrees) It's just hard isn't it? I wish I could do it really well now. It's just that I'm still learning and I know I can do it better and get more skilled. I'm never satisfied. (ambivalence about change, cautious optimism, self-deprecating)

S: You know that the more you practise, the better you'll get. (selective reinforcement of optimism for change)

M: Yeah. (agrees)

S: It's not that you don't think you do it well, you just want to do it better. (optimism – paraphrase)

M: (Nods, smiles looks relaxed) Yeah that's it. (agrees – appears to feel understood)

Now that the supervisor has helped the therapist to begin to acknowledge her good practice and feel good about it, there is a choice to be made about where the session goes next. One possibility is to attend to some of the less competent practice, so this could be covered now and risk the therapist reverting to criticising herself. Alternatively, time could first be spent building her self-efficacy before exploring areas of practice for improvement. The supervisor chose the latter option and asked for comments about another technique that she had employed.

M: Well again. He was able to generate positive aspects. (minimising therapist's role)
S: You helped him to generate positive aspects. (reinforcing therapist's role)
S: How do you know that technique worked? (open question)
M: Because I was able to help him identify the difference between the real him, and him as a heroin user and he said that the two sides of him didn't fit together. (recognition of competent practice and understanding)
S: It worked well. You developed a discrepancy, which he could then begin to resolve. (reinforcing therapist effectiveness)

The supervisor has elicited statements of optimism and self-efficacy from the therapist and now thinks she is in a stronger position to examine the parts of her practice that could be modified further. The supervisor had determined from viewing the video that the therapist's application of motivational interviewing skills was not consistent. He wanted to know whether the therapist was aware of this. Would she be able to identify how to maintain consistent practice? In order to explore the answers to these questions the supervisor asked a direct question.

S: You described using two different techniques, a decisional balance and developing discrepancy and you described feeling differently about them. Tell me more about that.
M: I feel less confident about developing discrepancy because I'm still trying to develop the language and the knowledge about it. (expression of concern)
S: You feel less confident about developing discrepancy. (simple reflection) How do you think that manifests itself? (open question)
M: It probably shows itself in the language I use. I'm probably doing more 'kind ofs' and being more woolly. My language is less sure. (problem recognition)
S: You're less specific, not as accurate as you want to be. (reframe to elicit desire to change)
M: Yeah. (agrees)
S: You'd like to change that round, and getting more confidence would help you achieve that.
M: Yeah.

The supervisor has elicited a desire to change practice and helped the therapist to identify that overcoming her lack of confidence may assist in this goal. The supervisor believes that helping the therapist to gain a more objective overview of her practice may help to increase her confidence. Telling her that her practice is good is not as effective a method as eliciting statements of self-efficacy from her about her practice. In these circumstances she may be more likely to believe it: the principle that she might 'learn what she believes as she hears herself speak' (Bem 1972). Rather than concentrating on the less good aspects of her practice the supervisor also seeks to focus on what she might do differently in future – firstly to ascertain that she understands the approach sufficiently well to achieve this and secondly as another mechanism to help improve her confidence.

S: We could have a look at the notes that I made when we watched your video and then see where you want to go from here.
M: OK.
S: This is a coding system that helps to record objectively what you've been doing. (shows her the coding system) I coded the first 50 statements that you made. Let's have a look at what it tells us. Could you read from the top? (engages therapist in a collaborative process)
M: Err, open question, reflection, reflection, open question . . .
S: They're mainly reflections with some questions. (reflection) How does that compare with what you would expect to see from a competent therapist? (open question)
M: It's what you'd expect to see I guess. (expression of confidence)
S: You're doing it well. (reframe to reinforce personal achievement)
M: Yeah. (sounds surprised and pleased)
S: There are a couple of closed questions, and I made a note of this one here when you were exploring the downsides of his heroin use and you asked 'Is there anything else?' (provides objective feedback)
M: Mmm. Not very open is it? (recognises problem)
S: The question led to him saying 'I can't think of anything'. (objective feedback to reinforce problem recognition)
M: It closed things down. (agreement)
S: Of course there might not have been anything else. (paradoxical reflection)
M: No but if I'd asked him an open question he would have been more likely to mention something. (acknowledges need to change)
S: Open questions are better to help you elicit more information. (reinforces understanding and need to alter practice)
M: Yeah.
S: The coding sheet tells us that you used that question three times during that technique. (objective feedback) What might you do differently in the future? (open question)
M: I could just ask 'What else?'

Having explored possible different responses to the situations highlighted by the coding sheet, the therapist attends to another area of practice that might be changed. To be consistent with the approach, and to improve self-esteem, good practice was reinforced before discussing areas that could be improved.

S: You can see that you start the next section with an open question followed by reflection, reflection, reflection, open question, reflection, reflection and amplified reflection. (selective objective feedback focusing on good practice)
M: Oh that's good. (expression of optimism)
S: It's just what you want to see. (reframe positive statement)
M: Mm. (smiles broadly)
S: Then in the next part you ask another open question about his personality followed by a closed question then followed by right, yep, right, yep, yep, closed question, yep. (selective objective feedback focusing on less good practice) I'm wondering what you make of that? What went on there? (direct open question)
M: I wasn't aware of what was going on there. It's quite a contrast. I seem to be losing control a bit there but I'm not sure why. I'm nodding quite a bit. (problem recognition)
S: You are not sure what was going on there. (reflection) Tell me what you remember about what you were trying to achieve in that passage. (open question)
M: I wanted him to hurry up, because I'd not asked him the right question, I'd asked him to focus on how heroin helps him instead of how he thinks of himself as a heroin user. (problem recognition)
S: You wanted to move back to your agenda. (reframe) Let's look at your body language here? You looked rather frustrated.
M. I was frustrated. That's why I wanted him to hurry up.
S: That's why you're nodding vigorously and saying yep, yep. (demonstrates understanding of therapist's intervention)
M: Yeah. (agrees)
S: What effect does that seem to have? (open question)
M: Well it's just reinforcing what he's saying. (accurately identifies problem)
S: Your response makes it more likely that he will continue talking. (reframe to reinforce therapist's awareness)
M: (Groans and smiles) Oh yeah. So I need to stop nodding and get him back to the question. (intention to change)

The supervisor has elicited an expression of self-efficacy and an understanding of what is going on. The supervisor has not highlighted every part of the session where practice might be changed, but instead has focused on a number of points for practice. Discussion of areas for improvement is likely to be easier when following positive feedback of achievements, thus maintaining self-esteem and enhancing self-efficacy. In motivational terms the supervisor has elicited from the therapist:

- a summary of what the therapist did well
- recognition of a number of areas where practice could be changed
- an understanding of how practice could be changed.

Before ending the session the supervisor aims to increase the therapist's motivation to change her practice by dealing with her remaining resistance and resolving any ambivalence she has about putting into practice the learning achieved during the session.

S: We're nearing the end of supervision for today. In light of what we've looked at and discussed, how do you think you are getting on so far? (refocus, open question)

M: Err (nervously, hesitantly) well looking at that coding sheet, I'm obviously better than I thought I was. (expression of self-efficacy)

S: You have achieved more than you realised. (reframed reflection)

M: Yes. I am improving, but is still doesn't feel anything like natural. (agreeing but minimising)

S: You haven't got used to this new way of practising yet, but you are getting there. (double sided reflection) Tell me what you feel you have achieved so far? (open question)

M: Well I think I know what I should be doing. It's just doing it. I want to be doing it properly now. I sort of get most of it and I can do it, but I'm not doing it as well as I want to be. (expresses accurate understanding of practice and desire to change)

S: You're frustrated that your practice isn't perfect yet; you can see that you're getting better and you're confident that you can improve. (double sided reflection to reframe towards increasing self-efficacy)

M: Yeah I know I will eventually. (agrees but minimises)

S: You're sure you'll get better the more you practise. (reframe to emphasise optimism for positive outcome)

M: Yeah. (agrees)

S: This is a brand new intervention to you and you've been practising for two months.

M: I guess it's early days. (expression of optimism)

S: It is not easy to say good things about one's own practice, and yet you're pretty sure you did well. (acknowledges difficult feelings and focuses on optimism)

M: Mmm. I suppose so. (reluctant agreement)

S: You want to do even better by the next time we meet up. (reframe and focus on future optimism)

M: Yes, I'll definitely bring a better video next time. (expression of intention to continue change)

Having resolved some resistance expressed as a lack of self-esteem and unrealistic expectation, the supervisor sought to reinforce the learning that had taken place during the session and to elicit a commitment from the therapist to changing future practice and to the supervision process.

S: Let me try and sum up what we've discussed today. You've been practising for two months so far. In the video we watched today, you've demonstrated your ability to stay in control, and be directive. You've used plenty of reflective listening skills and mainly used open questions. You've incorporated a number of techniques into your session and you've understood the rationale behind using them. You're a little frustrated that you're not doing it perfectly already and yet you know that realistically that's a bit much to ask of yourself. You have decided that using a variety of open questions would be a good idea, as would changing the closed questions into open ones. You would like to be more accurate and succinct with your reflections and to be careful about not reinforcing things that are not consistent with change with your body language. Finally you are confident that you will continue to get better with these points with more practice. Is that about right? (major summary ending with expression of self-efficacy)
M: Yeah that's it. (agreement)
S: In light of what we've looked at today, to what extent do you want to continue to practise in this way? (key question to boost commitment)
M: Oh I definitely want to do that. (affirms commitment)
S: You're really keen to get on with doing more motivational interviewing. (amplified reflection)
M: Oh yeah. (reaffirms commitment)
S: You definitely want to do more of it, so let's make an arrangement for us to meet up in a couple of weeks and we can look at the work you have been doing in the meantime. (boost commitment to practise and supervision)
M: Yeah. Good.

Concluding comments

The reader might like to ask whether there is merit in this approach and whether the example given above fulfils the criteria for motivational change? Did the supervisee reach her own conclusions about what she wanted to do, why she wanted to do it, that she was able to do it and that, having done it her treatment delivery would be better, that is to say more effective?

What are the general challenges the supervisor faces and which are specific to the development of motivational interviewing practice? We have often found that students of motivational interviewing and motivational enhancement therapy comment on the degree of attention required to deliver the intervention without missing opportunities for eliciting motivational statements or making helpful reflections that guide the client into more change talk. While it is true that, in order to use the material generated from your client for selective reflection and therefore move forward, the practitioner's constant attention is required, we cannot in all honesty think of an example of a therapeutic intervention that would depart from this principle.

Social and psychological circumstances may affect a therapist's ability to practise. Anecdotal evidence suggests that there is no exception to this when using a motivational interviewing style. Partnership breakdowns, moving house, promotion, changing jobs, awareness of previous questionable practice, feeling professionally challenged and frustration with a lack of progress are amongst those issues that get in the way of developing competent or consistent practice. Whilst it is important to attend to these potential problems in order to improve practice and to consider encouraging therapists to avoid practising if they are unable to perform to a satisfactory standard, the reality is that most therapists will inevitably continue to practise as many of these issues will come to light only after the event. It is important for the supervisor to be vigilant to the possibility of outside pressures, to encourage discussion where they provide a distraction and yet to remain focused on the core function of supervision – maintaining and improving the therapist's ability to practise. It cannot be assumed that simply because a therapist is having a difficult time, that they are unable to practise in a professionally competent way.

Finally while there may not be evidence for the superiority of one style of supervision over another, the case for the superiority of training followed by supervision compared to training with either self-directed learning or without subsequent supervision has been demonstrated (Miller *et al.* 2004). It makes intuitive sense that talking about practice in the classroom, even doing role-plays and feedback requires follow-up in the real world with real clients if competence is to be achieved.

References

Bem, D.J. (1972) 'Self Perception Theory' in I. Berkowitz (ed.), *Advances in Experimental Social Psychology*, Vol. 6, New York: Academic Press.

Miller, W.R., Yahne, C.E., Moyers, T.B., Martinez, J. and Pirritano, M. (2004) 'A randomised trial of methods to help clinicians learn motivational interviewing', *Journal of Consulting and Clinical Psychology*, 72: 1052–1062.

Prochaska, J.O. and DiClemente, C.C. (1984) *The Transtheoretical Approach: Crossing Traditional Boundaries of Therapy*, Homewood, Illinois: Dow Jones-Irwin.

Tober, G., Godfrey, C., Parrott, S., Copello, A., Farrin, A., Hodgson, R., Kenyon, R., Morton, V., Orford, J., Russell, I. and Slegg, G. on behalf of the UKATT Research Team (2005) 'Setting standards for training and competence: the UK Alcohol Treatment Trial', *Alcohol and Alcoholism*, 40(5): 413–418.

UKATT Research Team (2001) 'United Kingdom Alcohol Treatment Trial (UKATT): Hypotheses, design and methods', *Alcohol and Alcoholism*, 36(1): 11–21.

Section IV

Four studies of motivational therapy in practice

Chapter 8

A comparison of motivational interviewing with non-directive counselling

J. Douglas Sellman, Ian K. MacEwan, Daryle D. Deering and Simon J. Adamson

Introduction

Motivational interviewing (MI) is still a relatively new method of intervening psychologically. It was developed at a time and in a treatment context when overt, aggressive confrontation, particularly in group and family settings, was considered a key ingredient of successful psychotherapy. This was particularly so in the United States where 12-step approaches were dominant. MI has subsequently become popularised and has gained widespread support as a key psychotherapeutic intervention within the addictions field and beyond. However, the popularity of motivational approaches that now exists around the world is not reflected in a strong scientific literature attesting to its specific efficacy. In fact, to our knowledge, our study (Sellman *et al.* 2001), on which this chapter is based, was the only randomised controlled trial in the literature in which a motivational approach is directly compared with a non-directive psychotherapy.

This chapter provides a selective review of existing literature on the relative efficacy of MI compared with non-directive approaches. It then describes the purpose, findings and development of our study. Finally the chapter explores issues related to therapist training and reflects on the experience of delivering the two contrasting therapies from both training and therapist perspectives.

Background literature

In examining this literature the terms 'directive' and 'non-directive' are not used in consistent ways. The term 'directive' is referred to variously as meaning giving advice, direct confrontation, or, as is the case of MI, strategic questioning. MI also contains a number of elements that might be considered non-directive. These include being non-confrontational (avoiding argumentation), the therapist working alongside the patient rather than taking an explicitly expert role and the avoidance of giving direct advice. This range of interpretations means that caution is required in interpreting literature describing the clinical effectiveness of therapy in relation to level of directiveness.

Keijsers and colleagues (2002) review the impact of a variety of patient and therapist behaviour variables on treatment outcome primarily in cognitive behaviour therapy, with additional comment on insight-oriented therapy. This review considers a wide range of psychiatric disorders and the term directiveness is not operationalised, although the authors note that as opposed to insight-oriented psychotherapy, behavioural therapy is more focused on facilitating skills acquisition. Furthermore they report that the literature indicates that patients who undergo greater improvement rate therapist behaviour as being significantly different on a number of dimensions including being more 'directive and active', while the use of confrontation is addressed separately. In other instances, the term 'directive' has been used as indicating what could primarily be identified as a confrontational approach (e.g. Toma 2000).

A recent study, examining the interaction between therapeutic process and patient attributes with an alcohol treatment population, addressed the dimension of 'directiveness' (Karno *et al.* 2002). These authors however considered directiveness as being analogous with being confrontational, while being non-directive did not preclude some activities quite consistent with a motivational approach. They found that independently-rated therapist directiveness did not predict outcome. There was, however, an interaction such that those with high reactance, namely those who were more defensive and unwilling to be influenced by others, achieved better outcomes from therapists who were less directive while for those with low reactance the reverse was true. The authors suggest that this matching effect was congruent with one of the matching effects found in Project MATCH patients with high anger responded better to motivational enhancement therapy (MET) with its explicit avoidance of confrontation and focus on client control (Project MATCH Research Group 1998a).

Thus, in contrast to our study (Sellman *et al.* 2001), a motivational approach is typically described as non-directive with the term 'directive' usually denoting a confrontational style. Such a directive or confrontational style has been found to be rated as less helpful by drug and alcohol misusers (Toma 2000) and to predict poorer outcome for problem drinkers (Miller *et al.* 1993), although the findings of Karno and colleagues (2002) do not support this. There does not, however, appear to be any previous research comparing motivationally oriented therapy with a style that includes neither confrontation nor the more strategic 'directive' strategies which are central to motivational techniques.

Brief summary of the study

The detail of the study design and methods have been reported elsewhere (Sellman *et al.* 2001). The findings are simple albeit, we believe, important. We have, therefore, devoted most of this chapter to a discussion of the implications and learning points from the trial. We conducted a randomised controlled trial of MET, which utilised two control groups; non-directive counselling and no counselling at all. Following assessment, 125 alcohol dependent patients received an individualised educational feedback session based on assessment data and all patients subsequently received a 6-week review session, which again was conducted by their original assessor. During the 6-week period, two-thirds of patients received four sessions of counselling, either MET or non-directive counselling, and the final third received no counselling. Six-month follow up of 122 patients revealed a significantly lower rate of heavy drinking in the MET treated group (42 per cent) compared with both the non-directive counselling (62.5 per cent) and the no counselling (65.0 per cent) control groups (Sellman *et al.* 2001).

Background to planning this study

Project MATCH (Project MATCH Group 1993) was underway at the time we were planning and executing the study and was investigating a range of key clinical variables, chosen following careful literature review, which might predict which alcoholic patients do best with cognitive-behavioural therapy (CBT), twelve-step facilitation therapy (TSF) or motivational enhancement therapy (MET). The possible differences between the three therapies in treatment efficacy for clients with specific characteristics captured the imagination of those working in the field who had long held with the intuitive sense made by such hypotheses, namely that some treatments must work better for some people than for others. There was considerable evidence for the effectiveness of CBT, and TSF was the most popular approach with some evidence for its effectiveness. Furthermore, it was not just therapists who expressed preferences for practising different treatments, clients tended to express strong preferences one way or another, particularly when it came to 12-step approaches. A further question of interest to the field was that of the duration of treatment, hence interest in the 12 sessions versus 4 sessions dimension. The subsequent finding that only one of the a priori matching hypotheses yielded positive clinical guidelines for matching clients to different treatments which endured over time (Stout *et al.* 2003) further focused interest on the main treatment effects in the study. The findings were that no differences existed between the three therapies, 12 sessions of CBT, 12 sessions of TSF or 4 sessions of

MET, during follow-up in the two key drinking outcome measures (per cent days abstinent and number of drinks per drinking day) (Project MATCH Research Group 1998b).

We made a calculated guess that four sessions of MET would likely be similar in efficacy to 12 sessions of both CBT and TSF and that a point of interest post-Project MATCH would be whether lesser treatment than four MET sessions might yield similar treatment outcomes. Several years earlier the findings of the World Health Organisation (WHO) study of brief interventions in primary care settings were published (Babor and Grant 1992). This study focused on hazardous rather than dependent drinking and found that five minutes of counselling was just as effective as three 15-minute counselling sessions in effecting sustained reductions in drinking. We decided to compare four sessions of MET (as in Project MATCH) with both a 5-minute intervention (as in the WHO study) and a second control group, four sessions of non-directive counselling, to control for therapeutic venue and therapeutic time.

What is non-directive counselling?

We have already discussed the absence of any formal consensus on what constitutes non-directive counselling. For research purposes, our intention was to develop a 'placebo psychotherapy' to control for the possible therapeutic benefit of simply 'being in therapy' for four sessions, and therefore equivalent, time-wise, to being involved in MET for four sessions. Our intention was for therapists to believe they were conducting a form of psychotherapy and likewise for patients to believe they were receiving real psychotherapy. In reality the therapy consisted of a therapeutic venue, albeit one in which the client could talk about anything they wanted to, with a therapist who provided a confiding, caring relationship but only reflected back what had already been offered by the patient. No active advice, support or direction was given. Only one therapeutic technique was allowable – non-directive, reflective listening (NDRL).

Therapists were encouraged to reflect back words that were as close as possible to what had been immediately offered by the patient, while maintaining a therapeutic relationship. Constantly reflecting back exactly what the patient had just offered could have seriously undermined the therapeutic relationship and so the leeway of a degree of paraphrase was given to therapists to use particularly when the therapeutic relationship may have been threatened by 'purer' reflections. However, this paraphrase was to be non-strategic. Therapist reflections were to relate only to material that had just been offered by the patient. For example if the patient had spoken about cravings for alcohol and then moved directly on to talking about their low mood, the therapist would not be allowed to reflect back words related to alcohol cravings. The purpose of reflections was not to offer direction on what was important to talk about but simply to keep the conversation going and indicate to the patient that the therapist was listening very carefully to what they were saying, allowing any topic to be freely talked about by the patient, and to do so in an empathic and positive manner.

The integrity of the therapy, in terms of both therapists and patients believing it to be a legitimate psychotherapy, was facilitated by referring to the intervention as 'person-centred therapy' (PCT), a research variant of Rogerian counselling. A therapy manual was developed in similar manner to the MET manual used in the study. The specific principles of NDRL listed in the manual were the Rogerian triad of genuineness or congruence, unconditional positive regard and accurate empathy (Meador and Rogers 1979).

Therapists were instructed to take up this Rogerian stance in terms of therapeutic attitude but nevertheless to restrict their actual communications to simple NDRL. Thus genuineness (congruence) described as 'occurring when the therapist works in an open and honest way, when what the therapist says to the patient is an accurate and genuine reflection on what they are experiencing in reaction to the patient's concerns' was severely limited in its verbal expression. Similarly the expression of unconditional positive regard, described as 'the non judgemental acceptance of the patient's individuality, where the therapist aims to be honest and genuine in working with the patient, being warm and responsive, creating a climate in which feelings can be freely expressed' again was significantly curtailed. Finally, although therapists were encouraged to 'get into the shoes' of their patient, the verbalisation of empathic insights and experiences was not permitted. Only NDRL was permitted.

Key differences between a non-directive and a motivational approach

Three key differences between non-directive counselling and motivational interviewing outlined in the seminal book *Motivational Interviewing: Preparing People to Change Addictive Behaviour* (Miller and Rollnick 1991), were used as a further guide for differentiating the two therapies in the study. These are as follows:

1 direction of the therapy
2 advice and feedback
3 empathic reflection.

Direction of the therapy

Whereas a motivational approach strategically directs the patient towards motivation for change with a focus on drinking, non-directive therapy allows the patient to determine both the content and the direction of the sessions, which may or may not be related to drinking. This is well illustrated in the opening statement by the therapists. Each began with the following: 'Before we begin, I'd like briefly to explain the way we will be working together over the next six weeks. This is the first of four sessions, each of which will last about 45 minutes. During these sessions we will be taking a close look at your situation together and I will be helping you understand how you think and feel about your situation'. This was followed by a different comment for MET compared with PCT.

MET 'I want you to know I will not be trying to change you or your drinking, only you can do that. I may give you some advice along the way, but what you do with it will be completely up to you. Do you have any questions before we begin? . . . Perhaps we could start by you updating me about how you see your situation now in terms of your drinking'. The therapist assumes control from the outset while at the same time indicating to the patient that they, the patient, ultimately has responsibility for any change that might ensue.

PCT 'I want you to feel free to talk about any issues you want to, not necessarily ones related to your drinking. Do you have any questions before we begin? . . . Where would you like to start today?' In contrast to MET, the PCT therapist immediately hands control to the patient, where it remains for the remainder of the session.

Advice and feedback

Non-directive therapy avoids giving any advice or feedback to the patient in contrast to a motivational approach where therapist advice and feedback are given when judged to be likely to facilitate or consolidate behavioural change. For example, a motivational approach often begins with the therapist giving feedback about some aspect of the drinking history, especially when the patient is found to have lower levels of motivation to change.

Therapist: 'I was very interested to note that on average you've been drinking about three times more than the national drinking guidelines. What was your response when you first heard this feedback?' The therapist gently reminds the patient that their drinking is significantly over the national drinking guidelines, but more importantly immediately invites comments about how they felt about this feedback.

Empathic reflection

Empathic reflection is used selectively in a motivational approach to elicit self-motivational statements and reinforce intentions, which is in contrast to non-directive therapy where it is used non-contingently. In fact, for PCT, empathic reflection was not allowed unless it was simply reflecting back a person's own comments. For example:

Patient: 'I'm finding this therapy really frustrating'
PCT Therapist: 'You're finding this therapy really frustrating'

This contrasts with MET where the therapist may be sensing the patient's frustration with the therapy and the source of this frustration. Commonly it relates to the discomfort of facing consequences of heavy drinking and the need for drinking reductions. In contrast to PCT, the MET therapist could probe further. For instance, they could suggest empathically 'It's really difficult to talk about things that happen when you drink'.

NDRL and the five key principles of motivational interviewing

Miller and Rollnick (1991) outline five broad clinical principles underlying motivational interviewing, which we order into the acronym DEARS as follows:

1 Develop discrepancy
2 Express empathy
3 Avoid argumentation
4 Roll with resistance
5 Support self-efficacy.

Motivational interviewing utilises a variety of techniques to develop discrepancy between the person's current (drinking) behaviour and their broader life goals, present and future. Conversational wedges are strategically inserted by the therapist into the ongoing therapeutic talk to draw attention to the realities of the person's drinking consequences and how these might conflict with personal values and future goals. These techniques are the most differentiating aspect of motivational interviewing, whereas the remaining four principles could be considered entirely compatible with general Rogerian counselling. However, for NDRL in PCT, these remaining four principles were severely limited in their execution. Empathy was certainly actively felt by therapists but not strategically used in terms of active feedback to the patient by the therapist. Argumentation was avoided by the mandatory 'robotic' reflection of NDRL. Further, any resistance perceived by the PCT therapist could not be reacted to because of the constraint on therapist responses, so they were unable to utilise verbal techniques that would be needed for more reaction. Finally, self-efficacy was only implied by the lack of advice or direction that was forthcoming from the therapist. Some patients commented on this aspect by reporting that although initially the lack of active therapeutic help or direction was somewhat disarming and not what they were expecting, they nevertheless found this approach useful for sorting out a range of personal problems.

Equipoise

A significant threat to the validity of a randomised controlled trial investigating the efficacy of psychotherapy such as MET is bias in the performance of the staff delivering the alternative psychotherapies. It is not possible for competing psychotherapies to be delivered in a single blind, let alone a double blind fashion, as can be the case in pharmacotherapy trials. Bias in pharmacotherapy trials can be eliminated by making the experimental treatment look exactly the same as the control treatment (placebo or comparison medication) for both patients and research clinicians. Bias is not nearly so easily dealt with in psychotherapy trials but must nevertheless be addressed systematically and persistently in order for the trial to have validity. The need for equipoise on the part of the therapists, trainers and supervisors was faced by the research team at the outset and attended to during both the training and the ongoing supervision. This was particularly important as each therapist was involved in the delivery of both MET and NDRL and therefore the potential was always present that they may form their own preference for one of the therapies and then deliver it with greater conviction. The stance deliberately taken was that of emphasising the positive aspects of the two separate therapies and focusing on these as reasons why each is likely to be a very good treatment for alcohol dependence. For MET, the techniques and focus on alcohol use were emphasised, whereas for PCT, the opportunity and freedom to talk about any topic of importance in a confiding therapeutic situation was highlighted.

Training

Training began with a two day workshop attended by two locally recognised experts in MET and PCT, the research therapists and other members of the research team. This was an introduction to the overall concepts of the two therapies, identification of the key technical skills, demonstrations of these skills by video and role-play, and finalisation of the two therapy manuals.

The MET manual was based on the MET manual used in Project MATCH with minor alterations. The five key principles (DEARS) (Miller and Rollnick 1991) described above were outlined and then a series of specific strategies within two major phases of therapy: Phase 1 – Building motivation for change and Phase 2 – Strengthening commitment to change, were described. Two specific modifications to the original Project MATCH manual were: a focus on drinking within New Zealand national drinking guidelines, which could include abstinence if the subject chose; and the addition of six specific strategies to be used, at the discretion of the therapist within the two major phases of therapy, depending on the patient's stage of change. These were entitled: 'Problems and concerns', 'Good things – less good things' and 'Personal dissonance' in Phase 1 and 'Life satisfaction', 'Costs and benefits' and 'Construction of decisional balances' in Phase 2 (Miller *et al.* 1998), all therapeutic techniques based on the fundamental principle of developing discrepancy.

The PCT manual outlined a paired down version of Rogerian counselling, which was the starting point for the further cutting back of responses that therapists were allowed to make in order to define what we called non-directive reflective listening (NDRL) alone.

Five potential therapists were involved in the initial weekend workshop and four subsequently completed the follow-up training sessions involving practice in two pilot cases of MET and NDRL respectively until the required standard was achieved. During the study patients were randomised to either MET or NDRL or no counselling. All the therapy sessions for the study were to be audiotaped. Research therapists therefore had to master the use of a tape recorder, including being able to ignore its presence. These audiotapes were subsequently used mainly for the supervision sessions but also provided data for audit purposes.

NDRL

It turned out to be surprisingly difficult for such a simple therapeutic technique as non-directive reflective listening to be faithfully adhered to by the therapists chosen for the study. No doubt this related in large part to the keenness of the research therapists actively to help their patients. Each of the therapists selected was experienced in using a range of therapies including MET, CBT and traditional psychodynamic psychotherapy. Therapists found that limiting their therapeutic repertoire to NDRL alone made them more acutely aware of patient responses. NDRL required therapists to listen to what their patients were actually saying because that was the only cue they would get in terms of responding. Because of this, we now consider that initial training in NDRL is an excellent starting point, even for experienced psychotherapists, for training in MET because attentive listening is an expression of one of the key ingredients of therapy, namely expressing empathy. Empathy must be felt first, before it is expressed and active listening is a good place to start.

MET

The key was for therapists to move from the tight constraints of non-directive reflective listening into the challenging area of strategic reflective listening. Because experienced therapists were involved, generic therapeutic skills in asking open questions, listening reflectively, summarising and affirming were well established.

The new learning began with eliciting self-motivational statements. The goals of this overall strategy were to help patients first to recognise and weigh up their problems and concerns related to their drinking; secondly through eliciting self-motivational statements they would then voice these concerns and express the discomfort of the discrepancy between their desired role and their actual behaviour. Problems arising from their intentions to change, how important this might be to them and issues related to their confidence to make change would also be expressed. These skills were generally comfortably taken up by the therapists and were liberating post NDRL training.

The learning moved up a level in complexity when working with clients to make explicit, externalised motivational statements for change. This is often a critical period when 'blocks' may occur especially when working with patients for whom other people make their important decisions, or who generally feel they are the victims of circumstance. Therapists steeped in a style that frowned on direct questioning or challenging as being seen as disrespectful were initially reluctant to ask, 'Yes, but what do you think?' or 'But why is this important for you and why now?' or 'By not changing anything, whose needs are being met?' Potentially unsettling patients with such questioning did require an attitude shift towards more activity and directiveness than would be found in traditional Rogerian counselling. The therapists worked hard at developing this style, although subsequent auditing of the study audiotapes revealed a continuing tendency to refrain from reinforcing intrinsic motivation through these active therapeutic techniques.

Observing this difficulty with experienced counsellors raises the important question: does MET work as well with externally motivated people as it does with those more internally motivated? Do the former respond better to simpler explanations of addictive behaviour and to more practical and simple direction? Working with a client in terms of their focus of control involves working at a conceptual level that implies complexity in motivation and behaviour, which is not necessarily easy for everybody.

Similarly, MET highlights the importance of providing therapeutic options from which the client can choose. Some clients find options to be confusing and demoralising. Without simple direction, they can switch from one to the next and in so doing avoid taking determined action. Assisting with prioritising options did not always overcome this and for some, a single course of action raised their confidence in engaging with it.

'Rolling with resistance' also proved to be challenging for therapists at times. There was a tendency to roll using silence rather than strategic reflection. Though counsellors could accept intellectually that resistance was not necessarily a negative response to change, putting that into active practice and turning resistance into opportunities was not always achieved. Handling resistance was more difficult to master than any other strategy, as this requires both mental agility and therapeutic courage that comes with extensive practice. Because this was therapy within a research study where performance was being monitored carefully and the number of sessions were prescribed, the therapists' need for achievement appeared high and expectations may have inadvertently provoked a degree of resistance in the clients, which may not have appeared in more routine therapeutic settings. In some instances it was observed that if a positive engagement or outcome seemed less likely in the early stages, the therapist's expectations appeared to drop and this was reflected in a lowering of the client's expectations. The prescription of the number of sessions raised a tension between the spirit of MI that is about creating the conditions to encourage change and MET which was not only focused on outcomes but which also came with the expectations that this needed to be achieved in a limited amount of time.

Reflections on being a therapist in the study

One of the authors (DD) was a therapist in the study and reflects on this experience here.

MET

Fundamental to providing the MET was careful attention to the beginning phase of establishing the therapeutic relationship and the interpersonal context for change, including accepting and affirming the client's situation and developing a sense of collaborative partnership. Of primary importance, was 'being with' the person. As noted the four session limit promoted a pragmatic, strategic and directive approach. Maintaining active listening through selective reflection and attending to subtle feedback cues from the client was therefore essential, in order not to become out-of-step with the client. Being in front of the client tended to elicit resistance, being behind, or out-of-step, elicited queries about 'being heard'. Attending to the interpersonal context and being directive and strategic in approach required a 'relaxed' yet watchful approach: maintaining a therapeutic distance on the one hand while also being 'with the person'.

While it was expected that the focus of the initial sessions was on building motivation and strengthening commitment to change and that the third and fourth sessions involved subsequent check-ups of progress and reinforcement of commitment, the reality was not necessarily so, requiring an individualised approach. Maintaining an awareness that the degree of commitment to change may vary both from session to session as well as within sessions was essential. For some clients, acceptance of ambivalence in relation to sustaining their identified need for change was important, for others supporting the belief that change was both possible and sustainable was the key factor. It was also important to utilise strategies within the normal flow of the interview – not to introduce them as a checklist to be ticked off.

Finally, an emphasis on the ending of the therapeutic relationship was essential. It was important to take time to strategically review progress, emphasising the most important factors, acknowledging that ambivalence frequently remains an ongoing issue and affirming where the patient currently was in relation to his/her drinking behaviour. It was important to look to the future and to strategise with the patient around potentially concerning situations, likely issues and to identify avenues for support and further assistance if required.

NDRL

Careful attention to the beginning phase of establishing the therapeutic relationship and interpersonal context, including accepting and affirming the patient's situation, was fundamental. Perhaps even more so, was the importance of active listening and empathy through reflection and 'being with' the person. However, providing NDRL for some patients was difficult for a number of reasons. For some patients NDRL did not seem enough and more than a therapeutic, interpersonal context was required.

This seemed particularly so for patients who were feeling very ambivalent or demoralised about the need to change or were unsure about how to proceed. One particular patient who had to travel, take time from work and whose partner had high expectations seemed unable to see the point of the sessions and expressed frustration with the process. Faced with such issues, it was difficult as a therapist to 'sit on one's hands' and not be directive or strategic in approach. Patients' verbal and non-verbal expressions of frustration, helplessness and hopelessness required sensitive and considered reflection in order not to be strategic on the one hand and on the other hand genuinely to provide the patient with a sense of 'being heard' and of understanding his or her feelings. It was not unusual for some patients to run out of things to talk about and long, somewhat tense silences and clock watching sometimes occurred.

For some patients, however, providing a therapeutic environment within which they could explore issues relevant and important to them appeared most useful. These patients made use of the safe and supportive interpersonal context to review and clarify their position in relation to making changes to their drinking as well as to talk about other more general life concerns. Some patients would query as to whether it was all right to talk about something not specifically related to their drinking. It was important genuinely to affirm that it was their session and to reiterate the standard opening gambit of NDRL.

Concluding comments

This chapter began with a brief review of existing literature in which there is a lack of consistency in the use of the terms 'directive' and 'non-directive'. MI and MET are undoubtedly 'directive' compared with the NDRL we practised in our study and yet they are considered by some to be 'non-directive' compared with more overt confrontational styles.

We reported our study's finding that MET was superior in reducing unequivocal heavy drinking compared with NDRL. This is the first study of MET or MI to our knowledge which has controlled for the potential necessary and sufficient ingredient of providing a therapeutic venue and relationship (placebo psychotherapy). In demonstrating the effectiveness of MET in this way, the equivalent effectiveness of CBT and TSF in the treatment of alcohol problems are strengthened, given the lack of differences between these three therapies in Project MATCH. The criticism of Project MATCH that there was no control group is indirectly addressed through this study. Frank's (1972) proposed commonalities of successful psychotherapy persist despite three decades of scientific research.

We do not advocate NDRL as an effective psychotherapy for alcohol problems. However, our experience of training therapists for the study leads us to consider NDRL as an excellent starting point for training in MET. NDRL forces therapists to listen carefully and register precisely the words that patients say, which after all remain a fundamental stimulus to the development of empathy, understanding and subsequent therapeutic responses from the clinician engaged in effective psychotherapy.

References

Babor, T.F. and Grant, M. (eds) (1992) 'Project on identification and management of alcohol-related problems. Report on Phase II: A randomised clinical trial of brief interventions in primary health care', Geneva, Switzerland: World Health Organisation.

Frank, J.D. (1972) 'Common features of psychotherapy', *Australian and New Zealand Journal of Psychiatry*, 6: 34–40.

Karno, M.P., Beutler, L.E. and Harwood, T.M. (2002) 'Interactions between psychotherapy procedures and patient attributes that predict alcohol treatment effectiveness: A preliminary study', *Addictive Behaviours*, 27: 779–797.

Keijsers, G.P.J., Schapp, C.P.D.R. and Hoogduin, C.A.L (2002) 'Impact of interpersonal patient and therapist behaviour on outcome in cognitive-behaviour therapy', *Behaviour Modification*, 24: 264–297.

Meador, B.D. and Rogers, C.R. (1979) 'Person-centred therapy', in R.J. Corsini (ed.) *Current Psychotherapies*, Illinois: Peacock Publishers.

Miller, W.R. and Rollnick, S. (1991) *Motivational interviewing: preparing people to change addictive behavior*. New York: The Guilford Press.

Miller, W.R., Benefield, R.G. and Tonigan, J.S. (1993) 'Enhancing motivation for change in problem drinking: A controlled comparison of two therapist styles', *Journal of Consulting and Clinical Psychology*, 16: 455–461.

Miller, W.R., Rollnick, S. and Moyers, T.B. (1998) *Motivational Interviewing Training Videotape Series*. Albuquerque, New Mexico: University of New Mexico.

Project MATCH Research Group (1993) 'Project MATCH: Rationale and methods for a multisite clinical trial matching patients to alcoholism treatment', *Alcoholism: Clinical and Experimental Research*, 17: 1130–1145.

Project MATCH Research Group (1998a) 'Matching alcoholism treatments to client heterogeneity: Treatment main effects and matching effects on drinking during treatment', *Journal of Studies on Alcohol*, 59: 631–639.

Project MATCH Research Group (1998b) 'Matching alcoholism treatments to client heterogeneity: Project MATCH three-year drinking outcomes', *Alcoholism: Clinical and Experimental Research*, 22: 1300–1311.

Sellman, J.D., Sullivan, P., Dore, G.M., Adamson, S.J. and MacEwan, I. (2001) 'A randomised controlled trial of motivational enhancement therapy (MET) for alcohol dependence', *Journal of Studies on Alcohol*, 62: 389–396.

Stout, R., Del Boca, F.K., Carbonari, J., Rychtarik, R., Litt, M. and Cooney, N. (2003) 'Primary treatment outcomes and matching effects: Outpatient arm', in T.F. Babor and F.K. Del Boca (eds) *Treatment matching in alcoholism*, Cambridge: Cambridge University Press.

Toma, F. (2000) 'A comparison of the perception of drug and alcohol misusers on the helpfulness of therapeutic attitudes used by counsellors', *European Journal of Psychotherapy, Counselling and Health*, 3: 103–110.

Chapter 9

Motivational interviewing in the criminal justice system

Valter Spiller and Gian Paolo Guelfi

Introduction

In this chapter we describe a study which compares the training, implementation and outcomes of a motivational interviewing approach versus a confrontational approach in a coercive setting. We report perceptions of the effectiveness of the approach, differences in delivery between motivational interviewing and a standard approach and in outcome between the two approaches.

In the Italian legislative system, personal use of illegal drugs is a misdemeanour, not a criminal offence. Minor violations such as using or merely owning small amounts of illegal substances for personal use, although forbidden, are not punished by arrest or incarceration. Commonly violators are adolescents and young adults, whose average age ranges from 21 years to 25 years, and are caught by the police in possession of small amounts of illegal substances – 80 per cent with hashish or marijuana. They are subjected to administrative penalties, such as suspension of their driver's licence or passport for 2 months, unless they opt to be treated in a public drug agency. The decision to undergo treatment prevents the application of any penalties. At the end of a successful treatment programme, the case file is closed. The treatment is considered successful when no traces of illegal substances are detected on toxicology screening for a specific time period that, although not defined by the law, is usually 3 months. For a violation involving substances other than cannabis, or for a repeat violation, the entire procedure is managed at three levels:

1 the Prefecture at the Uffici Territoriali del Governo (UTG) – Government Territorial Offices, located in the country's major cities to which the police, who pick up offenders on the street, report;
2 the Nucleo Operativo Tossicodipendenze (NOT), an Addiction Operations Centre operated at each UTG, from which social workers summon the offenders, interview them, and decide whether to refer them for treatment or apply the administrative penalties;
3 SERT (Addiction Treatment Units) for treatment.

For a first violation involving substances in Schedule 2 (cannabis), the offender can simply be warned about the risks of using drugs and given a formal invitation not to use such substances again without applying any other penalty. Social workers are required to conduct just one interview which, in our opinion, makes its delivery particularly important. According to Italian law, the goals of the interview in the Government Territorial Offices Addiction Operations Centres are:

- to provide information
- to give support in thinking about one's situation
- to help people consider the need for change.

To achieve these objectives under coercion, with the predominant perception that the Government Territorial Offices social worker is a government agent assigned to control and punish, is difficult. A motivational type of counselling style was, therefore, perceived as a potentially important aid to achieve the legal objectives, to improve the satisfaction of the clients and to enhance the professional skills of the social work staff.

In 2000, the activities of the Addiction Operations Centres in Italy's Government Territorial Offices involved 22,212 people (20,886 males, 1,326 females) found to be in possession of illegal substances. Of the 23,142 proceedings filed, 18,366 involved the possession of hashish, marijuana, or both and most, 15,836 out of 26,728, interviews ended with a formal invitation, 5,749 with a request to participate in a treatment programme and 6,150 with the application of penalties. In 2000, 4,053 cases were dismissed (Italian Ministry of Work and Social Policies 2000).

A law passed by the Italian Government which came into force in 2006 reintroduces criminal prosecution for the possession of drugs for personal use. The ban on the personal use of illegal drugs is enforced through a modification in the police summons to the UTG drug unit. The modification consists of more severe administrative penalties – a ban on leaving the house at night, on attending specified places and on leaving the city even for work and signing in at the police station every day, are some examples. If a violation occurs, a criminal trial begins and the person involved may be incarcerated.

Background to the study

In November 1998 and May 1999, a group of social workers from the Italian UTGs in Arezzo, Campobasso, Florence, Perugia, Pisa, Prato, Rieti and Rome attended a 40-hour motivational interviewing training course. This stimulated interest in using motivational techniques during their interviews with illicit drug users summoned to the UTG, and in examining the effectiveness of such techniques. In order to determine whether the application of motivational interviewing techniques would improve the efficiency of the interview at the Prefecture, a study based on these considerations was planned in the eight aforementioned UTGs. The purpose of the study was to compare the use of motivational interviewing with standard interview techniques.

Designing the study

In designing this study, we hypothesised that the achievement of the specific goals of the interview would be enhanced with the creation of empathic relationships and impaired with confrontational relationships (Miller and Rollnick 2002) and that an empathic relationship would be more likely to be developed following training in motivational interviewing. To explore this, we decided to evaluate the subject's perception of being listened to, understood and helped, as well as the perception of being blamed, controlled and judged. We refer to these six aspects of the relationship as interactive attitudes.

The experimental hypothesis of the study was that offenders summoned to the Prefectures would have a perception of receiving more information, being more supported in thinking about their own situation and in considering the need for change if they were interviewed using a style that was more oriented toward listening, understanding and helping, that is to say an empathic and motivational style, rather than one through which they would be blamed, judged and controlled, in other words a confrontational style (Miller and Rollnick 2002; 1991).

Aim

The aim of the study was:

1 to examine whether a motivational interviewing style is perceived by subjects as a more efficient method to achieve the goals of the interview;
2 to examine the differences, if any, in interviewing style between the group of workers who took the motivational interviewing training course and the group of workers who did not, that is whether the interview was more motivational in the first group, and more confrontational in the second control group; and
3 to quantify the differences, if any, between the perceptions about the interview in the subset of subjects interviewed by the first group and the subset interviewed by the control group.

Thus, the basis of the study was for a group of social workers utilising motivational interviewing at a reasonable level of competence to be compared to a group of social workers administering the standard treatment.

Method

Training

The study design included several preparation phases, the first of which was the training of social workers in the experimental group. Each meeting was run by a pair of trainers from the Training Team consisting of Gian Paolo Guelfi, Valter Spiller and Maurizio Scaglia.

Eleven social workers from the NOTs of the eight Prefectures were randomly assigned to receive motivational interviewing training, the experimental group. In the same agencies, the remaining social workers were considered as the control group. In addition to the 40 hours of motivational interviewing training in 1998 and 1999, the experimental group also underwent intensive case supervision for 8 months for a total of 112 hours between September 2000 and April 2001. No additional actions were taken with the control group.

Training of the experimental group occurred in a number of steps: assessment by trainers and self-evaluation, followed by training sessions and repeated evaluation. The first meeting focused on assessing existing motivational interviewing skills by administering a questionnaire, known as the Eight Situations, which was to be evaluated by the trainers. As the name suggests the questionnaire consisted of eight situations, each the first sentence of an imaginary interview, with which the social workers had to interact in a motivational style. The answers were then evaluated separately by the three trainers and compared to determine an overall individual score. In this way, each trainee would have his or her own initial personal skill score on a scale of 0 to 10. Six of them scored < 6. The average of the initial evaluation was 6.1 out of 10. During the first meeting a self-evaluation questionnaire was also given to explore the trainees' self-perception of their motivational skills. The self-evaluation scores were quite low (4.4 out of 10) possibly because of the time that had elapsed since the previous training sessions.

The initial training sessions were dedicated exclusively to a review of motivational interviewing skills. Training was based on role-play of simulated interviews using clinical cases presented by the social workers under the direct supervision of trainers. In the last four meetings the trainers directly assessed the trainees' motivational skills, as demonstrated in role-play, using an evaluation form. Motivational skills, judged according to use of open-ended questions, reflective listening, summarising, affirming, eliciting change talk, and rolling with resistance, were considered to be consistent with a motivational approach, whereas confrontational attitudes and interactions, judged on the use of questions and answers, taking an expert stance, taking sides, and labelling, were considered as inconsistent. This procedure was used to conduct a field evaluation of training efficacy; three trainees still scored < 6 and the average score was 6.8 out of 10.

During the last meeting the trainees were again requested to fill out a new Eight Situations questionnaire. The assessment was carried out blind by the three trainers and the outcome was a significant increase in the trainees' motivational interviewing skills (Figure 9.1) which correlated with the field evaluation scores (Figure 9.2). The average score was 6.8 out of 10. The differences in the personal pre-training and post-training scores were statistically significant ($t = 4.3$; $p < .002$). In addition, in this assessment two out of the three trainees who scored < 6 in the previous evaluation, still scored < 6 and hence the work of these two workers was not considered in analysing the differences between the two groups. As expected, the self-evaluation scores regarding learned skills were higher, with an average of 6.4 out of 10.

Study participants

All offenders summoned to the NOT of the Prefectures in the first six months of 2001 were randomly assigned to one of the two groups. After giving informed consent, the participants were requested to fill out a questionnaire prior to the interview designed to explore their expectations of being listened to, understood, helped, judged, blamed and controlled. We defined empathic as the interactive style that makes the subjects feel more listened to, understood and helped. Conversely, we defined confrontational as the interactive style that makes the subjects feel more blamed, controlled and judged. The second section of the questionnaire was used to rate the expectation of receiving information, of being helped in thinking about one's own condition and in considering the need to change behaviour. They were requested to fill out another questionnaire designed to explore the same aspects after completing the interview.

The social workers in both groups were requested to complete a questionnaire the purpose of which was to assess client resistance at the beginning and at the end of the interview, their perception of the quality of the relationship, and their perception of giving information to help the offender to think about his or her condition and to evaluate the need to change his or her behaviour. Finally, they were requested to rate the perceived effectiveness of the interview.

Study population

All the offenders summoned for the interview were included in the study, with the exception of those who refused to participate, those who were already involved with SERT (Addiction Treatment Units) or who could not be interviewed according to the established protocol. The sample consisted

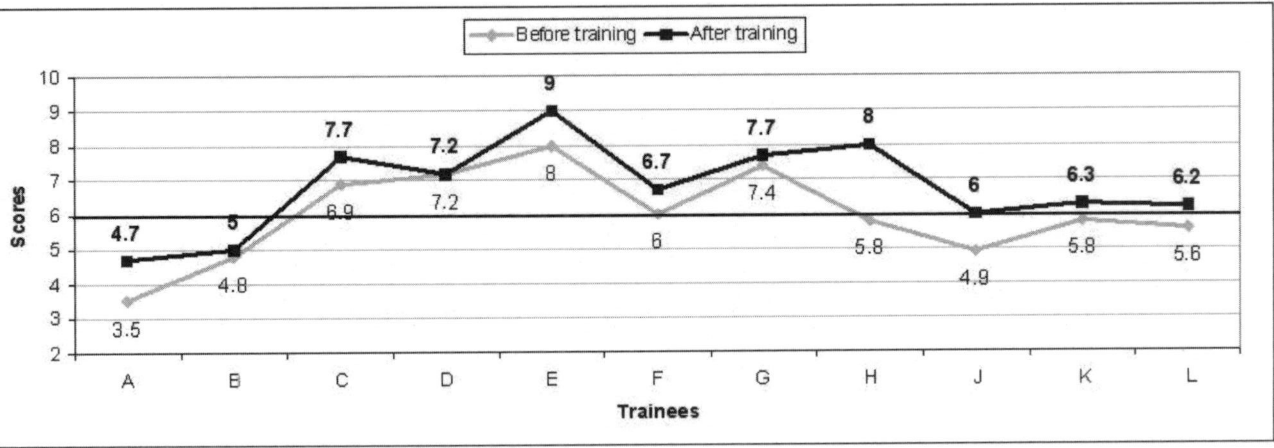

Figure 9.1 Evaluation of motivational interviewing skills before and after training using the Eight Situations questionnaire.

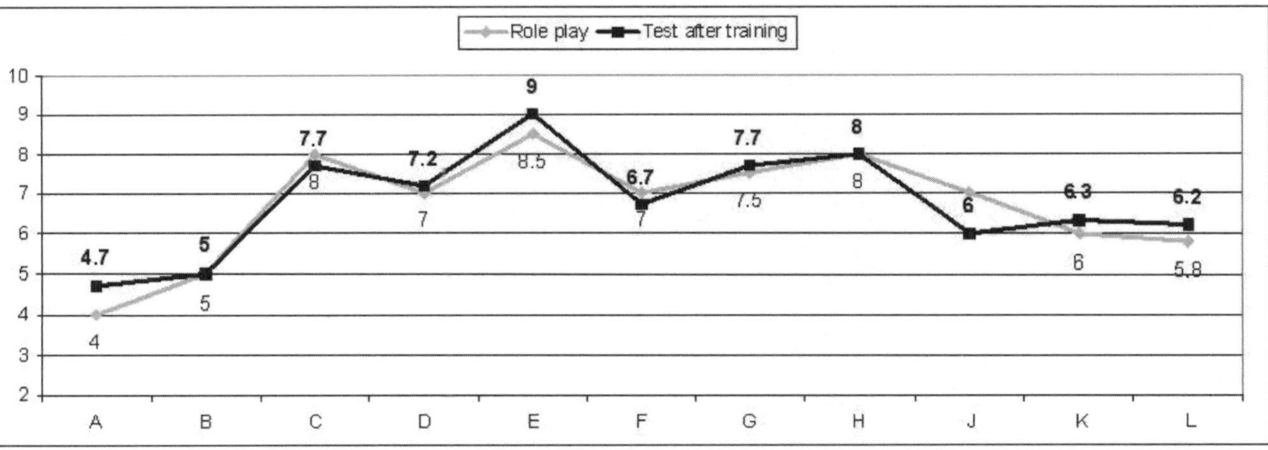

Figure 9.2 Evaluation of motivational interviewing skills assessed by role plays versus the Eight Situations questionnaire after training.

of 1,016 subjects summoned to the NOT of the Prefectures in central Italy, namely Arezzo, Campobasso, Florence, Perugia, Pisa, Prato, Rieti and Rome. One hundred and four questionnaires were discarded either because they were incomplete or incorrectly completed. The final sample consisted of 912 subjects, 83.9 per cent of whom were found in possession of cannabis derivatives.

Results

Key outcomes were analysed using the following statistical methods: factor analysis, analysis of variance, linear correlation analysis and study of difference between means (*t*-test). The analysis performed on the entire sample for the interactive attitudes showed two different and well-defined styles. Factor analysis (Varimax normalised) shows one factor including listening, understanding and helping, the empathic style, and another factor including blaming, controlling and judging, the confrontational style. This confirms the perception of two discrete attitudes in conducting the interview.

In order to explore which of the two styles is more consistent with the goals of the interview, we added them into the factorial model shown in Figure 9.3, and found that they strongly aggregate with factor one, the empathic style. An analysis of association, multiple regression, between

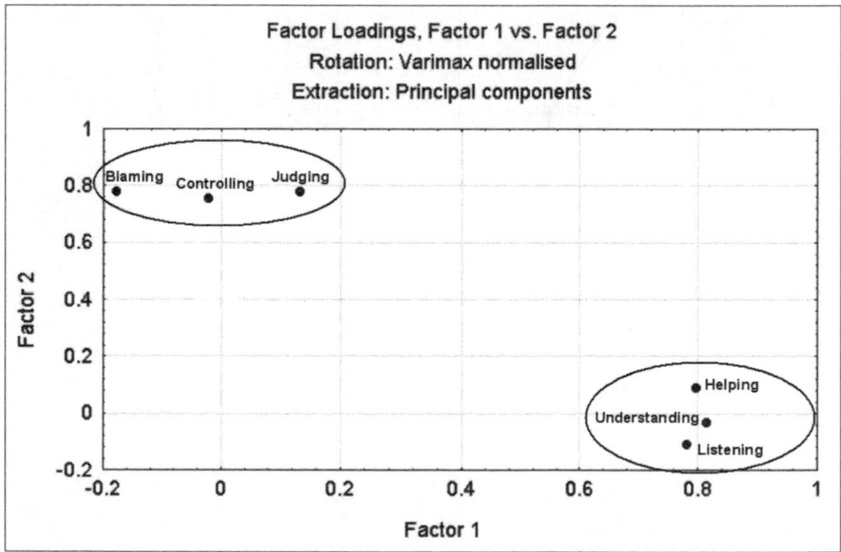

Figure 9.3 Plot of factor analysis: interactional attitude.

styles and goals showed a very strong correlation between empathic style and goals ($p < .0001$), whereas the correlation between confrontational style and goals is either not statistically significant or slightly significant ($p < .05$). These results confirm that an empathic style is consistent with achieving the goals of the interview, as defined by Italian law.

An initial confirmation of the effectiveness of in-depth training about motivational counselling was provided by the fact that we found a strong association between the final scores of motivational interviewing skills and the perception by the subjects of the quality of the relationship in the experimental group ($r = .797$, $p < .003$). In other words, the offenders who were interviewed by professionals with higher scores in motivational interviewing skills felt that they were listened to, understood and helped rather than blamed, judged and controlled.

Additional evidence in this sense was provided by the association between the training results and the effectiveness of the interview, perceived by the subjects, in relation to the specific purposes established by the law in providing information, giving support in thinking about one's own situation and helping people to consider the need for change (N = 11, $r = .774$, $p < .005$). The offenders interviewed by professionals with higher scores in motivational interviewing skills considered the interview as being more oriented to the goals of the legislation.

In the analysis of the differences between the two groups in expected and perceived interactive attitudes, we excluded the data from subjects interviewed by the two members of the experimental group who did not reach the score cut-off level. The final population consisted of 806 subjects. No difference between the two groups was detected in the expectations before the interview. Statistically significant differences emerged in four out of six perceived attitudes after interview (see Table 9.1).

Overall, the experimental, motivational interviewing group conducted the interview with perceived attitudes significantly more empathic ($p < .0005$) and less confrontational ($p < .0001$) than the control group. This point suggests that the motivational interviewing training may have enhanced the interactive attitudes that are characteristic of the empathic style and decreased the confrontational components of the social workers. The analysis of the outcome, considering the goals, shows no difference in the expectations between the two groups before interview, but statistically significant differences in two out of three variables after interview. The interview in the experimental group significantly increased the perceived help in thinking about their circumstances ($t = 2.56$; $p < .012$), and an increase in the perception of the need to change their behaviour ($t = 2.07$; $p < .039$). Both groups perceived similar levels of information giving in the interviews. This suggests that motivational interviewing training may have increased the efficacy of the experimental group in attaining the specific goals of the interview as defined by Italian law.

Table 9.1 Differences between the experimental and control groups on interactive attitudes

	Mean MI Group	*Mean Control Group*	*t-value*	df	P
Expectations before interview					
Judged	1.680	1.674	0.087	804	.930
Listened to	2.255	2.367	−1.846	804	.065
Blamed	1.329	1.459	−1.835	804	.067
Understood	1.791	1.870	−1.176	804	.240
Controlled	1.524	1.517	0.092	804	.927
Helped	1.764	1.881	−1.497	804	.135
Perceptions after interview					
Judged	1.225	1.293	−0.830	804	.407
Listened to	3.032	2.707	5.390	804	.000
Blamed	0.653	0.925	−4.544	804	.000
Understood	2.559	2.238	4.813	804	.000
Controlled	1.007	1.279	−3.831	804	.000
Helped	2.514	2.392	1.610	804	.108

Table 9.2 Differences between the experimental and control groups on the three goals of criminal justice intervention

	Mean MI Group	*Mean Control Group*	*t-value*	df	P
Expectations before interview					
Information giving	5.300	5.508	−1.157	804	.248
Support with situation	5.151	5.047	0.504	804	.614
Help to change	4.255	4.315	−0.295	804	.768
Perceptions after interview					
Information giving	6.232	6.514	−1.656	804	.098
Support with situation	6.385	5.923	2.561	804	.011
Help to change	5.444	5.033	2.075	804	.038

Conclusion

In this study (Spiller *et al.* 2002) the possibility of training a group of professionals to develop an empathic-motivational type of relationship to achieve the legally established objectives for conducting an interview in the UTG emerged in an original and satisfactory manner. It was demonstrated that a group of professionals with initial motivational interviewing training can be helped significantly to improve their capabilities, especially through training that focuses on direct supervision of the practical application of skills, in this case by role-playing real-life situations and professional cases. An important part of this process was found to be the evaluation by the trainers and self-evaluation. A majority of the social workers involved in the training process significantly improved their skills, as indicated by the difference in the before and after point totals. Such an improvement was confirmed by the substantial overlap between data from the evaluation combined with the abilities demonstrated in role-playing and by the result of the final evaluation using the Eight Situations tool. It was also demonstrated that there is significant congruence between the final competence level attained by the individual social workers and the quality of the relationship that was subsequently developed at a clinical level.

It was also noted that an increase in work skills with regard to motivation involves a significant improvement in the quality of the therapeutic relationship. This evaluation was obtained directly from the subjects summoned to the UTGs who were analysed during the study. It is interesting to note that such an improvement takes place within a context in which the satisfaction points indicated by the subjects in the control group, although significantly less than those expressed by the subjects in the experimental group, still indicate an overall outcome evaluation that exceeds initial expectations.

Finally, it was observed that the improvements deriving from the training of the social workers are associated with a clear increase in the clients' feeling of being helped to think about their situation, and encouraged to think of change, which satisfied two out of three of the key objectives established by Italian law, even without receiving a greater amount of information.

References

Miller, W.R. and Rollnick, S. (1991) *Motivational interviewing: preparing people to change addictive behavior*. New York: The Guilford Press.

Miller, W.R. and Rollnick, S. (2002) *Motivational interviewing: preparing people for change*. Second edition, New York: The Guilford Press.

Italian Ministry of Work and Social Policies (2000) *Annual Report to the Parliament on Drug Dependence in Italy* [Ministero del Lavoro e delle Politiche Sociali: Relazione annuale al Parlamento sullo stato delle tossicodipendenze in Italia anno 2000, p. 261].

Spiller, V., Scaglia, M., Guelfi, G.P. (eds) (2002) 'Il colloquio motivazionale nell'applicazione dell'art', 75 DPR 309/90, Genova: De Ferrari.

Chapter 10

Motivational enhancement therapy in the UK Alcohol Treatment Trial

Gillian Tober

Introduction

Growing numbers of practitioners in the UK who offer treatment to people with alcohol, drug and smoking dependence and related disorders have been trained to deliver motivational interviewing as a treatment. Motivational interviewing grew in popularity for a number of reasons: it was consistent in principle with the 'person-centred' style of counselling taught on many British counselling courses, it suited the more liberal approach to client self-determination of goals that had become standard practice with the widespread acceptance of controlled drinking and harm reduction as legitimate aims of treatment and, probably more universally, it relieved practitioners of the frequently experienced problem of getting into conflict with clients over drinking or drug using self-report and intention to change which, as described in Chapter 1, is likely to be the product of a more confrontational approach. However, by the 1990s there was still no study demonstrating the quality and outcome of motivational interviewing practice in the UK compared to other approaches.

The evidence base in the UK

In the mid-1990s, the Medical Research Council in the UK made funds available for a major trial of alcohol misuse treatment, which later became known as the UK Alcohol Treatment Trial (UKATT). The design of the trial (UKATT Research Team 2001) was heavily influenced by findings emerging from Project MATCH, a large multi-centre trial of treatment for alcohol misuse in the United States, which showed that a manual guided motivational treatment, Motivational Enhancement Therapy (MET), delivered over four sessions was as effective as twelve sessions of either Cognitive Behavioural Coping Skills Therapy (CBT) or Twelve Step Facilitation Therapy (TSF) in significantly reducing alcohol consumption and increasing abstinence in problem drinkers (Project MATCH Research Group 1997). For a number of reasons, the Principal Investigators in the

UKATT team decided that MET should be used as a gold standard, or reference, treatment against which to test a new treatment: (i) motivational treatments, albeit not necessarily MET, were commonly used in the UK and so there was an extensive practitioner base keen to develop MET skills; (ii) MET had been found to be more cost effective than the other treatments in Project MATCH (Holder *et al.* 2000); (iii) Both TSF and CBT were thought to be much more mainstream practice in the USA than in the UK.

The question was which new treatment to test? It was decided that the strongest contender was a social therapy that would integrate elements from the CBT family of treatments with a social network approach already established in the USA in the Network Therapy of Gallanter (1999) and modified in the UK with a less confrontational style into Social Behaviour and Network Therapy (SBNT) (Copello *et al.* 1997). A manual describing the theoretical and empirical background, the core skills and the principles of treatment, session outlines and examples of therapeutic dialogue was developed to form the basis of the delivery of SBNT and its application in clinical practice (Copello *et al.* 2002). SBNT was delivered in the UKATT in eight sessions of therapy made up of four core and four elective sessions over an 8–12-week period. The essential task in SBNT is to recruit and involve the client's social network in supporting change and so the first session is devoted to mapping out this network in order to identify those individuals who would be positive contributors to the change process. Topics for the four core SBNT sessions were: (i) communication, (ii) coping, (iii) relapse prevention and management and (iv) enhancing social support. Additional elective sessions, to be given on the basis of perceived need were chosen from the following: education on alcohol and drugs, employment or occupational counselling, increasing pleasant activities and developing positive support, both for the focal person (the client) and for network members. Both the SBNT and MET manuals had instructions on what to do in emergency situations and how to ensure that basic needs, such as housing, were adequately addressed.

MET as practised in the UKATT was adapted from the US version and changed in the following ways: the number of sessions was reduced from four to three and clients were discouraged from attending with a significant other beyond the first session. Minor adaptations to the MATCH treatment manual (Miller *et al.* 1995) focused primarily on modifying examples of therapeutic dialogue better to fit the English language as spoken in the UK. Beyond these changes the protocol adhered to the original version with the first session being the provision of feedback from the assessment battery given in a motivational interviewing style of eliciting concerns and intention to change. The second session included enhancing self-efficacy and optimism for change by means of recording plans in a Change Plan Worksheet and the third session focused on the benefits of change and strengthening commitment to maintain change in the future (UKATT Research Team

2001). The adapted treatment and its protocol were described in a new treatment manual, which included specification of session structure and content, samples of dialogue and guidelines for the delivery of each of the sessions in the treatment (Tober *et al.* 2001).

The trial was designed to be pragmatic which is to say that the investigators were concerned to know what happened in the 'real world' delivery of the two treatments (see Chapter 4). In a pragmatic trial it does not matter that one treatment is three and the other eight sessions, rather it is how well the two treatments perform overall. This design meant that findings would be generalisable to the average UK alcohol treatment agency, which typically is multi-disciplinary and located in the public sector, usually the National Health Service (NHS) or a social services department, the non-statutory or private sectors. Trial treatments would therefore be delivered by staff already practising in the agencies selected for participation in the trial.

Selection of clinical research sites was based upon an agency's ability to recruit sufficient numbers of clients, to provide sufficient accommodation for the conduct of the trial, a willingness for their staff to be taught and to practise one of two trial treatments to which they would be randomly assigned in line with trial procedures and treatment protocols, to have their staff supervised by specialists at a remote centre and to video record all treatment sessions for the purpose of supervision and independent monitoring and rating of their delivery (Tober *et al.* 2005).

Training staff to practise MET

Individual members of staff from the agencies selected for the UKATT were requested to express an interest to practise in the trial. The conditions for acceptance as a trainee were: willingness to be randomly assigned to train and practise in one, and only one of the trial treatments; demonstration of the ability to practise core motivational interviewing skills and separately the ability to practise with more than one person at the same time (because the therapist could be randomised to the SBNT treatment condition); and the ability to demonstrate approximately two years' experience working in the field by provision of a suitable curriculum vitae. Candidates were also required to make a commitment not to undertake concurrent training in a different treatment.

Detailed discussion of the overall outcomes of the study (UKATT Research Team 2005a) is beyond the scope of this chapter; suffice to say for our present purposes that significant reductions in drinking rates, in alcohol related problems and mental health problems were found, as were significant increases in abstinence rates. No significant differences were found in these outcomes between the two treatment groups. Nor did the treatments differ significantly in their cost effectiveness (UKATT Research Team 2005b). Some important lessons were learned about the requirements for training practitioners. Therapists had different professional backgrounds, different levels of educational achievement, varying duration of field experience, and had worked in a range of treatment settings. With a few exceptions therapists were successfully trained to a standard of practice of MET that was maintained over time (Tober *et al.* 2005).

The remainder of this chapter deals with training for the MET arm of the trial. The task turned out to be a greater challenge than originally anticipated, though responses to training varied a great deal. The training protocol for both trial treatments involved three days' initial training at the trial training centre. In the case of MET this was provided by the author and two additional trainers who were experienced in motivational interviewing practice, at teaching at the postgraduate level and members of the Motivational Interviewing Network of Training (MINT) described in Chapter 6. During the three days designated for MET training, in addition to familiarisation with trial procedures, trainees attended lectures and discussions on the evidence base for motivational interviewing and Motivational Enhancement Therapy, where the aim was to assure trainees that they would be offering the best possible treatment to their clients. They were invited to review motivational interviewing core skills with demonstration and practice in role plays, to study the treatment manual and to practise the core sessions, again with demonstration and role play. Concerns were aired and these primarily focused upon the unfamiliar habit of following a protocol (with particular reference to session timing and structure, and duration of treatment episode) and on using a treatment manual. For many participants this was a novel experience. Mainly the trainees came from a background where they were accustomed to selecting the treatment they thought best fitted the client's condition, motivation for change and preferred option. Some expressed fears that clinical autonomy might be eroded and individual style discouraged.

Following the initial three days participants returned to their place of work; they commenced video-recording their practice and participating in supervision of their video-recorded practice by sending a copy of their video-recording to the trial training centre, watching it while simultaneously discussing its contents with the supervisor by telephone. Attention was paid particularly to the development of competence in motivational interviewing core skills and following the protocol for the session. There was a requirement that supervised practice with a minimum of two training clients (i.e. clients who had been randomly assigned to receive MET) would be delivered by training therapists before moving to the assessment of their competence. Acceptance of the candidate to practise in the trial was decided by the Principal Investigator for training (the author) and the specialist supervisor, and was based upon assessment of competence against a checklist of core skills and session components derived from the treatment manuals by the authors of the UKATT version of those manuals and contained in the UKATT Process Rating Scale (Tober *et al.* 2006). Candidates were required to demonstrate competence in the core skills of asking open questions, reflecting selectively, summarising and affirming. They had to demonstrate their ability to adhere to the purpose of the session, its structure and content. They were expected to achieve at least average scores for quality of the delivery of the treatment components.

Thirty-one trainees commenced training, 68 per cent of them were female and their average age was 36; fifteen were nurses, mainly psychiatric nurses, eleven were counsellors or therapists and five were medical practitioners, mainly psychiatrists. Ten of the nurses, seven of the counsellors or therapists and all five of the medical practitioners successfully completed training. No differences were found in age and gender between those who did and did not achieve competence. The length of time people had been practising did not have a bearing on whether or not they achieved competence, but educational level and professional group did. Those who had a first (bachelor) degree or higher were more likely successfully to complete training than those who had lower educational achievement.

For those who successfully completed training, there were no interprofessional differences in the resource required to achieve completion as measured by the amount of time it took, the number of supervision sessions or the number of training clients seen, nor were any differences found on these measures between people who had different levels of educational achievement for the whole training cohort (Tober *et al.* 2005).

There was, however, considerable variation in the duration of training across the MET group of trainees, the total time to train in days ranging from 64 to 405, the number of supervision sessions required to complete training ranging from 4 to 15 and the number of training cases required ranging from 2 to 8. Site differences did have some bearing on this, with one site showing significantly shorter duration of training. There may have been different levels of acceptance of trial practices across the sites and different support for trial procedures though it is possible only to speculate as this information is not available. Age, educational level, professional background and duration of addiction work showed no effect on duration of training.

In addition to the duration of training in days and the number of supervision sessions attended during training, the number of training case clients seen was calculated to examine whether this provided a different dimension of the training resource required. Paradoxically (because it was the shorter treatment) it took significantly longer to train therapists to practise MET than to practise SBNT, when measured by the number of days required for the achievement of competence. This may however partially be explained by the finding that the number of training clients required to achieve competence in MET was significantly higher. As the treatment was so much shorter, less practice occurred with each client recruited and additional recruitment was therefore necessary, possibly accounting for the greater passage of time. When measured by the number of supervision sessions attended, however, the difference between treatment types was not significant.

Where people took a longer period of time to achieve competence, they had more training cases and more supervision sessions. We speculated, on the basis of conversations with trainees, that the differences were based in two individual factors that were not the result of different levels of therapeutic competence but resistance to practise and inability to pay attention. Where people felt that the choice to participate in the trial was not theirs but made under pressure from peers, and where people had other things going on in their lives, not any other things but negative sources of stress, they were unable to attend to training sufficiently to achieve competence. It was not that they were not able to practise, but did not do so sufficiently consistently to gain competence at an earlier stage.

Those who felt pressured or coerced into joining the trial were among the number that did not achieve competence at all; but as the data on duration of training suggest, we did not actually give up in our attempts to train people, rather they dropped out when they felt they were not getting there. On the one hand the necessity to continue to train staff until they achieve competence might be a realistic approach where staff are already employed in an agency, on the other hand it might substantially increase the cost of training, and therefore of treatment. However, in calculating the costs of training in the UKATT we found that, when costs were attributed over a whole year of practice, at £1.71 per MET treatment session they constituted a small fraction of the cost of providing the treatment itself. In a climate of growing concern about the loss of resources for adequate training of staff it may be useful to examine the ways this conclusion was reached.

The resources used to train therapists were calculated on the basis of both stages of training: the initial three days at the training centre, and training practice supervision in the workplace until competence to practise in the trial is achieved. Initial training costs were calculated from the cost of training premises, the cost of the trainers, and the opportunity cost of those being trained. The main cost of supervision was a 45-minute session, usually by telephone, every two weeks between training and competence. Travel and accommodation costs for the initial three days would not be incurred in normal practice if therapists train at, or close to, their base, so these were categorised as research costs rather than training costs. Selecting therapists for training required them to make videos of current practice and submit a CV and this was also categorised as a research cost.

A capital charge for the training suite and supervision premises including recurrent costs of heating, lighting and other facilities was calculated. The cost of trainers' and therapists' time was based on the time committed, estimated from actual salaries plus employers' costs for pensions and national insurance, with management overheads taken as 8 per cent of salary. Actual time spent in supervision by the supervisor and the trainee was added to the calculation of costs. The cost of therapist time in training was the largest component of the training costs.

The total costs of training can be expressed in different ways. Calculating averages per person trained yields an estimate of £895 per MET therapist trained (31 in all). Dividing the cost of incompetent therapists across all the competent therapists yields an estimate of £1,260 per competent MET therapist. Training is an investment expected to deliver benefits over a period of time. However in UKATT, therapists had opportunities to deliver the treatments which were limited to clients recruited into the trial and randomised to MET. The training cost per session delivered in UKATT is £35 for MET, but a more realistic assumption upon which to estimate the cost of training therapists for routine practice is based upon the delivery of 736 sessions per year (or 46 weeks multiplied by 16 sessions per week) with the effects of training enduring for a year. In this case, training costs would amount to £1.71 for MET (and £1.89 for SBNT with which it was compared). For a more detailed description of these calculations see Tober and colleagues (2005).

Practising MET in the UK Alcohol Treatment Trial

Once competent, therapists were required to maintain consistent practice in line with the treatment protocols throughout the trial. Even with an intensive period of training over two or more months (and the average was 244 days), the maintenance of consistent practice is a challenge. Learning atrophies where measures are not taken to prevent drift from treatment protocols. We therefore ensured that supervision continued on a fortnightly to monthly basis once training was complete, and, to gauge the success of this measure, we conducted independent blind ratings of therapist video-recorded practice. The findings from these ratings were that MET therapists did practise MET in a fashion which was highly distinguishable from the practice of SBNT therapists and with certain components practised more frequently than others. Giving feedback, eliciting concerns about drinking, eliciting optimism for change, eliciting commitment to a drinking goal, expressing empathy and reflective listening were the task and style components most commonly practised. There was a significant correlation between the amount of MET practised and the quality of practice and those therapists who saw more clients, that is who practised more frequently overall, delivered more MET consistent treatment components than those therapists who treated fewer clients. It is difficult to tease out the meaning of these data. As with the completion of training in general, it appeared to be the case that those therapists who were competent practitioners enjoyed their practice more and therefore stuck with it more than those who struggled. So while the maxim 'practice makes perfect' is probably relevant, the desire to practise seems to be determined in part at least by a sense of professional self-esteem and this has been shown elsewhere (for example Cartwright 1980).

As the two treatments were offered by therapists who were colleagues at the same agency and worked side by side, therapists were urged not to discuss the content of treatment across the two trial treatment conditions and it was consistently reported that this separation was maintained. Training in each treatment had been delivered separately and the style of delivery of each treatment taught was different. The delivery of both treatments was independently rated using a scale adapted from the Project MATCH rating scale and named the UKATT Process Rating Scale, which included ratings of both frequency and quality of treatment component delivery. The results of this rating showed the two treatments to be highly distinct and distinguishable from each other, though some of the MET task and style items were performed by therapists working in the SBNT condition albeit less frequently and less well than by those therapists who had been trained in the style. Far fewer SBNT task and style items were performed by therapists trained and working in the MET condition. The components of MET were not as unique to that treatment as were components of the more novel SBNT to that treatment. We took the view that this was testament to the ubiquity of this style of practice. We also found that those who practised SBNT in a motivational interviewing style, that is they were rated positively for MET style items, were no less likely to be rated positively for SBNT task and style items. We drew the tentative conclusion that a social and behavioural intervention can be delivered in a motivational interviewing style without compromising its integrity.

Empathy was one of the components rated. Empathy is a behaviour commonly taught to all those who engage in therapeutic relationships. In the UKATT empathy was emphasised to those training in the MET condition but not included in the training for SBNT. It was found to be performed in both treatments but less so in SBNT than in MET and when it was performed in SBNT it achieved lower quality ratings than in the MET condition. This goes some way to addressing the question of whether empathy is a unique characteristic of therapists or one that can be taught.

Responses of therapists

Focus groups with MET therapists conducted at the end of the trial yielded the following core themes and opinions.

Therapists expressed the view that, contrary to their concerns at the beginning of the trial that three sessions would not be sufficient for many clients, in the event the requirement for treatment to be time limited was helpful, as was the specification of treatment structure and content in manual form. They described this as giving a sense of urgency about getting on with the work and a sense of confidence that this could be done. They believed that clients were more likely to share their confidence when the number of sessions and their content was specified at the outset. With the exception of court-mandated treatments, it has more commonly been the case in the UK that treatment is open ended and its duration often decided upon by the client. Increasingly there is a requirement to specify the number of treatments to be offered and experiences such as these are likely to facilitate this change in practice by enhancing its acceptability with treatment staff. Further confidence in the time-limited treatment resulted from the finding that, in the event, the average attendance for MET sessions across the 422 clients assigned to this treatment was 1.9, with those 348 clients attending any MET sessions attending on average for 2.3 sessions.

Therapists also stated that the specification of session content prevented them from getting sidetracked, helping them to maintain focus on the subject of motivation to change drinking. Related to this were comments made on learning the basic skills of the approach. Therapists from non-directive counselling backgrounds found the reconciliation of a directive and a non-confrontational style to be difficult. Being directive had hitherto been interpreted as telling people what to do. They reported feeling more comfortable (by which they meant familiar) with practising in a non-directive way to ensure maintaining a non-confrontational stance. On the other hand those therapists who had been trained in a diagnostic and prescriptive approach to treatment found it more difficult to refrain from giving unsolicited advice and information. This was somewhat consistent with the finding of trainers that, despite being required to demonstrate basic motivational interviewing skills as part of the selection process, further training in the core skills of motivational dialogue was required. It may be that the need for further practice of these skills led to the greater than anticipated duration of training.

Therapists unanimously identified feedback as being the most potent component of the treatment in their view. They said that once they had mastered the principles and practice of using feedback to elicit concerns and heighten ambivalence about continued drinking (normally in the first session), discussion of the findings of tests constituted the most powerful method of eliciting intention to change. Further they expressed the view that of all the feedback they gave, it seemed that the results of liver function tests had the greatest potential to elicit concerns about drinking and intention to change. This was broadly attributed to the objective and relatively straightforward nature of the information and its implications. On the other hand therapists reported difficulty in implementing the change plan worksheet (normally in the second session) as a motivational intervention rather than a behavioural one. This claim suggests that more attention might be given to the distinction between behavioural planning designed primarily to enhance self-efficacy, and enhancement of self-efficacy as a by-product of implementing behaviour changes.

Much of the material elicited in the focus group attests to the fact that people do learn what they believe on the strength of their own experience; confidence to practise is gained through repeated practice and continuing supervision during practice seemed to be the means to achieve and maintain such confidence.

The implementation of evidence-based treatment which includes protocols determining duration as well as intensity is likely to be required in the UK by service commissioners. The conditions in which three sessions of MET are likely to be sufficient, or simply as good as another treatment of longer duration, as was found in the UKATT, need further investigation. Which are the individuals who will derive no further benefit from more extended treatment? And what about the further findings emerging, namely that those who had a longer duration of treatment did better overall? The confidence of the therapist in the treatment they were delivering was not measured in the UKATT and this would be a recommendation for future trials, given its apparent importance in commencing training and establishing practice, and the reported contribution of optimism to effectiveness (Miller *et al.* 1993).

Summary

Many positive experiences resulted from the training and supervision of therapists in the UKATT. With the benefit of hindsight we would have done some things differently. We would have measured therapists' confidence in the treatment to which they were assigned because, while a significant part of the introductory training was designed to develop confidence in the treatment, we did not measure the extent to which we were successful in achieving this or its subsequent influence on the duration and success of training. We would have looked more carefully at past training and addressed specific departures from learned practice rather than addressing these in a general way and allowing practitioners to draw their own conclusions. We would have alerted practitioners to the problems resulting from the intrusion of external preoccupations and difficulties (as described in Chapter 7) at an early stage and incorporated into the training protocol the need to be vigilant for the influence of these.

It was a general feeling from agencies that participation in the trial had improved practice markedly in many ways. The challenge is then to maintain these benefits in routine practice once the strictures of trial procedures have been removed.

References

Cartwright, A. (1980) 'The attitudes of helping agents towards the alcoholic client; the influence of experience, support, training and self esteem', *British Journal of Addiction*, 75: 413–431.

Copello, A., Moore, A. and Orford, J. (1997) *Network support therapy. Mobilising a positive network to support a change in drinking*, Birmingham, UK: University of Birmingham.

Copello, A., Orford, J., Hodgson, R., Tober, G. and Barrett, C. (2002) 'Social Behaviour and Network Therapy: basic principles and early experiences', *Addictive Behaviors*, 27: 345–366.

Gallanter, M. (1999) *Network therapy for alcohol and drug abuse*, New York: Guilford Press.

Holder, H.D., Cisler, R., Longabaugh, R., Stout, R.L., Treno, A.J. and Zweben, A. (2000) 'Alcoholism treatment and medical care costs from Project MATCH', *Addiction*, 95: 999–1013.

Miller, W.R., Benefield, R.G. and Tonigan, J.S. (1993) 'Enhancing motivation for change in problem drinking: a controlled comparison of two therapist styles', *Journal of Consulting and Clinical Psychology*, 61: 455–461.

Miller, W.R., Zweben, A., DiClemente, C.C. and Rychtarik, R.G. (1995) *Motivational enhancement therapy manual: a clinical research guide for therapists treating individuals with alcohol abuse and dependence*, Project MATCH Monograph 2, Rockville, Maryland: National Institute on Alcohol Abuse and Alcoholism.

Project MATCH Research Group (1997) 'Matching alcoholism treatment to client heterogeneity: project match research group post treatment drinking outcomes, *Journal for the Study of Alcohol*, 58: 7–29.

Tober, G., Kenyon, R., Heather, N. and Brodie, J. (2001) *Motivational Enhancement Therapy Manual*, Leeds Addiction Unit, UKATT.

Tober, G., Clyne, W., Finnegan, O., Farrin, A. and Russell, I. in collaboration with the UKATT Research Team (2006) 'Validation of a scale for rating the process of delivery of psycho-social treatments for alcohol dependence and misuse'.

Tober, G., Godfrey, C., Parrott, S., Copello, A., Farrin, A., Hodgson, R., Kenyon, R., Morton, V., Orford, J., Russell, I. and Slegg, G. on behalf of the UKATT Research Team (2005) 'Setting standards for training and competence: the UK Alcohol Treatment Trial', *Alcohol and Alcoholism*, 40: 413–418.

UKATT Research Team (2001) 'United Kingdom Alcohol Treatment Trial (UKATT): Hypotheses, design and methods', *Alcohol and Alcoholism*, 36: 11–21.

UKATT Research Team (2005a) 'Effectiveness of treatment for alcohol problems: findings of the randomised United Kingdom Alcohol Treatment Trial (UKATT)', *British Medical Journal*, 331: 541–544.

UKATT Research Team (2005b) 'Cost-effectiveness of treatment for alcohol problems: findings of the randomised United Kingdom Alcohol Treatment Trial (UKATT)', *British Medical Journal*, 331: 544–548.

Chapter 11

Motivational enhancement therapy for smoking cessation in primary care: a case study

Susi Harris and Gillian Tober

Motivational interviewing has been practised in the UK primary care setting over many years; a popular intervention because it enables the primary care doctor to address questions of behaviour change in a non-confrontational manner, exploring the reasons for change, eliciting and exploring concerns with the aim of creating a desire to change based upon confidence and optimism in its results. It departs from the practice of persuading the patient of the benefits of and need to change and has been applied to problems that require behavioural change in order to bring about improvements in health.

Smoking cessation interventions in the primary care and specialist setting in the UK have been based primarily upon motivational interviewing and behavioural interventions. Effects found in two studies (Butler *et al.* 1999; Colby *et al.* 1998) have been described as 'small but significant' and 'encouraging' (Dunn *et al.* 2001). In this chapter we document a single session, part of a three session structured Motivational Enhancement Therapy (MET) delivered by a primary care doctor to a patient for smoking cessation. This session follows the protocol for MET as delivered in the UK Alcohol Treatment Trial and described in Chapter 10. The transcript is a verbatim account derived from a video-recorded session and the patient gave written informed consent for use of the video content as a contribution to this book.

In the transcript, T denotes the therapist, in this case a primary care physician and P is the patient. The doctor begins with a summary of the current situation and the patient's previously completed decisional balance (describing the pros and cons of smoking). The commentary and description is provided at the end of the transcript of the dialogue, in order to avoid breaking up the flow.

T: Just quickly to recap what we went through yesterday, you had an assessment of your smoking. You've recently taken up smoking again after your dog died. We explored the pros and cons of you still smoking. There was not very much in favour of it really except that it was time by yourself in a corner with a cup of coffee, your breathing time, your head space, your special relaxation time, but there were a few things against it, in particular the smell on your clothes, in your house and the fact that when you are in the company of other people, the smoke billowing over them, you don't like them doing it to you and you don't like doing it to them. Some underlying concerns about your health, we particularly talked about the strokes and the fact that you could become dependent, which is not acceptable to you, so at the end of that we did some tests and you have come back today for the results.

P: Yeah, whether I'm still alive or not.

T: Well first of all I just want to check what your understanding of what the tests that we've done were about. Tell me what you understand we've tested for.

P: I think they are to make sure that my lungs are working as they should be, and there is enough elasticity there.

T: That's right.

P: And basically, oh yes the carbon monoxide one to see if I am poisoning myself which I probably am.

T: And what would it mean to you if there were any question that your lungs had been affected?

P: Well obviously there is not a great deal I can do about it to put it right because it's been going on so long, I wouldn't like to envisage myself not being able to go out and walk about and go up and down the stairs because I couldn't breathe and I certainly wouldn't like to be stuck with an oxygen mask so that I could get my breath. So looking at that side of it, if it was heading there, I think I would be getting a little bit panicky because then it would mean that other people would have to look after me.

T: A big concern is that you have made a serious dent on your lung function.

P: Yes, I don't feel as if I have but there are some days when I certainly do.

T: It's a fluctuating thought you have.

P: Yes but there again I don't think it's just that that had been making it particularly tight and hard to breathe. I think it is the outside factors that help towards it. I am not trying to make excuses, don't get me wrong, I know that sometimes I can't breathe because I have smoked a lot but if I cut back over the next couple of days I go back to being able to breathe and I feel OK but I do find that when I cut right down it is the frustrations of life really that, sort of have this tendency to tighten me up.

T: An interplay between the way smoking affects your chest and the general stresses in your life which I know are quite high as we talked about yesterday. I know things are quite difficult for you at the moment.

P: Well it is six of one and half a dozen of the other, if it is not the smoking then it is the stress so then you cannot draw this line of where it is coming from.

T: I understand. Let me tell you a bit about the tests you had, first of all before we tell you the results. First you had a test which is called forced vital capacity. This was when you breathed out into the tube for as long as you could and what we are measuring is the full capacity of your lungs, there is always a little bit of what we call 'dead space' you can't squeeze out but this is the amount anyone could possibly squeeze out without there being nothing left at all, and that is predicted for you to be level 2.91 and yours was 2.57 which means you are 88 per cent of the predicted total capacity. That can vary in normal people, this is corrected for your sex, height and race but it can vary from 2.20 to 3.62, I think it depends on build, etc. but in your case yours was predicted at 2.91 and yours is a bit below that. Now, how do you feel about that?

P: Well, it needs working on really.

T: It would be nice to improve on that.

P: To bring it more to what it should be. I think I'd feel better with that.

T: You would feel better if was a bit nearer to that.

P: Yes, but I have always been unpredictable. I have always been a stone under my predicted weight. No, I think that could be worked on, one way or another.

T: You want to do something about this.

P: I can't say I am happy about it; like everyone else I was considering myself to be reasonably fit then something like that happens and you realise you aren't as fit as you thought you were.

T: Now, the other part of the breathing test. That was the forced vital capacity; there was a measure of the elasticity of the lungs, and they also measure what we call the obstruction. There were two things that were both picked up and in your case your ability to breathe out fast is 82 per cent of what was predicted. You should be able to clear in one second 2.46 litres and you were clearing 2.01 litres, which is 82 per cent of the prediction. That implies that the elasticity was OK but there might be a little bit of a problem with the obstruction, that the air cannot escape so some of the linings of your tubes are a little bit thickened.

P: Hence the bronchitis every year.

T: That is very likely to be linked, yes.

P: I don't think I am quite surprised really, there has to be a reason I am getting this bronchitis year after year and when I was smoking I was always (clears throat) so that doesn't surprise me.

T: You had to clear your throat a lot when you smoke, there is always a lot of extra mucus at the back of your throat.

P: Of course there was the sinus trouble and the catarrh and all that is going down there so it doesn't surprise me at all.

T: I remember now. The sinus trouble was a problem for you when you were getting established again (with smoking).

P: And then when I get in a smoky atmosphere it always starts – runny nose, then it is blocked. And the eyes ache and the cheekbones ache.

T: You are very aware that your mucus membranes can be affected quite strongly by your smoking. I think this test is reflecting that too. Now the actual interpretation of the spirometer picture has been given by the computer as normal and it isn't quite but it only tells us its abnormal if it's less than 75 per cent, so the picture is it should be a fairly straight line and there is a little bit of a sag there and that is implying that little bit of obstruction we talked about but overall it's not giving a clinical diagnosis of chronic obstructive airways disease for you.

P: In other words, do something about it or get worse.

T: You feel it would be a good idea to make a move on this before it becomes more serious.

P: Oh yes, it is obviously saying to me 'Right, you are starting with problems so do something about it or else'.

T: Doing something about it now would be a sensible way forward.

P: But now you see, it becomes a problem, well OK so now what do you do about it?

T: Now we are in the business of deciding what to do. Well that's definitely the next step and we can come on to that. I would like first to quickly give you another few things. One is the way that the machine gives us a reading of the typical age of the lungs.

P: Go, on, what am I? About 75?

T: Well actually it was 73 so you were very very close there.

P: Well I keep on saying I feel 90.

T: And you are actually 58.

P: Yes. Well. That's not good. That is definitely not good. I hate that machine.

T: You don't like what the machine is telling you, you feel . . .?

P: No, I am only joking. Yes I mean I used to look around at other people and think 'They are younger than me and they are not as fit' and now I look at older people and think 'they are older than me and a lot fitter'. I do this now.

T: You compare yourself with other people and you feel like it is time to take some action.

P: I think this is why I decided I would give up smoking, I was not feeling ill, I just didn't feel fit so I thought 'well if I give up smoking perhaps I would feel fitter'. Everyone told me I would. So I hate to think what it was like 12 months ago.

T: It would have been very interesting to know what it was like then.

P: At least I have had some clean months, 16 months.

T: You said yesterday that you did get considerably fitter after giving up smoking. Little walks on the beach that suddenly became three miles.

P: I mean don't get me wrong, I can still do the same amount but probably do not do things as quickly as I did. I am slowing down a little bit again but I don't particularly feel as unfit as I did but I don't feel as fit as I did either.

T: There's been an effect of feeling less fit since you restarted smoking and your interpretation of these results you have been given here is that it is time to do something about that before things get more serious.

P: Last year it was a case of 'I don't feel well, I am just going to give up' because I know that it is the smoking that is doing it. Now it is confirmed, I really do, I really ought to have a really good start again.

T: This feedback has helped you to confirm something you were wondering about. 'Isn't it time to stop smoking?' Maybe it has helped to reflect that yes, it is time.

P: Yes, it is time something was done.

T: Right, well there is one other thing that . . .

P: It's surprised me has that.

T: It surprised you?

P: Yes.

T: You weren't really expecting it?

P: Well, I thought I was fitter than that's told me.

T: You were actually under the impression that you were keeping things higher up on the expected scale of things.

P: I must admit, I did say to my daughter a couple of months ago that it was time to take some better exercise than just walking. I do feel as if I really do need some stronger exercise but basically I am just lazy. I have never altered.

T: There is a general feeling of wanting to do something about your health, wanting to improve it.

P: Yes. I feel like I could do with a really good workout and feel shattered at the end of it and then sit down and have a cup of tea and then think 'At least I have done something today'. I would feel better for it tomorrow despite all the aches and pains.

T: Well when we have finished this session today and it is something we have been talking about I have got access to a referral scheme to help.

P: That's the way I feel right now. If I can get my circulation moving I would feel better.

T: Now with the other one, the carbon monoxide test.

P: You are going to tell me that I am dead, aren't you?

T: You are not looking forward to this one.

P: Not after that one, no!

T: Well just quickly to run through there are four possible results. The score of 0–6 for a non-smoker which is green, 7–10 light smoker which is amber, 11–20 heavy smoker which is red, 20 plus, heavy smoker flashing red alarm, OK?

P: So I didn't get an alarm.

T: No, you didn't get an alarm and in actual fact the result you came out with in 2 out of 3 was heavy smoker red.

P: Right. How can I be a heavy smoker if I am not smoking that much? What is a heavy smoker defined as?

T: This was defined as the amount of carbon monoxide that you have in your blood stream that a heavy smoker would have. It feels as though it couldn't be right because you don't think you smoke that much.

P: I would say I was smoking heavily before I gave up but not now. I don't feel that I am.

T: So a bit of a shock really.

P: Mmmmmm yes. I can't understand. It has right surprised me.

T: It can be affected by how recently you have had a cigarette. I don't know if you remember.

P: I think just before I came in actually.

T: Had you?

P: Yes, because I had one before I left home and then I drove and came in. So, about an hour.

T: Well that would probably tip it over. The other result was, as I said when I did the tests, I thought you were on a border line because you scored one on one of the results and two on the other but I think you are probably borderline.

P: There you go then, I know it is going to have to stop.

T: Feels like you really need to stop. You want to talk about how you might take this forward really.

P: Yes it is not worth carrying on like that.

T: It seems to be affecting you too much now. This is having too profound an effect on your body for it to carry on.

P: Yes because up to that it was a case of OK, I have smoked all of my life, I have given up, I can do it again but it is getting the time right and my head right but that could be tomorrow, next week, next year. Now that I have seen that it is going to be nearer next week than next year.

T: It has brought your stop date quite a bit forward.

P: Yes, I think it is going to have to be a definite stop date and there are people who aren't going to be very friendly because if I am not putting my own smoke in I am not putting theirs in either. I can understand. I tried not to be an ex-smoker. I tried very hard because I didn't want to be an ex-smoker. I didn't want to be 'Oh she has given up'. I didn't want that attitude but that puts a whole new light on the situation. I am going to be an ex-smoker.

T: Everybody's going to know that you've given up smoking, so you are going to talk to people about that and you are going to explain to them.

P: I am going to say to them 'I have stopped putting the smoke in to me because I am heading for my grave and I am not taking yours in either, just get out of my sight'.

T: You are not going to take in any smoke either yourself or from others.

P: I mean like when I was driving the car and I had smokers in the car and they would say 'Do you mind if we smoke' and I would say 'Pull the window down' but I could still smell it but then with something like this, it is going to be a case of 'Yes, I do mind', I'm going to become an ex-smoker.

T: You are going to go the whole hog.

P: I am going to have to and I think by going the whole hog it will be a bit easier this time and other folk will know that I am not accepting it. If it is doing that much damage to me, well their smoke isn't going to do it either.

T: You will make it very clear to them where you stand.

P: Yes because that surprised me, that basically is telling me it has knocked 18 years off my life and I am not prepared to accept that loss of 18 years because I am going to live till I am 94 but I am not going to be looked after.

T: You are not going to do yourself further damage at this point. Where do you want to go from here?

P: I mean having said that, I only used Zyban for a fortnight and you are supposed to use it for three months but I suffered terribly with wind, I was very uncomfortable and I had a couple of days off to see if it was this that was doing it.

T: You are not sure whether Zyban is where you want to go from here. You might want to look at different options. Let me give you some literature to look at. You have explored a lot of the problems to your health today. It is a difficult session for you considering the results of these tests; you have said that you have started to see things differently, you are thinking that now you have to stop smoking and you now want to think about the best way to do this. The test results have helped you decide that.

P: It's not just that, it has been the final decision making thing. Shall I? Shan't I? Can I? Can't I? And now, yes I will.

T: Now you are going to stop smoking. What concrete plans do you want to make?

P: I am going to start by reading the literature you give me and come back to discuss what to do.

When reading through the transcript, the experienced practitioner will have spotted that the session had structure and that feedback was the method used to elicit and heighten concerns and to direct these toward expressions of an intention to change. There was consistent use of open questions and reflective statements, some simple and some more elaborate, nudging the emphasis in the direction of change. Some readers might think they would have responded differently with some of the reflections. Generally in motivational interviewing there is no orthodoxy about the 'proper way of doing things' or right and wrong things to say. People are able to develop a personal style and we have seen great variations on these. The relevant question for assessing the quality of a motivational intervention is whether the practitioner manages to elicit statements about change, specifically statements about intention to change. Does the therapist elicit and heighten the patient's concerns about the behaviour to the point where some sort of change becomes inevitable? Does she successfully elicit intention to change, optimism about the outcome of change, self-efficacy for change? And finally does she elicit commitment to change?

A number of issues are raised in the example described above. The patient seems to some extent to be expressing low self-esteem at the beginning of the session, and a pessimistic feeling about the damage she might have caused to date. Central to the idea of enhancing optimism for change must be the possibility of improvement as a result of change. Where there is a feeling that it is too late to reverse damage caused, or at the very least to arrest further deterioration, there will be little incentive to go through the discomfort of changing the behaviour. A point to remember is precisely this distinction, is it the case that, if irreversible damage has been done, is this degree of damage static or might further, additional damage still be prevented? Knowing the answer to these questions at the outset and when planning the session, part of being knowledgeable and authoritative in the subject area, is an important aspect of being able to encourage optimism for change. In a motivational interviewing approach the therapist aims to elicit and reinforce statements expressing optimism for change. In order to do this, she needs to be convinced of the point of making a change herself.

There is then the question of how to give the results of tests, how to maximise their potential for raising concerns about the smoking and to direct these concerns towards a decision to change. Whether or not the purpose of the tests and the meaning of their results were explained at the time they were administered, the process is so emotionally charged that the information may not have been stored correctly, or at all. The physician repeated the explanation of the tests, explained how they worked, the sort of results you might get and what they mean. The results then have more immediate impact when given.

On examining the transcript, it appeared that a number of gains had been made. It sounded to be the case that a therapeutic alliance had been developed, working out together why quitting smoking was a good idea, what might be gained from it, what might be prevented, ending with a commitment to stop smoking with at least the possibility of proceeding to the action required on a collaborative basis. A core ingredient of a motivational interviewing approach, empathy, expressed in the reflective statements and reinforcement of thoughts about change, seems to be at the centre of this therapeutic alliance. Initial statements of low self-esteem and low self-efficacy changed into statements of determination; belief in the patient's ability to change was explored by examining methods of helping her with quitting.

There is a question about the patient's commitment to change at two points; the first is when the patient begins to think that increasing exercise might be the better route to improve her health. At this point the therapist refocuses the discussion on quitting smoking by feeding back another smoking related test result. She avoids using any confrontation in redirecting the patient's thoughts. The second is at the end when, instead of proceeding to a plan right away, the patient opts to read the literature first and return to make a plan to quit. The session thus ends with an expression of commitment to explore methods to assist in her quitting smoking. In developing a theoretical basis for motivational interviewing, Hettema *et al.* (2004) refer to the work of Amrhein *et al.* (2003) in highlighting the importance of ending the session with a commitment to change, with the strength of commitment utterances predicting the likelihood of subsequent behaviour change. How strong was the commitment expressed by this patient? Did she backtrack at the end of the session when faced with making concrete behavioural plans? Hettema *et al.* exhort sensitivity to the patient's motivational state in order to avoid eliciting resistance at this point. There appears to be a risk that the momentum for change may be lost by the time of the next appointment, and raises the question of whether there was scope to elicit a concrete immediate plan to quit.

The physician is able to describe in everyday language how the respiratory system works, the way tests measure its health and function and the meaning of results. An authoritative style is an important component of the therapist's ability to be perceived as a competent and trustworthy practitioner (Miller *et al.* 1993; 1988; Sanchez-Craig *et al.* 1991). Such authoritativeness has been demonstrated in studies of Motivational Enhancement Therapy which include feedback as a central plank for eliciting concern and heightening ambivalence (Project MATCH Research Group 1997; UKATT Research Team 2001), highlighting the need to ensure that knowledge about the condition forms the platform upon which the skills of motivational dialogue are built.

The average primary care doctor might claim that there is not enough time in a typical primary care consultation to conduct such a session; however, this real life example demonstrates the benefits of allocating more than routine time; if the session is effective and does result in a successful quit attempt, the time spent in future smoking related disease management could be reduced.

References

Amrhein, P.C., Miller, W.R., Yahne, C.E., Palmer, M. and Fulcher, L. (2003) 'Patient commitment language during motivational interviewing predicts drug use outcomes', *Journal of Consulting and Clinical Psychology*, 71: 862–878.

Butler, C.C., Rollnick, S., Cohen, D., Russell, I., Bachmann, M. and Stott, N. (1999) 'Motivational consulting versus brief intervention for smokers in general practice: a randomised trial', *British Journal of General Practice*, 49: 611–616.

Colby, S.M., Monti, P.M., Barnett, N.P., Rohsenow, D.J., Weissman, K., Spirito, A., Woolard, R.H. and Lewander, W.J. (1998) 'Brief motivational interviewing in a hospital setting for adolescent smoking: a preliminary study', *Journal of Consulting and Clinical Psychology*, 66: 574–578.

Dunn, C., Deroo, L. and Rivara, F.P. (2001) 'The use of brief interventions adapted from motivational interviewing across behavioral domains: a systematic review', *Addiction*, 96: 1725–1742.

Hettema, J., Steele, J. and Miller, W.R. (2004) 'Motivational Interviewing', *Annual Review of Clinical Psychology*, 1: 91–111.

Miller, W.R., Benefield, R.G. and Tonigan, J.S. (1993) 'Enhancing motivation for change in problem drinking: a controlled comparison of two therapist styles', *Journal of Consulting and Clinical Psychology*, 61: 455–461.

Miller, W.R., Sovereign, R.G. and Krege, B. (1988) 'Motivational Interviewing with Problem Drinkers: II. The Drinker's Check-up as a preventive intervention', *Behavioural Psychotherapy*, 16: 251–268.

Project MATCH Research Group (1997) 'Matching alcoholism treatment to patient heterogeneity: Project MATCH research group post treatment drinking outcomes', *Journal for the Study of Alcohol*, 58: 7–29.

Sanchez-Craig, M., Spivak, K. and Davila, R. (1991) 'Superior outcome of females over males after brief treatment for the reduction of heavy drinking: replication and report of therapist effects', *British Journal of Addiction*, 86: 867–876.

UKATT Research Team (2001) 'The United Kingdom Alcohol Treatment Trial (UKATT): hypotheses, design and methods', *Alcohol and Alcoholism*, 36: 11–21.

Section V

Motivational dialogue and stepped care

Chapter 12

Motivational dialogue 1 – core interventions

Gillian Tober and Duncan Raistrick

Introduction

In this chapter we propose a protocol for integrating motivational dialogue into routine treatment of alcohol and drug dependence using a stepped care approach. In earlier chapters we have explored the evidence for using a motivational style of counselling problem drinkers as compared with a confrontational approach (see Chapter 1) and with a non-directive approach (see Chapter 8). In Chapter 5, Kadden and colleagues reviewed the evidence for using motivational interviewing as a stand-alone treatment with different substance problems in different permutations and as a treatment combined with other treatments. In this chapter we suggest a further integration whereby all interventions are delivered using a stepped care framework starting with assessment and simple advice and working up through increasingly intensive interventions. The point of this book, and the two final chapters in particular, is to demonstrate the potential benefits and the feasibility of delivering all these interventions in the style of motivational dialogue. It is a way of putting together all the evidence we have assembled into a logical interpretation and then into practice.

Stepped care

Before going on to describe the requisite set of skills and some thoughts about the style of delivery we first turn to a description of an organisational method of treatment delivery called stepped care. The stepped care approach described in the UK Review of the Effectiveness of Treatment for Alcohol Problems (Raistrick *et al.* 2006) provided the scientific underpinning for Models of Care for Alcohol Misuse (MoCAM), a framework for service delivery (National Treatment Agency 2006). Models of Care for Alcohol Misuse and Models of Care for Drug Misuse both describe a four-tier framework for commissioning treatment services:

- Tier 1: Non-substance misuse specific services requiring interface with drug and alcohol treatment

- Tier 2: Open access drug and alcohol treatment services
- Tier 3: Structured community-based drug and alcohol treatment services
- Tier 4: Residential services for drug and alcohol misusers.

The tiers of services are about degrees of specialisation whereas stepped care is about degrees of intensity of treatment. The concepts are different but there is a correlation between the two. The steps of stepped care are designed to be significantly different clinically (see Figure 12.1) and to have an evidence base supporting the difference.

The basic principles of stepped care have long been practised by clinicians albeit without giving a name to the approach. The essential principle is that the least intensive treatment, which is usually also the least intrusive and least costly treatment, is given first – only if this treatment fails is a more intensive, next step, treatment given. The approach is particularly relevant to substance misuse treatments for two reasons: (i) pre-treatment variables and therapist assessments are poor predictors of who will do well in treatment; (ii) there is a variety of effective treatments which result in similar outcomes across different client groups – many of these treatments differ in intensity and therefore also in cost. It follows that the interventions selected for stepped care must all have strong evidence of effectiveness and there should be clinically significant differences between the interventions chosen for each step. Stepped care is justified on the grounds that it is a rational, rather than evidence based way to deliver treatment.

Stepped care can be applied both across different tiers of services within an integrated treatment system and also within a specialist treatment agency. Stepped care interventions begin following identification of a problem behaviour, in this case substance use, which may occur by opportunistic means, by formal screening or by help-seeking on the part of the individual. It is important to note that clients do not have to start at the lowest step, rather, where it is clear that a more intensive treatment is indicated then this should be the starting point. If matching clients to treatment were a more precise science then the rationale for stepped care would all but disappear. In fact the evidence is that drinking or drug taking during treatment and life events that occur after treatment are stronger predictors of treatment outcome than any pre-treatment variables; it is likely that stepped care is here to stay. The cost effectiveness and client acceptability of a stepped care approach have not been evaluated, however there is promising research, for example STEPWICE (Drummond *et al.* 2003), demonstrating its feasibility.

The core skills of motivational dialogue

In motivational dialogue there are concrete things to do and there are less concrete ways of doing them. The concrete things to do are the two essential and core skills of: (i) asking open questions and (ii) selective reflective

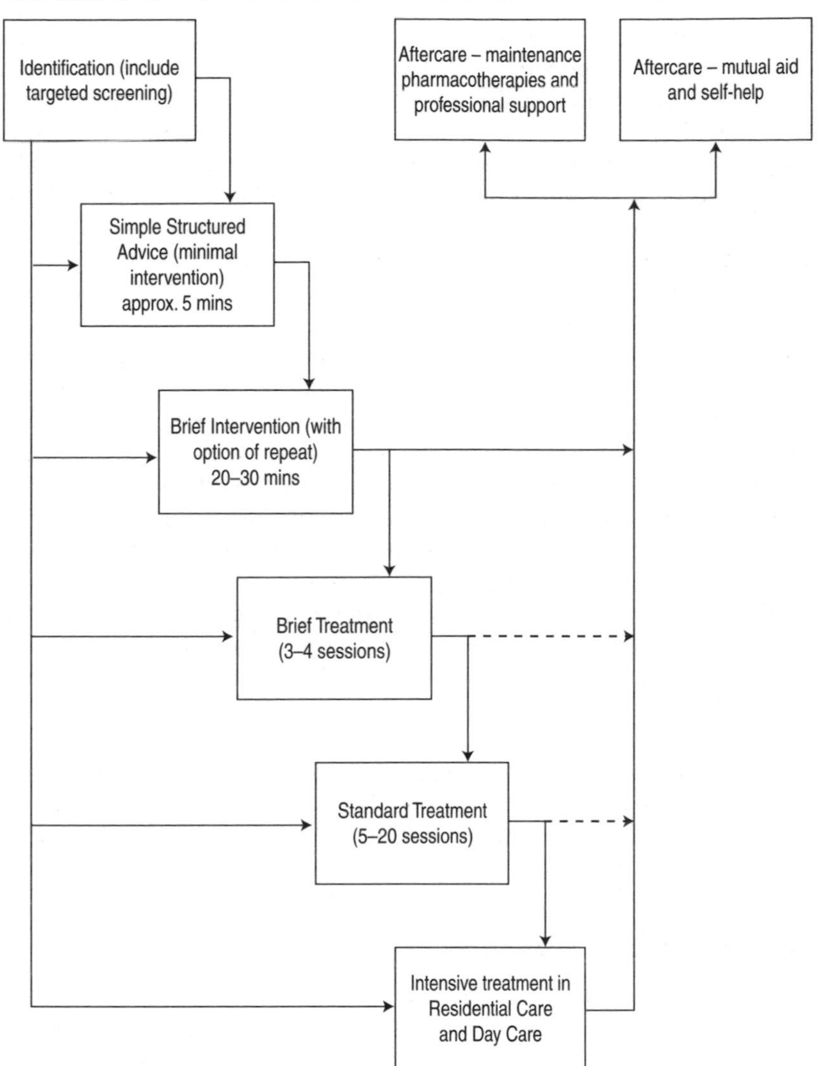

Figure 12.1 Stepped care.

listening. Asking open questions can be done in different ways with a simple defining principle: the reply cannot be determined by the question. An open question allows any sort of a reply as well as none. In reality it is a question that might be put as an invitation to respond thus allowing phrases like 'tell me about . . .' delivered as an invitation not a command. Giving options, no matter how many, narrows the scope of the response, indeed defines the response.

The art of asking open questions serves many purposes. At its most basic it ensures at least the possibility of getting a good account, getting at what is really going on, getting at the truth of the matter. Why this might be the case is that if the person asking the question does not communicate the expectation of a particular reply the recipient will be less tied to fulfilling this expectation. It communicates interest in the other person, in what they have to say. It shifts focus to the other person and away from the questioner. This is one of the essential ingredients of empathy and a way to communicate empathy, a simple way of saying 'I am interested to hear what you have to say'.

So, this core skill is going to be the basic method of eliciting, which will apply whether the goal is to elicit concerns about the problem behaviour, to elicit optimism about change, or to elicit intention to change.

Selective reflective listening is about being directive in the sense of 'steering a course' and, combined with asking open questions, is the method whereby the therapist pursues the agenda for the session. Miller and Rollnick (1991) have defined categories of reflections, which the reader might find helpful in extending their understanding of the breadth of the ways this skill can be applied. The overarching principles are that it is not only words and statements that can be reflected, but also expressions of feeling and behaviours; that present and past material can usefully be reflected, that contrasting feelings can be reflected and that reflections can be used for selective emphasis. Selective reflection is used to guide the discourse along its agenda from expressing concerns about a behaviour to expressing intention to change. It is the therapist's response to the material elicited by asking open questions. Reflections are then followed by further open questions so that the dialogue progresses.

What else does a therapist need to do?

The research tells us that there are ways of being and ways of doing things that are more effective than other ways. Therapist style is of great importance. You can ask open questions and listen reflectively in different ways, because it is not just what comes out of our mouths that is interpreted as communicating interest. Empathy is not communicated solely by what we say, though it is to a large extent. The accuracy of reflective statements communicates to the client that the therapist 'gets it', is able to make sense of what the client is saying and this is the very essence of empathy. Facial expression, eye contact, posture and general demeanour are our additional tools in communicating warmth or coldness, positive or negative regard, patience or impatience.

Thus there is an interdependence of skills and style at the most basic level of practice. What is done with this is often likened to the challenge of driving a car. The skills required to operate the machinery need to be learned and practised in isolation of the demands of the road to the point where they become automatic responses to stimuli. This will be the result of repeated rehearsal until confidence and competence are achieved. Once achieved on the disused airfield, the road map should be studied before embarking upon the journey. This is the art of deciding on an agenda before the session commences, in its outline form (for example the agenda for the session will be to elicit concerns about a behaviour, to arrive at a decision to change and so on). One has to be prepared for the change of plan brought about by road closures and diversions, but the automatic application of basic skills frees up attention to be alert to these, and to whatever else happens, the sudden braking of the car in front, the person crossing the road without looking. The analogy is that the therapist is then free to address whatever the client brings with them, whatever motivational stage the client is in, the level of resistance they might encounter, the other matters (other than the problem drinking or drug use) that might intrude.

The agenda can be set in the broadest way. The goal is to effect change in the problem behaviour that is consistent with improvement in health and social functioning. The milestones required to get there will vary from individual to individual; some will travel directly and some will take steps forward, steps back or seem to stand still. The detail of the journey, the cognitive and behavioural challenges that need to be addressed are unique to each client and will be elicited from and defined by the client. The treatment protocol provides the strategies that can be used in pursuit of this task in each session.

In the next section we are going to illustrate motivational dialogue applied to the delivery of four interventions of different intensities from the stepped care model:

- Assessment
- Simple advice
- Motivational enhancement therapy
- Social behaviour and network therapy

In each example we have written some text to suggest how the conversation might flow. Here are some notes to guide the reader through the 'scripts':

1. Obviously the examples are somewhat contrived but make sure you can pick out the two core skills of asking open questions and selective reflective listening.
2. Make sure you can see the therapist's agenda and how motivational dialogue guides the client towards the preferred treatment choices. You would probably use different words which suit your own style, so translate the text we have written into questions and statements with which you feel comfortable and rehearse using them in your head or

role playing with a colleague, until you do not have to think about them.

3 Notice that we frequently draw upon leaflets or worksheets or self-completion questionnaires to deal with giving and collecting simple factual information.
4 In the examples below we have used the abbreviations: T = therapist; C = client; D = doctor.

Motivational dialogue in practice

Conducting an assessment in the style of motivational dialogue

With rapidly changing political priorities and the demands for ever more information on clients and on the outcomes of treatment, staff in training and supervision are often heard to lament 'this motivational dialogue is all very well but it will not help with the mountains of factual information we have to collect'. We understand the problem but believe that there are sound reasons to approach the assessment of new clients using motivational dialogue.

Our goal at the outset is for every encounter to have therapeutic benefit for the help seeker, whether they are seeking help for an alcohol or drug problem or for a sore throat. We would always take the view that to gather information for its own sake is intrusive. We can do better than setting out to get as much information as possible 'in case I need it later' or for some ill defined thought that it will help to make sense of the case. The requirements of information gathering put many workers in a dilemma: this form says that I have to collect information on x, y and z but I really do not know to what use this information is to be put. How can we maintain in practice the principle that the task of gathering information for anything other than a specific therapeutic purpose is to be avoided?

We put great store in the practice of preparing for the session before it begins; this would be the case no matter how short the session is to be. The first preparatory step is to ensure familiarity with data collection instruments in all their detail, to understand for what purpose each piece of information is collected, not to accept the collection of data for its own sake or for the bureaucratic needs of an organisation or political goal. After all it is the person who asks the questions who will be responsible for the intrusion, if this is how it is perceived.

Once such familiarity with the data required is achieved, the therapist is then free to give their full attention to the task of engaging the client and developing rapport by getting the client's account of the problem behaviour, eliciting the client's concerns about this behaviour and strengthening the client's belief in their ability to change it. How does this work? People often say that their memory is not good enough to remember what the client is saying to them and so they have to write things down while the client is speaking. We would urge you to try two things. First you could video record your assessment session and observe what you look like writing things down when the client is talking to you. Certainly it is difficult to communicate warmth, interest and positive regard without making eye contact and tracking the dialogue with complete concentration. Secondly, more constructively and more reassuringly, try it. Put down your pen and give the client 100 per cent of your attention. While they are speaking, attempt to make sense of what they are saying, create as much of a visual image of what they are describing as you can. If you give this 100 per cent of your attention you will find that you will recall what they have said in all its detail. If there are details that you have not achieved you can go back at the end, with your last summing up and say 'let's just check that we have down all the information that we need to have' without having disrupted the flow of the dialogue earlier.

T: Good morning, welcome, take a seat and tell me what brings you here today.
C: I have been feeling very low and depressed in the morning. I can't get myself going and do not want to go out of the house. I never used to be like this.
T: Tell me more about these feelings; how long have you been having them?
C: (responds with a description of anxieties)
T: Tell me what other things you have noticed, perhaps how you have been feeling more physically.
C: (responds with a description of physical symptoms)
T: What have you noticed about other sorts of changes: things that have happened in you life recently?

With further directed open questions you will be able to get a drinking pattern and its consequences, you can get information about how the drinking fits into the routine day, what are its usual and its worst consequences, and you will have begun to formulate some hypotheses about those things that are of greatest concern to the client. This you will do by paying attention not just to the content of their speech, but to the tone and volume, their body language; by this time you will also have elicited information you seek on what a typical day is like, who is in the social network, how they respond to the drinking.

Once you have elicited a description of the problem behaviour you begin to gauge the client's feelings about it by asking questions like:

T: Tell me what you get out of it? What sorts of things do you feel after drinking or when you are drinking?

You then pick up on any negative connotation in the client's account and ask them to elaborate on that. For example:

T: You said that it does not always relax you. Tell me more about the times when it doesn't.
T: Tell me about the worst thing that has happened.
Or
T: Tell me about the worst time that happened when . . .

When you have an account of the negative consequences of the behaviour you begin to gauge the client's feelings about them, for example does she or he play them down, or sound concerned about them and this can act as a trigger to asking

T: How would you prefer things to be?
Or
T: What would you like to happen?

You can then go on to the question of what might help to bring this about. Much of the literature on resistance in the therapeutic process focuses on the ease with which the therapist can inadvertently elicit resistance by talking about change prematurely. However, this caution need not result in the opposite, that is, never talking about change lest it elicit resistance. It is worth trying to move along as quickly as you can because you will develop the skills of defusing resistance when you do encounter it. One of the important skills to develop is your level of perceptiveness regarding the pace at which your particular client is going to move and of course this will vary with every individual.

What then are we hoping to get from the first assessment and what do we aim for the client to get out of it? It is our view that a good benchmark for evaluating the point of any encounter is to ask yourself the question: Is this person in any different, more advanced-toward-change state at the end of the session than they were at the beginning of the session? If all the client has done is to impart a whole lot of information about themselves they arc going to be taking away very few of those ingredients of the therapeutic alliance which contribute to the building of what is perceived to be a helping relationship. If, on the other hand, they have gained some insight into the nature of their behaviour, what maintains it and what things would look like if it changed, combined with a feeling of optimism about change then, even if behavioural change has yet to occur, there is a greater likelihood that some of the groundwork has been laid.

This then is the sort of agenda we would set for the first appointment, the first discussion about the problem behaviour:

1 Bringing it up and getting enough of an account of the behaviour to draw conclusions about its consequences
2 Eliciting the client's perceived concerns about it, whether the client's own or those of other people for whom the client has some concern
3 Eliciting a vision of what change would look like, what its outcomes might be, optimism in the achievement of those outcomes and confidence to effect change.

This agenda is our primary concern and if it is achieved the likelihood is that all information needed will have been collected along the way. The only thing that can convince you of this is the experience of it.

Simple advice in the style of motivational dialogue

On the face of it, motivational dialogue is the very antithesis of giving advice, and yet if we stick to the principle that we can elicit a description of where the client is now and where they want to be, we can also elicit a response to the question 'What do you think would help you to get there?'

We are fairly convinced that giving unsolicited advice about almost anything will elicit resistance, because it carries with it the implication that what you are doing now is wrong, in other words it will be perceived as a criticism and is likely to provoke a defensive reaction. Even if this does not invariably happen it is probably not worth taking the risk that it might. Stick to the safer method of finding out what the individual thinks.

Many advice giving situations are designed to exploit opportunities to target a given behaviour in the hope at least of diminishing the damage resulting from it. At the other end of the spectrum they are designed to bring about a behavioural change which will not require too much effort or involve too much difficulty. Motivation is no less important an aspect of change in these situations and exactly the same principles apply as in those situations where change is perceived as being difficult. The individual has to believe that they can accomplish the change and that it will be worthwhile. The change can be an important one to achieve even when the current behaviour is not causing too great a problem. In other words, change can be desired for overall positive reasons, as well as for both positive and negative reasons. An example might be where an individual takes up with a non-drug using partner and decides they want to quit using drugs because their use is no longer consistent with their new life style.

The purpose of advice giving then can be to limit harm or to effect behaviour change. The bottom line is that when the recipient remains completely resistant to identifying drug or alcohol related harms resulting from their behaviour then it is incumbent upon the professional to give information about the consequences of the behaviour whether these are in the health, social or legal spheres. Merely carrying out our professional responsibilities in such a way is less rewarding than assisting a person to believe that change is in their (as opposed to our) interests.

The simple advice-giving situation is one in which, by definition, we are not conducting an assessment. It may be an opportunistic event in which a specific aspect of behaviour has come to light. Let's take the ubiquitous example of injecting drugs in the context of a drop-in for injecting equipment exchange.

T: Hi Bob. How are you today? Tell me how you have been injecting in the last week since you were here.

C: I couldn't find a vein in my arms anymore. This girl showed me how to go into my groin.

T: Tell me what you know about injecting there. Where are you trying to get in? What else is going on in that part of your body? Tell me how that works. What have you heard about this from your mates?

C: I've heard that lots of people do it. I've seen people do it.

T: What else have you heard?

C: People say that you can lose your leg if you aren't careful but all my mates seem to have both their legs.

T: Seems that losing legs is not that common. What have you noticed about people who inject into their groin?

C: Seems like quite a few of them limp sometimes.

T: Tell me what you make of that.

C: Dunno. I heard they get blood clots or something. Then you have to take medicine to get rid of it.

T: We could go over some of the things that might happen. I have got a picture here of that whole part of the body so we can see what is happening. I know that you are in a hurry and it will only take a couple of minutes. We might be able to prevent anything bad happening before the next time you come in when we can make sure we have a bit more time to talk about it.

All this is done in the spirit of an alliance, and at the same time there is an insistence on the part of the therapist that the information is given. Once this has occurred the therapist proceeds to elicit specific, personal concerns about the behaviour with questions like

T: Where does this leave you?

Or

T: What are your thoughts now having looked at this information?

T: How would you like things to go from here?

The purpose of these questions is to elicit a request for advice on change. When giving such advice it is worth remembering that small manageable incremental tasks are the way forward. We also know from many studies over the years that brief advice works better when there is a follow-up appointment to check progress.

Brief treatment in the style of motivational dialogue

The intervention we describe below is based upon Motivational Enhancement Therapy (MET) as practised in the UK Alcohol Treatment Trial (UKATT) (UKATT Research Team 2001; Tober *et al.* 2001) in three sessions, which in turn was based upon Motivational Enhancement Therapy as practised in Project MATCH in four sessions (Miller *et al.* 1995). We are not suggesting being prescriptive about the number of sessions offered under this heading; it is the content and the principles that are important. The three-session treatment is distinguished from simple advice, described above as being given in one session with a possible follow-up to report back on progress, by virtue of having different specific tasks for each session. It might be that more time is required to achieve these tasks. It could be that less time is required. Some of the difference will be determined by the stage of change and the amount of resistance to change encountered. Moreover it is distinguished from what we would call longer term, more intensive treatment which requires the recruitment of significant others with inter-session tasks to perform, practice to be done and feedback to be given.

In both Project MATCH and the UKATT, the first session consisted in the giving of feedback from assessments. In order to adapt this process to different agencies and contexts, a variety of assessment instruments can be used for this purpose. At one end of the spectrum is the hour-long battery of questionnaires used in the UKATT for the purpose of feeding back in MET. At the other end is the screening tool that is the Alcohol Use Disorders Toolkit (AUDIT) (Babor *et al.* 2001), a now widely known screening tool used in a variety of primary care and hospital settings. It yields information on recent drinking and life-time problems or concerns. Using the latter example, the pattern of recent drinking can be put in the context of population norms and risk categories for drinking. But the challenge is to do this in a non-confrontational style, when the content of the intervention is, by definition, quite confrontational, the underlying message being, for example 'you drink more than 90 per cent of the population', 'your drinking puts you into the highest risk category'.

An example of the dialogue that might be used is given in Chapter 11 when the doctor explains the nature of the test to the patient before she feeds back the results. An equivalent example with feedback from liver function tests might look like this

D: You remember that we ran some tests when you said that you wanted to know whether you had incurred any harm to your liver as a result of your drinking. Tell me what you remember about how those tests work and what they are going to tell us?

C: Something to do with how well my liver was coping with my drinking, something about showing whether the liver was working abnormally and had to work extra hard.

D: (Confirms and repeats explanation. Shows the normal range so that the individual can see themselves in relation to the normal range.)

C: That's way above what it should be. Does that mean that my liver is badly damaged?

D: You can see that your tests results are not normal and you are worried about what amount of damage you might already have done. Would it be helpful to explore exactly what might be implied by these results and what courses of action are open to you?

The simpler and more everyday example that is more likely to occur outside the medical consulting room is with the screening questions:

T: Let's start by looking at what we might call population norms for drinking. This is the question of how many people in the population drink which amounts of alcohol. We can then look at what the science tells us about the potential risks from different levels of drinking so that you can gauge where your own drinking fits in.

It is probably a good idea to have a simple chart to hand for the purpose of this explanation. It is easier to have a visual representation to which you can refer. Manuals for MET provide such visual aids.

T: You have recorded drinking more than twelve standard drinks per day. Where does that put you in relation to the rest of the population?

That sounds like an open enough question but in fact there is only one right answer and this is therefore the point in the feedback that is likely to elicit the strongest resistance, like:

C: I don't know where they get these figures from. I don't know anyone who drinks two or three drinks per day.

Or

C: Everyone I know drinks like I do and they are not having problems.

T: These figures are pretty difficult to relate to. You haven't come across thinking about them like this before. It might be more helpful to focus on what your drinking means to you and come back to this later.

Where population drinking levels and norms do not have much meaning for people in their drinking milieu, there is no point in pressing the matter.

One of the guiding principles of motivational interviewing is to combine objective information with that which has personal meaning. For this reason it is useful to have a range of assessment data; each individual will have their own unique preoccupations and concerns and the art is to tease these out rather than to impose them, no matter how obvious a particular sort of damage might be.

In Chapter 11 the author demonstrated the way this worked with a smoker; with problem drinkers there is a wide array of potential problem areas to identify in eliciting concerns and we have found that nothing substitutes for eliciting those from the individual; experience has taught us that there is no way that the therapist can guess what will be of greatest concern. What is also true though is that the skilled therapist will be sufficiently knowledgeable about the consequences of excessive drinking to guide the client along the most likely lines of enquiry. As we described in Chapter 10, MET therapists in the UK Alcohol Treatment Trial took the view that, of the whole range of feedback given, the results of liver function tests were the most likely to have an impact on identification of concerns about drinking and to constitute the basis for motivational change.

In the three-session treatment, the goal by the end of the first session is to elicit an intention to change based upon the client's confidence in their ability to change and their belief that things will improve if they do change. Feedback from assessment questionnaires can be used to identify and elicit concerns. Where such data are not available, the therapist can elicit a report of recent drinking, smoking or drug use and elicit concerns from information given on the pattern and frequency or the methods of use. The knowledgeable therapist will be able to form hypotheses about likely adverse consequences experienced by the client from this account. There will be considerable individual variation in what will be achieved: some people will start the session with a fully formed intention to change, some will have difficulty arriving at this point by the end of the session. It is, however, important that the therapist starts the session with this purpose driving their agenda.

Modifications in the subsequent sessions will follow the achievements of the first session. The goal in the second session is to establish commitment for change in the light of change plans and for this purpose a change plan worksheet might be used. Examples of such an instrument are given in both the Project MATCH and the UKATT MET manuals (Miller *et al.* 1995; Tober *et al.* 2001). The change plan worksheet has been confused with a behavioural planning approach; the emphasis in MET is on the building of confidence. It is perhaps useful to think of the earlier work of Annis and colleagues on self-efficacy in the prevention of relapse (Annis and Davis 1988). Several clinical tools have emanated from this work, encouraging people to think about what they need to have in place to increase their belief in their ability to remain abstinent or to adhere to some other treatment goal.

In the style of motivational dialogue the therapist asks

T: What sorts of things do you need to put in place to help you with this?

Or

T: What would be useful in making you feel more confident that this would work? Can you think of who or what might be able to help you with this?

Thus the emphasis in a change plan worksheet is on the way in which the plans made enhance confidence and on eliciting from the client a description of how they do this. It is worth remembering two important principles from the motivational interviewing literature here: that the client knows what they think as they hear themselves speak (Bem 1972) and related to this the principle that rather than the therapist persuading the client of which factors might help, the client persuades the therapist of what they perceive is going to be useful. What is it that persuades the therapist in this way? Attending not just to the content of speech but also to its expression, to the tone and tenor, the enthusiasm or passion which accompanies the words, or alternatively the lack of conviction which might be denoted by a lowering of the volume of speech. We are not looking just to hear the client say particular things, but we are looking to hear them say these things in a particular way.

The third session concentrates on building motivation for changed behaviour where change has occurred. In this session the therapist gets the client to give an account of achievements so far. Emphasis is placed on positive achievements; setbacks or incomplete achievement of goals are acknowledged and de-emphasised. For example:

C: I only managed to stop drinking for two days.

T: You stopped drinking for two days.

C: I didn't drink as much as before but I was really determined I was not going to drink at all.

T: You have decided you don't want to drink at all and you are making progress towards that goal. It might be helpful to look back at the week and decide what needs to be in place to make further headway in the direction you want to go. Let's talk about some of the challenges you encountered and we can then take a look at the change plan worksheet we wrote out last time and decide what needs to change.

Many people have asked what to do in the third session if everything has gone according to plan. Change rarely occurs as a one off event or a short series of events. Kent (1991) described the importance of addressing motivation after change has occurred for the reasons that all sorts of challenges can arise. The initial sense of euphoria at having achieved the change may be replaced with frustration that significant others might not have accepted the changes, might be incredulous and untrusting, or conversely might put pressure on the individual, particularly in the case of drinking that, now that the problem drinking is solved, 'normal' drinking can be resumed. People may have frustrations that life style changes they wanted to effect are slow in materialising. The health consequences may have been resolved in the short term and the point of stopping is less prominent in the individual's daily experience, or simply they may miss some of the vicarious rewards of the previous behaviour, like peer group sanction, pharmacological rewards and excitement. Identifying motivation for maintaining change and for continued change can be like starting the whole process from the beginning, except that people may have learnt how to think differently. They may have learnt from their therapist about looking to the future, about positive emphasis, about developing and enhancing self-efficacy. There are a number of research findings that encourage us to think that motivational interviewing helps people to think differently. For example, Butler *et al.* (1999) found that motivational interviewing compared with brief advice resulted in changes in motivational stage of change towards greater readiness to change and in people making more attempts to stop smoking. The results of the Drinker's Check-up (Miller *et al.* 1988) were also notable for the way that the intervention encouraged people to engage in treatment, to think about and embark upon a journey of change.

In the third session the therapist will be able to check motivation to consolidate or improve on changes already made. A decisional balance, like a balance sheet, can be drawn up graphically or just verbally, identifying the benefits of changes already achieved compared to losses likely to be sustained in the event of reversing changes. For example

T: Let's have a look at what you feel you have gained so far. Perhaps we can list the benefits to you of giving up using heroin.

The decisional balance needs to contain all the perceived benefits of the changed behaviour that the client can think of.

T: And how do you want change to continue from here? / What sorts of things do you want to see in the future? / Where would you like to see yourself in a month's time? / What will help you to get from here to there?

The downside of change can be reframed in a positive way by being registered as the benefits that will be derived from further change. Boredom and sleep problems are common complaints in those giving up alcohol and drugs. Weight gain and inability to concentrate are common complaints in those giving up smoking. The therapist reframes these as things that are currently a problem that the client wants to change, building motivation to sustain and improve on changes already made by exploring what needs to be put in place to enhance self-efficacy in tackling these challenges.

Standard treatment in the style of motivational dialogue

Some of the studies of motivational interviewing suggest that this approach gets people thinking differently about their problem drinking, drug use or their smoking. It must be the case that all treatments that have an effect are going to get people to think differently about the target behaviour and are therefore going to affect motivation to continue and motivation to change. Tober (2002) described the components of each of the Project MATCH treatments that were designed to target motivational change and there is no question that whether one adopts a cognitive behavioural approach to treatment, a twelve-step approach or a community or milieu therapy, motivation to continue and motivation to change are targeted, albeit in different ways, by environmental pressure and contingency management, in other words by external factors. Delivering milieu therapies in the style of motivational dialogue has the advantage of capitalising on the principles of both. The therapist resists the temptation to tell people what to do, to give unsolicited advice and thus to run the risk of eliciting resistance while at the same time putting in place those external environmental factors that have been shown to be equally effective in achieving improved outcomes.

We want therefore to look at the provision of Social Behaviour and Network Therapy (SBNT) (Copello *et al.* 2002) in the style of motivational dialogue. The reasons we have chosen this relatively recently developed treatment are that we have discussed the widely practised Cognitive Behavioural Approaches elsewhere in the book and because SBNT has been shown to be as effective as MET in reducing drinking and associated problems and improving mental health in the UK Alcohol Treatment Trial (UKATT Research Team 2005). Both in the UKATT and in pilot studies of treatment of drug misuse, SBNT has been shown to be popular with practitioners, able to be learnt and practised to a standard level of competence by a range of professional groups and suitable for application in a variety of settings (Tober *et al.* 2005).

SBNT fulfils our criteria for standard treatment as its prototypical presentation was eight sessions. We have examined the therapist core skills as practised by the SBNT therapist and found no reason why these should not be practised in the style of motivational dialogue. These core skills are described as: 'thinking network', focusing on positive support, being an active agent for change, and a task oriented team leader. At first sight the latter two core skills might seem to be at odds with the more eliciting than doing approach taken in motivational dialogue; however it is a good idea to interpret them as the formation of a therapeutic alliance which, in SBNT goes beyond the therapist and extends to members of the social network. The skill of thinking network is the art of getting away from thinking that all change has to occur in the individual drinker or drug user. Rather change needs to occur in and be supported by the whole network. SBNT has a future focus, explicitly making plans for future functioning of the network in the absence of the treatment agency and the therapist, in much the same way as motivational interviewing is future oriented in its attempt to get people to think differently about their substance use and questions of control over it. The same would be true for Cognitive Behavioural Coping Skills training and those similar approaches that have a present and future focus.

In its standard protocol, there is an introductory session during which the treatment goal is negotiated and a network supportive of positive change is planned. The four core sessions then follow, in which the focal person (as the client is called) and the assembled network examine first their patterns of communication, then their coping strategies and plan and implement improvements to these, make relapse prevention and management plans and enhance social support networks, in order to extend the network and recruit further sources of support both for the focal person and for the network members. There are then a number of elective sessions that are decided upon according to need and specific deficits. These cover education on alcohol and drugs, employment or occupational counselling, increasing pleasant activities, minimising support for problem drinking/drug use and active development of positive support. The point of the treatment is to create an environment supportive of positive change.

The principles of motivational dialogue that we would apply to SBNT are those of ensuring that the client or focal person is the one to determine which sort of environmental changes need to occur, what sort of communication methods are going to be helpful, which ways of coping both with drinking and with abstinence are going to be supportive, what alternative activities are going to be rewarding and so on. The problems and the solutions are defined by the focal person and their social network; the art is in eliciting rather than telling (even though the style prescribed in the original protocol for SBNT does allow the therapist to make suggestions and give unsolicited advice). It is arguably every bit as effective to use this approach to establish where it is that the client wants to be and how they want to get there, in other words what support they wish the network to put in place. This can be done with open questions, reflective listening and summarising. The skill of reflective listening is particularly helpful; for example, where the network is keen to impose a goal of abstinence when the focal person has not yet made the decision to take this route reflective listening is the method most likely to diffuse the ensuing resistance.

It is beyond the scope of the chapter to go into the detail of each session and this is to be found in manual form (Copello *et al.* in press). However, some illustrative dialogue might be helpful. Starting with the first session in which the aim is to agree the appropriate drinking goal and to identify a social network that is supportive of it, the therapist commences with an introduction in which the goals and method of treatment are spelled out and the purpose of the first session is explained. The therapist might then proceed as follows:

T: The first thing we need to establish is where you want to be with regard to your drinking, say in six months time.

C: I want to be able to drink normally. I want to go to the pub and have a couple of pints with my mates.

T: Your feeling is that in the future you would like to be able to go out with your friends in the way that you see them doing. And you have also said, when we discussed your recent pattern of drinking, that the way things are at the moment is that once you start drinking you have not been able to stop. What is your view about the way forward in the immediate future?

C: Well I can't go on as I am and I cannot imagine never having another drink, so I could think about not drinking for the next few weeks.

T: Not drinking at the moment seems to you to be the way forward. Now, if we were to look at the people around you, who do you think might give you support in staying away from alcohol? Can we make a list of all the people you know, who are concerned about you? We can then decide which of those would be able to give you active support in staying away from alcohol altogether.

The next bit is fairly straightforward as all the information is generated from the client. The therapist uses open questions to find out whether the proposed network member supports the goal of abstinence, whether they have any problems with alcohol themselves, what sort of support (practical, emotional) they are able to give, whether they would be able to come to sessions or at least be available on the phone. The session ends with an agreed plan to contact people to become network members, agreement always being reached by questions like 'What needs to happen next?' 'What (or who) would help to make that happen?' The details of the plan will be determined by the focal person and the way that they wish to proceed. The therapist in SBNT is expected to be an active agent for change so that, if the focal person requires help in contacting people with whom they may have lost contact or previously fallen out, the therapist can, at the request of the focal person, make this contact on their behalf. Another principle in SBNT is that the treatment can be delivered even if the network is not present. It is possible to adhere to the principles of being guided by what the client wishes even when this includes not wanting to assemble the network. The therapist is able to discuss with the client or focal person what it is they want absent network members to do and then to rehearse with the therapist how to communicate these wishes to them. The complementary process of conducting sessions with the network in the absence of the focal person requires client consent at the outset, at the time when the nature and processes of the treatment are being described. In order to avoid provoking resistance later on in the course of treatment, it is advisable to return to reiterate this agreement at frequent intervals.

The skills of open questions and reflective listening are used to pursue the agenda and keep the focal person on track. When the network, or some members of it, is assembled for subsequent sessions, the therapist may encounter resistance from any of the members at any time and will use the same core skills to deal with this.

The communication skills session might look like this:

T: We have looked at different patterns of communicating with each other that people tend to get into. I wonder whether any of these sounded familiar to you and whether you feel that you have got into patterns of communicating, that is the general way things tend to go when you speak to each other, perhaps when you are feeling upset or emotional in some way.

T: Tell me a bit about the sorts of things you might say to each other? What sorts of things might your husband say to you when you are drinking? What sorts of things does he say that you find helpful? What are the things that he might do differently?

T: What are the things you think go well? Tell me about the things you think could be different? In what way could they be different? What sorts of things might your wife say that you would find helpful?

The therapist can then encourage the network members to speak directly to each other and to have a discussion about communicating with each other, culminating in reaching an understanding about the effects of different styles of communicating on their feelings about each other and about what they are doing. The therapist then attempts to get the network to reach an agreement about what to say and what to try to avoid saying. If the network members get stuck, it might be useful to suggest something like

T: Would it be helpful to look at things that other people have said they find helpful? Of course not everyone is the same and everyone has to find the way they are most comfortable with. Sometimes looking at what other people do helps us to think of what we might do ourselves.

T: I wonder if it would be helpful to have a go at trying that out, like a sort of practice, you could see what happens, how you feel when you talk to each other like that.

The same principles apply to the coping session. The purpose of this session is to explore the network's coping style, whether this is coping with the focal person's drinking, with their craving and fears about drinking or with their abstinence, and to put in place coping styles that are likely to be supportive of achieving and maintaining abstinence or control and that are not supportive of drinking.

The session will commence in much the same way as the communication session

T: Let's explore some of the ways that people in the network deal with your drug use. It might be helpful to look at a recent occasion when you used and describe what people did. Perhaps you [the focal person] could then tell us how that made you feel. Was it helpful? Did it make you feel like stopping using? Did it make you feel that you could turn to them for help with stopping using? What do you think would have been a more helpful response?

T: [Directed at network members] What sorts of things do you see yourself doing when [the focal person] looks as if they have had some heroin? What sort of effect do you think that might have? What would you want to happen? What sorts of things do you think you might do instead?

Described like this, it looks like a barrage of questions. However, for our purposes here we are simply listing some lines of questioning that the therapist can pursue, interspersed with reflective statements, summaries, affirming statements addressed to different members of the network. Once different coping styles have been explored, the ones perceived to be most effective can be agreed. Using open questions about how this might be done, the therapist then wants to plan some practice (for 'homework') tasks to be attempted in between sessions. These tasks will be reviewed at the beginning of the next session.

The sessions on relapse prevention and management will follow the same routine, with the therapist asking the focal person and network members what are the risks for relapse and what sort of steps would be useful to take in order to put in place an early warning system and to galvanise the network into supportive action to prevent relapse from happening. This session also requires the network to plan giving support to each other in the event of relapse and the steps they can all take to minimise the duration and severity of the relapse. While the focal person is in the central position in deciding what would be helpful, the network members are encouraged through open questions and reflective listening to identify the support that they might need from each other.

Looking for additional sources of support is a constant theme throughout the treatment. In addition to this, an elective session is described in the SBNT protocol whose purpose is to focus specifically upon it. Network members may be partners, relatives and friends who have been dealing with the problem themselves often for years and often feeling unsupported in doing so. Feedback from interviews with network members (Williamson *et al.* submitted) illuminate the importance of enhancing people's potential for giving support into methods they believe to be constructive. The claim that they did not know whether what they were doing was the right thing to do, coupled with the perceived isolation and absence of support has driven many a partner to leave if they have not found a route into *Al Anon* or a similar support group. Using the style of motivational dialogue, the therapist can elicit from the focal person and the network members an account of additional sources of support. The therapist suggests ways of thinking about this that other people have found helpful once again, if such input is required.

We do not need to go through each of the sessions of SBNT to illustrate the point that it can be delivered in the style of motivational dialogue. We have found that practitioners previously successfully trained in motivational interviewing skills are likely to adopt these as a matter of course in their SBNT practice and this may have many benefits. To the extent that the principles of motivational interviewing practice, namely the communication of positive regard and a non-judgemental approach, form the bedrock of the therapeutic alliance and that the therapeutic alliance is associated with engagement and retention in treatment, we can assume that practising other treatments in this style will equally enhance the likelihood of engagement and retention in those treatments. A further benefit is that the more practice practitioners get, the better they will become in the performance of motivational interviewing core skills. Thus where such skills do not directly conflict with the style of delivery required for the treatment, it seems that the consistent practice of them must be a good thing.

Conclusion

This chapter should be read in conjunction with the next, which covers the use of motivational dialogue in special treatment situations such as the delivery of pharmacotherapies and the treatment of people with dual diagnosis. Here we have demonstrated how treatments with different theoretical underpinning can be delivered in a motivational dialogue style. We have also shown that an assessment can usefully be conducted using the same style. The skill requires a considerable amount of practice to master to the point of being as automatic as driving a car. We touched on the importance of therapist style in Chapter 2 and noted that the way any treatment is delivered may be just as important as what is delivered in terms of achieving measurable outcomes. If 50 per cent of treatment outcome depends on how well the treatment is given then therapist style becomes a legitimate issue for staff supervision and development.

References

Annis, H.M. and Davis, C.S. (1988) 'Self-efficacy and the prevention of alcoholic relapse: Initial findings from a treatment trial', in T.B. Baker and D. Cannon (eds) *Assessment and Treatment of Addictive Disorders*, New York, Praeger.

Babor, T.F., Higgins-Biddle, J.C., Saunders, J.B. and Monteiro, M.G. (2001) *The Alcohol Use Disorders Identification Test – guidelines for use in primary care*. Second edition. Geneva: World Health Organisation Department of Mental Health and Substance Dependence.

Bem, D.J. (1972) 'Self perception theory', in I. Berkowitz (ed.) *Advances in Experimental Social Psychology*, vol. 6, New York: Academic Press.

Butler, C.C., Rollnick, S., Cohen, D., Bachmann, M., Russell, I. and Stott, N. (1999) 'Motivational consulting versus brief advice for smokers in general practice: a randomised trial', *British Journal of General Practice*, 49: 611–616.

Copello, A., Orford, J., Hodgson, R. and Tober, G. (in press) *Social Behaviour and Network Therapy. A Clinical Research Guide for Clinicians Treating People with Addiction Problems*, London: Brunner-Routledge.

Copello, A., Orford, J., Hodgson, R., Tober, G. and Barrett, C. (2002) 'Social Behaviour and Network Therapy: basic principles and early experiences', *Addictive Behaviors*, 27: 345–366.

Drummond, C., James, D., Coulton, S., Parrot, S., Baxter, J., Ford, J., Godfrey, C., Lervy, B., Peters, T., Russell, I. and Williams, J. (2003) 'The effectiveness and cost-effectiveness of screening and stepped-care intervention for alcohol use disorders in the primary care setting (STEPWICE Project)', final report to the Wales Office for Research and Development, London: St. George's Hospital Medical School.

Kent, R. (1991) 'Motivational interviewing and the maintenance of change', in W.R. Miller and S. Rollnick (eds) *Motivational Interviewing: Preparing People to Change Addictive Behaviour*, New York: Guilford Press.

Miller, W.R. and Rollnick, S. (1991) *Motivational Interviewing: Preparing People to Change Addictive Behavior*, New York: The Guilford Press.

Miller, W.R., Sovereign, R.G. and Krege, B. (1988) 'Motivational interviewing with problem drinkers: II the drinker's check-up as a preventive intervention', *Behavioural Psychotherapy*, 16: 251–268.

Miller, W.R., Zweben, A., DiClemente, C.C. and Rychtarik, R.G. (1995) *Motivational Enhancement Therapy Manual: A Clinical Research Guide for Therapists Treating Individuals with Alcohol Abuse and Dependence*, Project MATCH Monograph 2, Rockville, Maryland: National Institute on Alcohol Abuse and Alcoholism.

Raistrick, D., Heather, N. and Godfrey, C. (2006) *Review of the Effectiveness of Treatment for Alcohol Problems*. London: National Treatment Agency.

The National Treatment Agency for Substance Misuse (2006) *Models of Care for Alcohol Misusers* (MoCAM), London: National Treatment Agency.

Tober, G. (2002) 'Evidence based practice – still a bridge too far for addiction counsellors?' *Drugs: Education, Prevention and Policy*, 9: 17–20.

Tober, G., Kenyon, R., Heather, N. and Brodie, J. (2001) *Motivational Enhancement Therapy Manual*, Leeds Addiction Unit, UKATT.

Tober, G., Godfrey, C., Parrott, S., Copello, A., Farrin, A., Hodgson, R., Kenyon, R., Morton, V., Orford, J., Russell, I. and Slegg, G. on behalf of the UKATT Research Team (2005) 'Setting standards for training and competence: the UK Alcohol Treatment Trial', *Alcohol and Alcoholism*, 40(5): 413–418.

UKATT Research Team (2001) 'The United Kingdom Alcohol Treatment Trial (UKATT): hypotheses, design and methods', *Alcohol and Alcoholism*, 36: 11–21.

UKATT Research Team (2005) 'Effectiveness of treatment for alcohol problems: findings of the randomised UK alcohol treatment trial', *British Medical Journal*, 331: 541–544.

Williamson, E., Smith, M., Orford, J., Copello, A. and Day, E. (submitted) 'Social Behaviour and Network Therapy for drug problems: analysis of qualitative data from a feasibility study'.

Chapter 13

Motivational dialogue 2 – special treatment situations

Duncan Raistrick and Gillian Tober

Introduction

This chapter follows from Chapter 12; the reader will benefit from reading Chapter 12 before tackling this one. Here we are going to illustrate motivational dialogue applied to three particular treatment situations that commonly arise within the context of core stepped care interventions as described in the previous chapter:

- Prescribing
- Investigations
- Comorbidity

As for Chapter 12 we have written some text to suggest how the conversation might flow in each example. For convenience we will repeat the guidance notes for reading the 'scripts':

1 Obviously the examples are somewhat contrived but make sure you can pick out the two core skills of asking open questions and selective reflective listening.
2 Make sure you can see the therapist's agenda and how motivational dialogue guides the client towards the preferred treatment choices. You would probably use different words which suit your own style, so translate the text we have written into questions and statements with which you feel comfortable and rehearse using them in your head or role playing with a colleague, until you do not have to think about them.
3 Notice that we frequently draw upon leaflets or worksheets or self-completion questionnaires to deal with giving and collecting simple factual information.
4 In the examples below we have used the abbreviations: T = therapist; C = client; D = doctor.

Motivational dialogue in practice

Pharmacological interventions in the style of motivational dialogue

Pharmacotherapies are normally used as enhancements to psychosocial treatments. Probably the only exception is detoxification, which may be a stand-alone procedure. Much of what was said about assessment applies to a prescribing intervention: there is an element of information gathering followed by some negotiation with the client for the purpose of agreeing the best medication. The prescriber will normally be working to a protocol and will need a familiarity with both protocols and medications in order to use motivational dialogue successfully, that is in automatic mode.

The prescriber has a duty to ensure both that any medication prescribed is safe for a particular client and also that it is likely to be of benefit to the client. These considerations should apply to any kind of treatment, however there are rarely lawsuits claiming that the wrong psychosocial treatment was given whereas the opposite is true for pharmacotherapies. Clearly one reason for this is that drugs, whether prescribed medications or self-administered street drugs, can have serious and immediate side effects. So, the challenge is for motivational dialogue to accommodate the legal as well as the clinical requirements of a prescribing intervention.

A prescriber will need to have either personal knowledge of a client, information from a suitably qualified practitioner, or routine assessment data in order to reach a prescribing decision. From any of these starting points the prescriber will have formed an initial impression of what medications might be suitable for a particular client and what risks might apply. There are few absolute contraindications to prescribing on medical grounds – a definite allergy would be one but a potentially high risk situation, such as prescribing disulfiram to someone with a history of myocardial infarction, might be agreed should the client give written informed consent. A common difficulty to which a prescribing risk is attached occurs where there is mismatch between the client's expressed belief in the efficacy, or at least desirability, of a particular medication as compared to the prescriber's knowledge that the medication is inappropriate, for example requests for benzodiazepines as hypnotics. What lies behind the request from the patient is often the continued desire for a drug effect, expressed as a need for medication for a particular ailment and this is a common cause of conflict between client and prescribing doctor. How to avoid conflict in a situation like this?

We will look at some specific prescribing examples but, before doing so, a few words on timing. Motivational dialogue is a directive, but not challenging, style of delivering interventions and it is, therefore, well suited to the needs of prescribers. Each prescriber will have their own 'comfort zone', that is the risk level beyond which they will not go. The question is whether to declare the limits at the outset, which raises the question of how this might be done in the style of motivational dialogue, or to negotiate with the client, which risks failing to achieve the desired agreement and ending a consultation in conflict. Some guiding principles are useful here.

Every ethical practitioner needs to set out boundaries as part of an introduction to treatment. These boundaries will relate to confidentiality, the scope of the professional's practice and will include reasons for prescribing. While describing reasons for prescribing, the rules for prescribing can also be explained, thus making sense of the rules by setting them in the context of reasons, or goals and objectives for prescribing. All these rules and routines can be given in a positive tone, emphasising duty of care and the pursuit of the best outcome for the patient. Much emphasis has been placed in the motivational interviewing literature, and in the psychological literature on behaviour change, on the importance of choice and the client's perception of choice and it is this which should be emphasised. There is rarely one way to deal with a problem and the practitioner starts the session by emphasising both the exploratory nature of the decision-making process and the alliance which will be the basis of arriving at the decision which is right for the problems identified and defined by the client.

Thus it is possible to identify a problem with sleep while also identifying accurately those medications, where they exist, that are effective in dealing with this problem. In the therapeutic alliance, the client is the expert in understanding the nature of the problem and the way the substance use impinges upon their life, albeit that it is the job of the skilled therapist to elicit the description and definition, while the practitioner is the expert in knowledge about the efficacy of different treatments. There follow some examples of prescribing in practice – where the task for the practitioner is to arrive at agreement about the best pharmacological course of action while avoiding the conflict often inherent in these situations where the client's reasons for taking the medication may be at odds with the doctor's reasons for prescribing it. It is assumed the dialogue is between a doctor and a client.

A common request encountered by addiction specialists is for a high tariff prescription, such as diamorphine (heroin) or amphetamine.

C: Hello doctor. My keyworker said I should come and see you to get a diamorphine scrip.

D: Yes, I spoke to your key worker and suggested we talked about what you are thinking. Tell me about what you are currently doing and how things are going for you.

C: I am doing fine most of the time, but I come home from work and don't know what to do with myself. Then I just start thinking about gear and one thing leads to another and I go and get some. I keep thinking about it and if I had something to take in the evening as well as the morning then I think it would be easier. I'd stop using on top of my methadone.

D: You are finding the methadone helpful in getting you through the day.

C: Yeah and it's only in the evenings that it's not enough. If I had a diamorphine scrip then it would be better.

D: You want things to be better than they are. You want to stop going out and getting heroin in the evenings after work. This was what you wanted to move away from when you first came here for treatment.

C: Yeah, I really want to stop using street gear. My mum says she won't have me in the house if I carry on like this plus I want to save money anyway to get my own place. I think that a scrip for diamorphine is going to be better than methadone for stopping me going out and scoring.

D: We have been over all the reasons why you came for treatment in the first place and once you got started on the methadone you stopped using street heroin for a while. Now things have changed again. Let's just go over the reasons for not using street heroin now.

C: (lists original reasons and adds reasons of not wanting to lose achievements made, like the job and relationship stability)

D: What other risks can you think of that might come up?

C: Well there was the other business we first talked about when you don't really know what you are taking and you could be taking anything and you could overdose.

D: You could overdose with using on top when you never really know what you are taking or what exact dose it might be. Of all the things that you have mentioned here, what is the thing that most worries you about taking the heroin?

C: That I am going backwards and I'll end up where I started. I thought I was making progress and now I am not so sure.

D: Tell me what are you thinking about how you think things would improve if you had diamorphine, over and above the benefits you are currently getting from your methadone scrip?

C: (responds with perceived benefits)

D: (Reflects back the client's perceived benefits) What else have you heard about diamorphine?

C: Nothing really. My friend Peter gets it and I think it would be good for me.

D: Well, let's explore whether it is the right solution for you; we need to do some more work on this. What you are telling me is that you cannot see any down side to diamorphine – and yet as you have said from your own previous use of street heroin, there is a catch to most things. One way we could do this is to look at all the advantages and disadvantages by way of using this decision making worksheet, you might want to discuss this with your family or friends who know what is going on and come and see me next week. We can then decide which is the best way forward to get to where you want to be.

The doctor has gained some impression about the reasons for the client requesting diamorphine by using open-ended questions and has reflected back the need for more careful thought. She has taken care not to rush into an important decision on either part. In the next sequence the client is once more talking to the specialist:

D: Hello, thanks for coming back. Last time we were talking about the question of changing your scrip from methadone to diamorphine. There are certain things we needed to look at in order to make a decision about whether this is the correct course of action for you. Each patient is different and individual and it is important to get the treatment right for each individual. We looked at your present circumstances, at your plans and at how your treatment fits into and helps you to achieve your goals. Let's start from going over what you hope to get out of treatment overall.

C: Overall I want to get myself sorted out and back on track. I want to stop using street heroin so that I can get my own place and the things I need for it. I cannot do that when all my money is going on heroin. I want to get back to college.

D: (Reflects positive plans) Tell me where you see yourself in a year's time?

C: I hope that I will have moved into my own place and got back to the college course that I started. My grades were good and I was really interested in the subject before I started using.

D: Using heroin got in the way of completing your studies, which you were enjoying.

C: Yeah, and I was good at.

D: And you are keen to get back to them. Tell me how you see a diamorphine scrip fitting in with this plan.

C: It's not as addictive as methadone and it's easier to get off.

D: It's easier to get off than methadone. Now tell me where this particular plan to come off fits into your plans for the future. What sort of time scale are you looking at?

C: (responds)

D: Now perhaps we can look at that piece of homework I gave you where I asked you to list what you thought are the pros and cons of diamorphine and decide whether this course of action fulfils your needs at this point.

The doctor is using the basic techniques of open-ended questions followed by reflections. In this case the reflection is elaborated in order to introduce material that the doctor needs to discuss. The sorts of considerations needed for making a decision are stated at the outset, so the client is then in the position of persuading the doctor that they want to have the diamorphine the better to pursue their ultimate goal of abstinence. If the rationale for deciding the goal is clearly stated at the outset it is more likely to be the case that the doctor and client will reach the same decision. Moreover, the decision reached will then be able to be tested for its efficacy against these stated goals of treatment. A similar kind of interaction would be expected for any substitute prescribing.

Another common prescribing situation is a client requesting detoxification. The example here is an opiate detoxification.

D: Hello, my name is Dr Jones. I understand that you have requested a detox.

C: Yeah but I don't want them blockers I want that lofexidine detox

D: That's fine. Can I just check what you know about all the methods that are available to do a detox so that we can arrive at the best way forward for you?

C: Some people get that drug that has a blocker [buprenorphine] – my friend had that and it made her ill.

D: You have decided that you want to go with lofexidine because you are worried that another route might make you ill. It is important to you to feel confident in any medical course of action we might pursue. What is it that makes you think that the same thing might happen to you as happened to your friend? Have you heard of anyone else who has had a successful experience with either, or any other course of detox?

C: I tried to do one myself before with subby's [buprenorphine] that I got off a mate. I felt really ill too.

D: You have tried them before though not in a clinic. But you are keen to try something different that you hope will work better. I need to be sure that this is going to be safe, so I need to check out if you are taking any other medication or if you have had any serious illnesses?

C: (responds none of these)

D: You aren't taking anything else at the moment, and you have not had any serious illnesses. Have you thought about any plans for what you would do during the detox week?

C: Yea. My support worker got me to write it down on this detox prep thing.

D: Tell me how you found that. Let's just go through it together and you can tell me which bits you found helpful and how you are going to get started.

In this case the support worker has done a lot of preparation work and has used the detoxification preparation tool to elicit from the client what sorts of things he thinks he can put in place that will make him feel more confident to get through the withdrawal successfully. If this had not been done, the prescribing doctor will need to gather this information by asking open-ended questions.

D: What sorts of things do you anticipate feeling as you withdraw?
C: I really can't handle hanging out. I need to be sure that the medication is going to stop me hanging out.
D: You are worried about hanging out and you want to be sure that the medication you get will stop that happening. What else do you think will help you to deal with your worries about withdrawing?
C: Being able to talk to someone about it. Knowing I can see you if it isn't working. Not having to go back out on the street.
D: Who are the people apart from myself that you will want to be able to talk to?
C: (Lists mother and support worker)
D: Once you have made the arrangements with them for who is going to be there with you through the detox days we can get started. How confident do you feel that you can get through it with this assistance? [and then] What else would help to make you feel more confident?
C: (responds with some ideas)

As described earlier, the doctor should continue to elicit ideas from the client that are described with conviction and enthusiasm. The goal is for the client to convince the doctor, both with the tone of their voice and the content of their speech that they believe what they are saying. As in the previous example reflection is elaborated in order to check key pieces of information, namely other medications and previous medical history.

Another challenge for the medical practitioner is to engage the client in taking relapse prevention medication. The example here is for disulfiram (Antabuse).

C: Hello doctor, Jane [client's keyworker] said I had to come and see you about getting some tablets but I'm fine – I haven't had a drink for three weeks now.
D: You are doing really well in that you feel fine and have not had a drink for three weeks. I am wondering what you talked about with Jane to make her worry so much?
C: (defensive response repeating that everything is OK)
D: Tell me what Jane would say if she were sitting here now?
C: Well I told her that one day I was out with my friends and one of them offered me a drink. I was very tempted to have one.

D: You came close to saying yes. What would have happened if you had taken the drink you were offered?

C: It would not have been just one drink. If I started again now, that would be it. I would be back on it all the time like I was before. My wife would really throw me out and I would be back where I was with trouble at work. I can't see any future if I start drinking again.

D: If you had taken that drink you would have continued drinking that night and the following day. You are then not sure you would have stopped. You are saying that maintaining abstinence is really important to you and you need to stay off the drink to keep hold of the gains that you have made. Your wife is giving you another chance depending on staying away from drinking.

C: I just feel I shouldn't put myself into those situations. I can't take the risk. I thought my friends would respect the fact that I had given up drinking but it seems I cannot rely on them. I am going to have to give up having any social life.

D: Giving up your social life is one way to avoid the risk of drinking. By the way you say it that is not an option you are looking forward to. Have you heard of anything else that might help you to deal with those unexpected situations that arise when suddenly you are faced with the risk of having a drink?

C: My wife said I should try that medicine that makes you sick if you have a drink.

D: What have you heard about it?

C: I've heard that you can't have a drink after you've taken it because it is too dangerous.

D: What else have you heard about it?

C: I knew someone at the office once who swore by it.

D: I could tell you a bit about how it works and then you could decide whether you think it would be helpful to you either in the short term or the longer term. At least if you have some clear information then you can make up your mind.

The clue to the client's interest is in the fact that he brought up the subject of disulfiram himself, and depending upon the way the doctor describes its utility and the precautions to ensure its safety, the likelihood is that he will give it a try. Remember that an important principle in the eliciting style of counselling associated with greater reductions in drinking is optimism, as identified by Miller and colleagues (1993). This is the principle that the therapist believes in the efficacy of the treatment and in the client's ability to benefit from it and to do well.

Clients may express resistance to the idea of taking medication when they are not committed to pursuing or to maintaining a goal of abstinence. Reflecting back statements that might be a sign of resistance ('I want to do this by myself'; 'I don't like taking tablets') and exploring alternatives so that the client perceives that they have a choice are likely to reduce resistance and open up the discussion about a positive way forward. Medication can be presented to the client as one option among many. It may be that going over the ground to arrive once more at the commitment to the goal of abstinence is necessary and once this goal is again affirmed the discussion can refocus on what things would help to maintain abstinence.

Investigations in the style of motivational dialogue

Health concerns are the most frequently cited reasons for stopping or moderating drinking and are commonly given as reasons for stopping illicit drug use. It follows that investigations are not only helpful in making a diagnosis and assessing the extent of substance related problems but also have important potential as sources of motivation for change. There are three stages to undertaking any investigations: first, an explanation of the reasons and possible gains, second an explanation of the tests themselves, how they work, what they do and do not detect and what the results might mean and third, feedback of the results and discussion of any implications. We had a detailed description of such an intervention in Chapter 11. We give another one, albeit in less detail, here.

Investigations are typically undertaken at assessment or follow-up though there may be some particular reason at other times. This example is a client who comes for assessment of an alcohol problem.

D: What we are doing today is trying to get to grips with the consequences of your drinking. You have described to me a lot of the things that have happened after drinking and we have put together a list of the concerns you have about what has happened and what might happen in the future. We have based all this on the things that you have experienced, on the things you know about. We could also look a bit deeper into the things that might be going on beneath the skin, the things that are not always so obvious until we take tests. An example of this is taking a blood test to get some idea of how your liver is coping with your drinking.

C: I hate having blood taken – do I have to?

D: Having blood taken is not something you like doing.

C: I hate needles. But the worst thing is you never know what you are going to be told.

D: You are worried about what the results might tell us. Tell me what sorts of things you are worried about.

C: My uncle died of liver cirrhosis.

D: Tell me what you understand about that.

C: Well he was quite old and he just drank the whole time. I never saw him when he wasn't drunk.

D: Your uncle was older than you and had been drinking for much longer. Tell me what you know about how alcohol affects the liver.

C: Don't really know.

D: Perhaps we could just go over some facts about that and then you could decide whether this was a worry to you. [describes the mechanism for liver damage] Where does this leave you with regard to your own health and recent drinking?

C: Not sure I really want to know but I definitely don't want to get as far as having liver cirrhosis. I want to keep my options open and be able to drink normally again one day.

D: You are saying that there are some worries about your health and you really want to stop things deteriorating to the stage they got with your uncle. If I could explain a little bit about how these tests work and what they tell us, we can then decide whether having them is going to be the best way to proceed. [explains the tests and what they show] It might be helpful if you took this leaflet to read if you want to think further about it. As I have explained, the tests will not tell us anything definitive but we can use the results to decide on the next best step. If we detect an abnormality in your liver function it will act as a helpful warning that action needs to be taken. If we do not, there will be a sense of relief, which might help you to decide how to keep things that way. The decision is yours.

C: You make it sound like a good idea.

D: If you are happy for me to take some blood then we will do the screening tests and they will alert us to any potential health problems from drinking. I will go through the results next time when you will have had time to read the leaflet.

The doctor's goal was to secure informed consent to undertake some routine investigations. Initially the client was a little frightened of blood tests. The doctor used open-ended questions to elicit health concerns and agreement that the blood tests would be of interest when fed back to the client as in the next sequence:

D: Hello, how are you?

C: Well, I decided I had best stop drinking and so I haven't had anything since I last saw you.

D: What was it that made you decide that?

C: Well I was a bit worried about my blood tests and also when I saw your nurse for my health check she said I was quite a lot overweight. My partner has been saying I should lose some weight too and she wants me to stop drinking.

D: What do you think about it?
C: (responds in general terms about a healthier lifestyle)
D: You want to get fitter and you see stopping drinking and doing other things to lose weight as the next step. There is good news on the blood tests that we did, your blood sugar is slightly raised but all the other tests were normal. Is there anything that you wanted to ask about any of the tests?
C: That is a relief. You are saying that I have not damaged my liver.
D: As I explained to you last time, as far as we can see from the results of these tests, it seems that your liver has been coping with your drinking to date. You have decided to stop drinking in the meantime so future damage to your liver from drinking is not going to be a concern at the moment.
C: That's one thing less to worry about.
D: It's a relief that you don't have to worry about that. You are now thinking of making a fairly big change in your lifestyle. You have got off to a good start – it's always easier to keep things going well than to have to start from getting there first. The results of the investigations were all normal except for the sugar. We could repeat the sugar when you have started your new diet as it's most likely to do with your being overweight. How would you feel about bringing your partner along next time we meet?

It seems that the health check and investigations have brought about some commitment to a change of lifestyle. Open questions can further be used to elicit the benefits of lifestyle change rather than just focusing on the drinking. The fact that the results were essentially normal is used as an encouraging point to start from, something to maintain – and thus can be used to reinforce the need for change.

Many clients attending substance misuse services will request blood borne virus testing.

C: Doctor, can you do a hepatitis test?
D: What has made you decide that you want to be tested?
C: Someone told me that a friend I shared needles with is positive for Hepatitis C.
D: You have some worries having shared with someone who has hepatitis. Tell me what exactly happened to make you think you may be at risk.
C: (responds with some drug use and needle sharing history)
D: That's really helpful to know exactly where your fears come from. Tell me what else you know about what puts you at risk?
C: I don't know. How else can you get it?
D: Certain sorts of sexual behaviours. For example not using condoms would be one way.

C: I've done that a couple of times with a bloke I used to go out with.
D: How do you want to tell him that he might also be at risk?

Open-ended questions are used to explore the client's level of risk and find out if others may also be at risk. It would be usual to give out a leaflet with information about blood borne viruses. In this case the doctor asks an open-ended question that makes clear what needs to be done – '*how will you tell the person you had sex with?*'. Before testing, the doctor would need to be assured that the client understood the implications of positive results, as in the following sequence:

D: Hello, how are you doing?
C: (responds indicating continued high risk drug using and sexual behaviours)
D: Well, last time we met you asked whether we could check out whether you had been infected with any blood borne viruses. I am sorry to say that you are positive for Hepatitis C but not for Hepatitis B or HIV. Lets just deal with the Hepatitis C – what do you know already?
C: (responds with no real knowledge and a question about treatments for Hepatitis C)
D: OK, it's important that you are thinking about treatment because treatment will certainly improve the chances of a good outcome. For the hepatitis treatment to work there are a few things that also need to happen. These have to do with drinking, drug taking and risky sex as we talked about last time. How do you see the way forward?

This is difficult feedback but the role of motivational dialogue is nonetheless important. It is an opportunity to explore in an empathic manner how the client feels about the bad news. It is an opportunity to raise and enhance optimism for treatment and an improved outcome. It is particularly important to enhance engagement in treatment for these diseases where high rates of non-attendance are one of the biggest challenges for the public and individual health. The agenda of this session is to give information about Hepatitis C in an empathic manner and to highlight the benefits of treatment for the individual; at the same time there is a need to elicit concerns about continuing high risk behaviours and again to focus upon their implications for the individual. Public health risks may be high on the agenda of the health professional, but it is optimism at the individual level that will enhance motivation to engage in hepatitis treatment.

Motivational dialogue for people with mental health problems

It is very common for substance misuse and mental illness to co-occur. There are of course many forms of mental illness with wholly different manifestations and each liable to fluctuations in severity of symptoms over time. Readers are referred to the standard diagnostic manuals, ICD-10 (World Health Organisation 1993) and DSM-IV (American Psychiatric Association 1994), for full descriptions. For the purpose of demonstrating how motivational dialogue might be used with people who have both substance misuse and mental illness problems we shall consider three major categories of mental illness: (i) psychosis – such as schizophrenia or manic depressive disorder; (ii) moderate severity mental illness – such as depression, anxiety states or obsessive compulsive disorder and (iii) personality disorder – such as emotionally unstable or paranoid.

There is nothing about mental illness that contradicts the use of motivational dialogue. Even people who suffer from severe mental illness, such as schizophrenia, usually have intact cognitions. The added complexity is that the substance misuse problem and mental illness problem become intertwined and often the substance use is seen as a solution to the mental illness. It follows that the two problems need to be tackled together and not as separate entities. There is a further need for caution in that an individual's mental state at the time of a therapy session may lead to misinterpretations – for example injudicious statements or questions from the therapist may feed paranoid thoughts, may further entrench negative or depressive thoughts, or may excite symptoms of anxiety or volatile emotions.

Pharmacological treatments are often helpful and sometimes essential components of the care plan for a person who has a mental illness. Equally people with mental illness often look to pharmacological solutions when these are known to be ineffective or even harmful. The cognitive behavioural family of therapies is generally accepted as the mainstream psychological treatment for most mental illness. We have already stressed the importance of clinicians having a clear agenda in mind before starting any therapy session and this is crucial when working with comorbidity. The therapist will be using motivational dialogue to engage the client generally but in particular to engage the client in a cognitive behavioural therapy, which will then be conducted in a motivational style; in addition the therapist will be seeking to encourage either compliance with medication or avoidance of medication as might be appropriate to the mental illness in question.

In the following examples it is assumed that the client's history, at least a comprehensive assessment, is well understood by the therapist. We are illustrating particular barriers that might be overcome using motivational dialogue and in each case the aim is to engage the client in some form of cognitive behavioural therapy. It is unusual for people with a psychotic illness to use 'hard' drugs but commonly they use alcohol or cannabis. This example is a client who suffers from schizophrenia and is a heavy user of cannabis.

T: Good to see you again. We said last time that we would talk a bit more about your cannabis use. Can you tell me some of the good things that you get from smoking cannabis?
C: Everyone smokes weed – I like it 'cos it makes my voices go away.
T: It seems to take away the voices. Is there anything else?
C: I've always smoked it, it makes me feel more relaxed.
T: It helps you to relax. It feels like something you have always done, and it seems like something that everyone does. What else have you experienced?
C: That's it really. I think it's OK –
T: You like to smoke because your friends do, it relaxes you and the voices are not so troubling. Tell me about the times you have been in hospital.
C: There have been times when I feel much better in hospital.
T: Describe to me what you think is different about when you are in hospital feeling better than when you are home when things are not so good. Can we use this workbook, which you can keep, so we can write down the things you say and keep track of our discussions.
C: I feel safe in hospital. I know what's going to happen and I don't get those paranoid thoughts that I get after smoking cannabis.
T: Feeling safe and protected from unexpected things happening and not smoking cannabis are the things that are different. You are also saying that if you don't smoke cannabis you don't get the paranoid thoughts.

The workbook referred to would be the client's homework as part of a cognitive behavioural programme. The therapist is attempting to elicit statements connecting cannabis use and symptoms of schizophrenia that lead to hospital admission. The therapist would also want to make connections between taking prescribed medication and symptom reduction. The purpose of the workbook is to put the specific mental illness and substance related problems into a more holistic view of the client's lifestyle.

Depression and anxiety symptoms are ubiquitous and often difficult to assess. The example is of a client with a drinking problem and depression.

T: There are a number of options for treatment to tackle your depression. I would like to discuss these with you so that we can agree on the best way to proceed. One of these is a treatment called cognitive therapy, which focuses on looking at your thoughts and the way those thoughts make you feel and behave.
C: Do you mean you're not going to give me antidepressants?
T: Antidepressant medication is one of a number of treatments we can look at. Depending upon the nature of the depression they may or may not work well. We have looked at the way you have turned to drink to

deal with your depression and you have said this works for you in the short term, and that is for shorter and shorter periods of time and sometimes not at all. What do you see to be the advantages of taking a tablet over drinking in making you feel better?

C: Well I wouldn't get hangovers, I wouldn't be going out to the pub, it wouldn't be costing me so much.

T: There are several advantages for you. You have said that you are worried about your health because of your drinking and we have agreed that you have decided to be abstinent at least for the next month. You want to stay away from your drinking friends during that time. Apart from going to the pub, what do you like to do with your time?

C: I don't really do anything anymore.

T: You don't do anything anymore. What are the sorts of things that you used to do that you enjoy doing?

C: I used to help my friend with his market stall every day and I really enjoyed doing that. Then I just started feeling so low that I couldn't face going out of the house. Once I started staying at home every day I just seemed to feel worse and worse, except when I managed to get to the pub and started drinking.

T: What we want to do is to find the best way to help to improve your mood and this depression that you experience. One of the things you have thought of is antidepressant medication. You are also saying that when you do things you enjoy you do not get these feelings of depression. But the antidepressants cannot replace doing things that you enjoy. One of the ways forward might be to use your workbook to start planning doing some of the things you enjoy, writing down what things need to be in place to help you get started with doing them again. You can then also record how your mood varies depending on what you are doing and we can see whether there are things that are better to do and things that are not so good in improving your mood. If this does not get to the heart of the matter we have other possible courses of action to explore and one of the ones you have mentioned is the medication route. How would you like to proceed from here?

The therapist's preference is to engage in mood monitoring with a view to increasing enjoyable activities, namely a cognitive behavioural programme. However, in this case there is a relatively inexpensive and low risk option of trying the client's choice, an antidepressant, which may yield benefits in terms of building the therapeutic alliance. It is important that the client has a perception of choice and a therapeutic alliance in deciding the way forward.

The final example is of a client with an emotionally unstable personality disorder and heroin use.

T: Hello Felicity, nice to see you again. I'm pleased that you feel more settled with your methadone but you cut your arm quite badly again this week. Tell me about what was going on leading up to that.

C: (describes the sequence of events)

T: Tell me how you felt when you cut yourself.

C: (responds by describing some pleasure and tension relief from cutting)

T: Those are some of the things that you said about taking heroin. Is there anything that you particularly like about cutting yourself?

C: I love watching the knife go in slowly and then the blood starting to come out.

T: And is there anything you don't like about it?

C: I don't like going to hospital – people are horrible to me. I don't like all these scars on my arms and I just feel depressed the next day.

T: You seem to have cut yourself more often since you have been on the methadone.

C: Yea, I don't really do it if I've injected stuff.

T: Can I just check out then what you are saying. You said you don't like injecting heroin because of all the trouble with the police and you don't want to cut yourself because people stare at your arms and it all makes you feel bad. Injecting heroin and cutting yourself both seem to give you some kind of good feeling but it is short lived and you also say that in fact you end up feeling worse.

C: (responds by confirming the therapist's understanding is essentially correct)

T: You have given me a good understanding of how you see things at the moment. You have got into a pattern of doing things that you know you can do and that relieve your bad feelings very quickly. You also say that you do not like doing them because they make you feel worse in the long term. Tell me how you would like things to be.

C: I really want to stop feeling so awful about myself. I want to be able to enjoy myself and not feel embarrassed all the time. I just don't know how to stop myself doing all these stupid things.

T: Tell me about a time you felt good about yourself.

The therapist then begins to get an idea of the sorts of things that need to be put in place to enhance self-esteem and as a first positive step the therapist's agenda is to engage the client in supportive, problem solving, behavioural work in order to stop the self-mutilation and achieve stability on methadone. The way to do this will be agreed through open questions, reflective statements and summaries. There may be many deep-seated psychological problems yet to come to light. Getting to grips with the immediately problematic behaviour will either reveal what these are or may result in improved every day functioning, which minimises the need to address them.

Conclusion

In these last two chapters we have described the way that motivational dialogue can be used across the spectrum of treatments for substance misuse problems. We have looked at the way that motivation needs to be addressed at each of the stages of change and with reference to different elements of a stepped care approach. Whether the treatment is a motivational therapy, a behavioural or a pharmacological treatment, the principles of eliciting problem recognition and problem definition from the client, the need to elicit client-defined solutions, to raise self-efficacy, positive outcome expectancy and self-esteem all apply. The core skills of asking open questions and responding with selective reflective listening, summaries and affirmation are used to communicate to the client with empathy, positive regard and a non-judgemental approach that it is the client's perspective and choice of the way forward that will form the basis of the particular treatment which is pursued. It is our hope that practitioners of all kinds will adopt motivational dialogue as their preferred style of delivering interventions whether these are motivational therapies, from the 12-step or cognitive behavioural families of treatments, or supplementary interventions, such as pharmacotherapies. We hope that in the process of achieving professional competence, practitioners will enjoy spin-off benefits from practising motivational dialogue with their children, family and friends.

References

American Psychiatric Association (1994) *Diagnostic and statistical manual of mental disorders (DSM-IV)*, 4th edn, Washington, DC: APA.

Miller, W.R., Benefield, R.G. and Tonigan, J.S. (1993) 'Enhancing motivation for change in problem drinking: a controlled comparison of two therapist styles', *Journal of Consulting and Clinical Psychology*, 61: 455–461.

World Health Organisation (1993) *International statistical classification of disease and health-related problems – ICD-10*, Geneva: WHO.

Subject index

Note: page numbers in **bold** refer to diagrams, page numbers in *italics* refer to information contained in boxes.